D0143444

Baudrillard and Signs

This book documents Baudrillard's tempestuous encounters with semiology and structuralism. Genosko illuminates in detail his efforts to destroy structural analyses from the inside by setting signification ablaze with his concept of symbolic exchange. Simultaneously, the book shows that Baudrillard's project to go beyond signification is fraught with difficulties which return him to a semiotic scene saturated with all kinds of signs. Through this illumination, Baudrillard's work is situated in the broad spectrum of European and American semiotic traditions. His key concept of symbolic exchange is critically examined and is traced through its maturation and development over some thirty years of theorizing.

Also examined are Baudrillard's engagements with and debts to French theatre and literature with reference to Antonin Artaud, Alfred Jarry and Victor Segalen. Discussion of Baudrillard's relation to the thought of Deleuze, Guattari, Lacan, de Certeau and Lyotard casts light on many neglected features of his work.

Gary Genosko is Visiting Research Fellow, Department of Sociology, Goldsmiths' College, University of London.

Baudrillard and Signs

Signification Ablaze

Gary Genosko

London and New York

First published 1994
by Routledge
11 New Fetter Lane, London EC4P 4EE

Simultaneously published in the USA and Canada
by Routledge
29 West 35th Street, New York, NY 10001

© 1994 Gary Genosko

Typeset in Palatino by
Florencetype Limited, Kewstoke, Avon

Printed and bound in Great Britain by
Biddles Ltd, Guildford and King's Lynn

British Library Cataloguing in Publication Data
A catalogue record for this book is available from the British
Library.

ISBN 0–415–11256–7
ISBN 0–415–11257–5 (pbk)

Library of Congress Cataloging in Publication Data
Genosko, Gary.
    Baudrillard and signs: signification ablaze / Gary Genosko.
        p.   cm.
    Includes bibliographical references and index.
    ISBN 0–415–11256–7 : $50.00 – ISBN 0–415–11257–5 (pbk.) : $16.50
    1. Baudrillard, Jean – Contributions in semiotics.   2. Semiotics.
3. Structuralism.   4. France – Intellectual life – 20th century.
I. Title.
P85.B36G46   1994
302.2 – dc20   93–49039
                                                              CIP

For Hannah

Contents

Figures and tables

Acknowledgements

I began to think seriously about Baudrillard while I was a doctoral student in the Graduate Programme in Social and Political Thought at York University in Toronto, Canada. Sitting around the dining room table at John O'Neill's house during his Monday evening seminars was conducive to dispelling as much as distilling the theoretical fictions of Baudrillard. I would also like to thank Ioan Davies, with whom I have worked for many years on the editorial collective of *Borderlines* and who read an early version of this book, for his encouragement. I also wish to acknowledge the critical advice I received along the way from Brian Massumi, Brian Singer, Marie-Christine Leps, and Ray Morris. In addition, I have learned so much about semiotics from Paul Bouissac that a mere acknowledgement seems to diminish his contribution. Jean-François Côté helped me when Baudrillard's French became overwhelming, and Baudrillard himself deserves mention for letting a virtual stranger into his apartment. Finally, this book could not have been completed without the support of my partner Rachel Ariss.

Much of my work on this book was made possible by awards from the Social Sciences and Humanities Research Council of Canada and the Queen Elizabeth II Fellowship Program in the Province of Ontario. Derrick de Kerckhove, Director of the McLuhan Program at the University of Toronto, and Chris Jenks, Deputy Head of the Department of Sociology at Goldsmiths' College, University of London, both provided me with institutional, intellectual, and convivial social support while I was research fellow in both cities in 1992–93 and 1993–94 respectively.

Introduction
Signs must burn!

Born at Reims in 1929, Jean Baudrillard has been active in French
intellectual circles for thirty years. He began his career in the
early 1960s as a book reviewer of German and Italian literature
for *Les temps modernes* (Baudrillard, 1962, 1962a, 1962b; and
Gane, 1991a: 6–15). Trained as a Germanist, he translated into
French major works by German playwright Peter Weiss, in
addition to writings by Bertolt Brecht, social anthropologist
Wilhelm E. Mühlmann, and Friedrich Engels, among others.
Before the publication of his first major theoretical statement in
Le Système des objets in 1968, Baudrillard had produced a significant number of translations of quite diverse texts, many of
which remain standard works. The bulk of his work in
translation was in the area of theatre and, in particular, the
revolutionary *'théâtre-document'* of Weiss.[1] Moreover, before his
university career began, Baudrillard was a secondary school
(*enseignement secondaire*) teacher. He arrived in Paris at the
Université de Nanterre (Université de Paris X) in 1966 and took
up the position of *assistant de Sociologie* (assistant lecturer), a post
in *enseignement supérieur* (university teaching) below that of
Maître-assistant (junior lecturer), to which he rose in the early
1970s in the Faculté des Lettres et Sciences Humaines at
Nanterre. He retired from his teaching post in 1987.

From 1967 into the 1970s Baudrillard was associated with the
sociology of urbanism group around the journal *Utopie*, and in
1975 he joined the founding editorial board of the cultural
theory journal *Traverses* of the Centre Georges Pompidou in
Paris. He withdrew from the latter journal in the late 1980s.
Despite Baudrillard's much commented upon disdain for many
of the theoretical inroads made by his contemporaries in France

over the last thirty years, he has on at least two occasions, in interviews given during the 1980s, remarked upon the positive nature of his experiences with *Utopie*. In an interview 'Intellectuals, Commitment and Political Power' (Baudrillard, 1984–85: 166), Baudrillard reflects upon the energy generated by the social movements of the 1960s and what he calls the 'favourable critical position' which the journal enjoyed since it drew upon the energy of revolt. By the 1970s, however, this energy was used up. Speaking a year earlier (Baudrillard, 1983i: 32–3), Baudrillard described this dissipation of energy with reference to *Utopie* as well as, *circa* 1975, his new post on *Traverses*. While at one time a small review like *Utopie* could consider itself to be part of a movement which gave its members the impression that 'things were relatively clear' vis-à-vis the 'Other, Society and Power', Baudrillard explains that 'with the society which developed around the liberalism of Giscard in 1975–76, it became suddenly evident that these little reviews had waned'.[2]

In 1975, together with Michel de Certeau, Gilbert Lascault, Marc Le Bot, Louis Marin and Paul Virilio, Baudrillard founded *Traverses*, although he did so without the clarity of vision which had helped to carry *Utopie*. *Traverses* was born from 'a kind of transversality, no longer a transgression, so as to regain a negativity of another type, one which was more interstitial, floating halfway in the institution. Significantly, *Traverses* is Beaubourg. But it is anti-Beaubourg as well' (Baudrillard, 1983i: 32). Even though *Traverses* is still published, it has exhausted itself by enduring beyond its years, in Baudrillard's estimation, since its play with collusion and the protection and cultivation of a scene is no longer tenable. If one has an interest in drawing a line between Baudrillard's early and later works, I suggest that the articles contained in *Utopie* and *Traverses*, many of which became parts of books which have been translated into English, enable one to establish two coherent bodies of writing toward which two distinct attitudes are clearly marked out by Baudrillard.

Further, from 1969 to 1973 Baudrillard was associated with the Centre d'Etudes des Communications de Masse at the Ecole Pratique des Hautes Etudes, in Paris. Under the auspices of this Centre Baudrillard conducted seminars in addition to those he gave at Nanterre, Vincennes, and numerous other institutions and organizations in and around Paris. Founded in 1960 by Georges Friedmann at the Ecole Pratique des Hautes Etudes, the

Centre d'Etudes des Communications de Masse publishes a yearly report of its activities in its journal *Communications*. These reports provide a clear indication of Baudrillard's activities under the auspices of the Centre and other organizations from 1969–73. His courses at the Ecole Pratique des Hautes Etudes, other teaching assignments around Paris and abroad, papers delivered and conferences attended, and publications are all included for this period. What emerges most clearly for the years 1969–70 and 1970–71 is Baudrillard's interest in design; a complement, in short, to the urbanism of *Utopie*. He lectured on the 'Social Problems of Design' at the Chambre de Commerce de Reims, and on 'The Critique of the Concept of Environment' at the Institut de l'Environnement in Paris. In 1970, Baudrillard served on the jury of the 'Compasso d'oro' design prize in Milan, and attended the World Design Congress in Aspen, Colorado. Baudrillard's seminar (1970–71) at Vincennes included much of the material which would appear in *Pour une critique de l'économie politique du signe* (1972), and he gave a paper on 'Design' at the Ecole des Hautes Etudes Commerciales in 1971. Subsequently in 1972, Baudrillard would hold a seminar in the Département d'Urbanisme at Vincennes. By 1972, the Centre had been renamed the Centre d'Etudes Trans-disciplinaires (Sociologie, Anthropologie, Sémiologie). Roland Barthes and Edgar Morin shared the directorship with Friedmann.

With these biblio-biographical remarks in mind, a brief overview of Baudrillard's major theoretical concerns over the course of his career to date will allow me to situate the semiotic problematic at issue in this book.

Baudrillard set himself the task of defining consumption in his first two major studies, *Le Système des objets* (1968) and *La Société de consommation* (1970). He argued that the place of consumption in the new consumer society is everyday life. Social life is mediated and radically alienated by a controlled logic of merchandise in which consumption has nothing to do with principles of reality and the satisfaction of needs. Modern consumers are 'cyberneticians' enagaged in a 'calculus of objects' which have been liberated from their functions and materiality. Baudrillard's central claim is that objects have become signs whose value is determined by a disciplinary cultural code. In this code the idea of the relation between signs is consumed.

Modern monopolistic production produces the signs of differentiation by means of which social standing is established and personalization accomplished, thus fully integrating the consumer into the system. Like Henri Lefebvre, Baudrillard used structuralist method to criticize the structural logic of the society of consumption, but unlike Lefebvre, he claimed that revolution was impossible at the level of a total system which thinks and speaks of itself through consumption (Baudrillard, 1968a, 1969a).

Baudrillard published a series of books in the 1970s in which he developed and criticized key concepts from his first studies. *Pour une critique de l'économie politique du signe* (1972) described the collapse of the parallel orders of production and consumption into a general political economy. By demonstrating the homology between material and sign production, Baudrillard was able to define the stage at which commodities are immediately produced as signs and signs as commodities. Use value, exchange value and sign exchange value converge in two-sided 'object forms' integrated into a functional syntax and controlled by a code which determines their circulation. At once structural and anti-structuralist, *Pour une critique* remains Baudrillard's most tightly argued attempt to come to terms with formalist readings of signification as a symptom of repression.

In *Le Miroir de la production* (1973), Baudrillard took leave of Marxism by arguing that its categories mirror the capitalist mode of production and are uncritically dependent upon bourgeois political economy. Marxism is a 'repressive simulation' of capitalism and therefore incapable of describing life before and after the era of production and of presenting a genuine revolutionary alternative. Baudrillard criticized structural Marxist anthropology because it projects its own categories, without critically transforming them, onto 'primitive' societies (Baudrillard prefers the even more objectionable term 'savage'). This criticism was made for the sake of his theory of primitive societies based upon 'symbolic exchange', a concept he adapted from Georges Bataille's notion of a general anti-productivist economy of expenditure and Marcel Mauss's analysis of the potlatch and the gift.

Baudrillard invests pre-capitalist societies with principles non-recoupable to any economic or semiological logic of value. Eschewing ethnographic detail, Baudrillard defines symbolic exchange as an incessant cycle of giving and receiving at odds with accumulation, scarcity, production, necessity, surplus and even survival. Accordingly, commodities and signs are produced and consumed under the illusion of 'symbolic participation'. The political economy of the sign reproduces the exploitative power relations of capitalism, themselves unwittingly mirrored by Marxism. In *Le Miroir de la production*, Baudrillard emphasizes that the respective relations of producer and product, producer and user, the producer's labour power and needs, and the product and its utility, are not autonomized in the primitive relation of symbolic reciprocity.

Baudrillard developed his concepts of simulation and symbolic exchange in *L'Echange symbolique et la mort* (1976), where he claims that a 'structural revolution of value' has abolished and surpassed Saussure's and Marx's laws of value. He explains the social and historical mutations leading to this new era of simulation in a well-known model of the three orders of simulacra. In *La Transparence du Mal* (1990), written fourteen years later, he adds a fourth order. Simulacra emerge from the annihilation, and subsequent higher order reproductions, of reference to the real in a pure structural system whose terms commutate indeterminably among themselves.

Each order has a law (natural, market, structural, fractal), a dominant form (counterfeit, production, simulation, proliferation), displays certain semiotic features (arbitrariness, seriality, codification, viral metonymy) and, despite Baudrillard's general critique of systems of value, suggests the successive predominance of different types of semiotic processes (corrupt symbol, icon, linguistic sign, index).

The sure and referential symbols of an endogamous society were corrupted by the emergence in the Renaissance of arbitrary signs freed from their referential obligation. These exogamous signs counterfeited an extra-systemic referent as they played together 'democratically'. With the Industrial Revolution, the extermination of reference made possible the machinic replication of serial signs. These iconic simulacra of one another were dull, repetitive and operational. In the post-Industrial era of simulation, mechanical reproduction gave way to a universal semiotic operating according to the metaphysical models of the code. Conceived in terms of their reproducibility, and given the impertinence of the referent, the signs of this order are simulations of second order iconic simulacra. Today, Baudrillard adds, a fourth fractal order has emerged. The simulation of the simulation of reference has imploded into an uncontrollable metonymic and 'viral' proliferation in all directions to infinity. Promiscuity reigns in an unstable condition of transsignification and transversal contamination which erases all distinctions and differences. Baudrillard exploits Benoit Mandelbrot's concept of the fractal and concepts from biology but without, he thinks, transposing them from their disciplines to his description of the fourth order's 'Xerox degree of culture', because they too are subject to universal commutation.

In *L'Echange symbolique* Baudrillard also criticized – in order to reclaim in a refigured form – Freud's idea of wit, linguistic interpretations of Saussure's anagrams and, most controversially, the fetishistic disjunction of life/death through symbolic exchange. His goal was to reclaim death from its 'social exile', making it a condition of social being in a reciprocal symbolic relation between the living and the dead. No longer an end nor an individual fatality mourned through melancholy, death is a 'gift' received from the cultural Thanatos system which must be returned to it as a radical 'counter-gift' if death is to become a symbolic act breaking the system's control over it.

In *L'Effet Beaubourg* and *A l'ombre des majorités silencieuses*, two short books published in 1977 and 1978, Baudrillard elaborated further symbolic counter-gifts based upon the potlatch-like behaviour of the masses. They return the gifts of modern culture and the simulations of the social by bringing their critical mass to bear upon Beaubourg and by the pathological manipulation and sumptuary hyperconsumption of signs. During this period, Baudrillard turned his critical concepts of symbolic reversibility and cancellation against Michel Foucault's analyses of power and sexuality in *Oublier Foucault* (1977a).

Baudrillard gave symbolic exchange a new face in *De la séduction* (1979), although the principle of seduction retained all the features he had invested in the radical alterity of primitive societies. Seduction is still recoverable today despite being transfigured and simulated in a universe incommensurable with the primitive world. Seduction is symbolically effective because it replaces production and challenges 'representative signs' bound to transcendent meanings by means of 'ritual signs' establishing symbolic pacts. Free from the dictates of an abstract digital code, these signs bind themselves together so strongly that their 'senseless unfolding' leaves no room for meaning. Seduction is an agonistic, non-diacritical, anti-semiological principle.

Baudrillard renewed his interest in objects in *Les Stratégies fatales* (1983) after which he has published mostly sociological diaries (*Amérique* (1986), *Cool Memories I & II* (1987a and1990a), *La Guerre du golfe n'a pas eu lieu* (1991)) and essays on contemporary trends in social and political theory (*L'Illusion de la fin* (1992)). In delineating all the senses of 'fatality', Baudrillard theorized a world of wily objects potentiating their passions, fulfilling their destinies and thwarting the subject's will to know them. Baudrillard's theoretical debts to the theatres of Antonin Artaud and Alfred Jarry are much in evidence here in the cruel 'revenge of things' and the 'pataphysical delicacy' of a world he thinks must be seen in the place of the traditional one at whose centre subjectivity once stood.

Baudrillard's concern with a postmodern world of simulacra uncontrollably hyperrealizing themselves has manifested itself in his equally extreme style of theorizing. His guiding principle that only a response equal to or greater than the message issued by the system can in theory effectively challenge it, has been especially influential among art critics and critical theorists. Baudrillard's long-standing critical engagement with signs has been, however, insufficiently analyzed hitherto, although therein lie his most perspicacious and disputatious claims to date. His contributions to poststructuralism are, in fact, best understood in this context.

It may appear strange to locate Baudrillard's work in relation to poststructuralism because it has been labelled 'postmodern' by the first wave of North American readers. Recently, however, the label has begun to peel with the demonstration of the contradictions of its initial application as well as with the clarification of Baudrillard's explicit struggle against postmodernism. Baudrillard is not complicitous with the depthless and soft ideologies of late capitalism. He theorizes from the radical perspective of the symbolic. One should not confuse his effort to render the genesis and the condition of contemporary society (metropolitan and Western to be sure) in the stages of his well-known model of simulation with capitulation.[3] Baudrillard is not an advocate of the 'dead sign' and 'semiological implosion'.

Rather, if one understands postmodernity in terms of this abject semiotic condition, then Baudrillard is an anti-semiological and an anti-postmodern thinker, with the proviso that the two concepts are not identical.

Semiotically minded thinkers have on the whole shown little interest in Baudrillard's work. I am not assuming that they should 'know their enemy' and may come to do so by reading Baudrillard. After all, Baudrillard's battle cry *circa* 1972 that *'les signes doivent brûler'* did not endear him to semioticians. His anti-semiological arguments and insistence that symbolic exchange has nothing to do with signs does, however, clarify theoretical transitions and conflicts of interpretation central to an appreciation of the complexity of the ongoing issues raised by Saussure and his French readers. In the decade from 1964 to 1976, that is to say, from the publication of Roland Barthes's *Eléments de sémiologie* to Baudrillard's *L'Echange symbolique*, the divide between semiology and poststructuralism broke under the pressure of critical practices which sought to dismantle the structure of the sign in the institutional settings of structural interpretation, whether they were Marxist, psychoanalytic, anthropological, linguistic, etc. Despite all this, my reading does not tell the story of Baudrillard's Saussure, as opposed to a presentation of Baudrillard's Marx; neither does my analysis of Baudrillard's Saussure supplement the much covered ground of his readings of Marx. On the contrary, I explore in some detail the homology between the sign and the commodity in the context of Baudrillard's separation of systems of value from the symbolic domain by means of several different kinds of semiological bars. This exploration does not ask after the ways in which Baudrillard has misunderstood Marx, but instead concerns itself with the ways he has had to read Marx and semiology in order to produce a homology within a structural analysis which is also deconstructable from the perspective of the symbolic. In addition, Baudrillard does not reduce Saussure to his structural linguistics. He reads Saussure's concept of the anagram against the so-called 'structural' Saussure. Further, this does not mean that he adopts Saussure's perspective on the anagram. On the contrary, Baudrillard finds in this concept a radical element which Saussure could not have seen.

The semiotic credos which inform my approach may be described in the following ways. My semiotic perspective develops a dimension of Baudrillard's work well known to all of his readers. His encounters with the sign have been duly noted in the expositions of his writings as well as in the studies of his engagements with Marxism, but these notes have not burgeoned into a full scale analysis. My semiotics is ecumenical in that I pay close attention to the work of sign types in Baudrillard's descriptions of the four stages of value in his model of simulation. I also touch upon the semiotic investigations of C.S. Peirce and the Prague School. This general semiotic perspective finds in Baudrillard's theorizing, despite the fact that it is imbued with uses of and attacks on semiolinguistics, several of the semiotic relations included in Peirce's taxonomy. Although Baudrillard criticizes the kind of sign found in the linguistic tradition, he employs in quite explicit ways processes which are semiotic in a Peircean sense. To read Baudrillard semiotically is to recognize this tension at the heart of his theorizing. This tension is irreducible to the distinction between semiology and semiotics, that is to say, between an attack on Saussure and support for Peirce. For in Baudrillard's oeuvre there is no explicit recognition of Peirce. There is, however, both a use and abuse of semiology. Peirce is not included in my work simply for the sake of appearances, nor in order to explain away appearances. My inclusion of sign types and processes from Peirce's system highlights and problematizes Baudrillard's adherence to certain features and suppositions of the tradition of Euro-semiology even as he struggled against it. I reject, however, the contention that Peirce's semiotics is superior to Euro-semiology because Peirce believed in the existence of referents. As far as this claim goes, it is maintained that since Euro-semiology does not believe in the referent it is false, as false as a radically textualist postion would be in discourse analysis. While this continues to be an unfortunate sore point between some ungenerous Greimassians and Peirceans, for instance, the former's response to the effect that the existence of the referent is not pertinent in semio-structural analysis in no way throws the game in favour of the latter. It would be crudely reductive to treat Peirce's complex conception of the object in semiosis as a referent. In fact, such reductionism adds nothing to the debates concerning the so-called 'metaphysical' status of the referent in relation to the kinds of claims one may want to make about simulation.

Every reader of Baudrillard must at some point ask themselves the following twofold question: what is the symbolic and how does it function? It does not suffice to claim that this concept has been replaced in Baudrillard's so-called 'later' writings by seduction, for instance. Not only is the matter of (re)placement crucial from a critical perspective, but the symbolic has taken numerous forms over the course of Baudrillard's theorizing.

In Baudrillard's writings, the semiotic and the symbolic are normally at odds with one another (there is one exception to this general rule). The orders of simulacra serve as a reminder that the symbolic has passed into the semiotic, thus gaining a kind of fatal independence from the concrete relationship between persons it once, for Baudrillard, so transparently sealed. The symbolic was once a sure sign: transparent, motivated, presimulacral, expressing an obligatory, reciprocal and antagonistic relationship. Baudrillard shifts the symbolic from its association with archaic societies into the cold, abstract and opaque world of codes. Symbolic relations are said by Baudrillard to be 'primitive' and 'cruel' (these terms, he recognizes, flirt dangerously with stereotypes, but he retains them for the sake of their power to upset). The symbolic inspires in him a flood of cool memories ('cool' in Marshall McLuhan's sense of participatory and 'tribal') about this origin – not to which he wants contemporary Western societies to return, but in virtue of which he evokes a revolutionary anthropology with sufficent symbolic violence to destroy the prevailing semiocracy, at least in theory.

By far the most common figure of the symbolic in relation to the semiotic in Baudrillard's writings is that of its break and entry into the latter. The symbolic breaks through the semiotic. Nothing in principle can re-fuse the signifiers and the signifieds after the symbolic has opened a crack in them. If the result of this break and entry is that signs will have burned, one wonders whether it is possible to signify what one means by the symbolic.

Baudrillard critically attacks signs and structures in order to ameliorate the condition of the symbolic in a world of simulacra and autonomized relations. In addition to such attacks, but closely related to them, one also finds a series of weak tactics in support of the symbolic running through Baudrillard's work. Such textual banditti infest and destabilize magisterial systems.

Weak strokes, as opposed to strong, vigorous and robust blows, cancel the great biological 'power bar' between life/death by opening the way to a non-diacritical 'unsplit world' or an asemiological, barless imaginary world of symbolic exchanges unchecked by the dichotomania of structural systems. Although Baudrillard attempts to maintain a position of positive weakness so that he neither falls back upon the strength of that which he struggles against (the semiotic, or the economic), nor slips into a kind of mysticism regarding the post-signifying nature of the symbolic (what may be called a proto-new-age, oceanic feeling about communication after signs), his reliance on the idea of agonistic reciprocity forces him to oscillate between both poles of the disjunction, thus making a variety of strong and mystical claims. Indeed, in the realm of the weak, the strongest (rather than the strong) are dead. If one's goal is to overcome the system which disbars the dead from the living by means of the 'power bar' between life/death, one is best on the side of the dead – Baudrillard's clever observation is well taken that in the West it is not normal to be dead. In the agonistic relation of reciprocity which is symbolic exchange, one must at some point in the reciprocal relation take the position of death, having broken through the bar in a way which defies 'normality' and cannot be easily stripped of its symbolic attributes by the semiocrats who erect bars between all of the dichotomies which can make life a living death. The goal is, of course, not to die in a revolutionary action, but to force the system to kill itself. Symbolic violence against the system requires that the principle of its own power (the impossibility of response and retaliation) must be turned against it, even if the system is not beholden to an archaic symbolic relation. The counter-gift of death functions symbolically by trapping the system in the obligatory circuit of returning this counter-gift in kind or with interest: 'Scorpinization of the system encircled by the challenge of death. For the thing to which it is summoned to respond, under the pain of losing face, can be obviously only death. It is necessary that the system commit suicide in response to the increased challenge of death and suicide' (Baudrillard, 1976: 64). Baudrillard's textual imaginary of the strength of a symbolic or ritual death is closely tied to fictional notions from the 'science' of imaginary solutions which have also inspired pataphysical bar games. What Baudrillard does not explain is how the system will be made to suffer the weight of the symbolic obligation and give up its will to think in terms of simulated reciprocity and contractual relations at best, and more commonly in the interest of isolated, autonomous poles of social networks of communication.

'Wh   ; *fait bander*], theoreticians . . . is
the (... ...stinct', Jean-François Lyotard has
prov   ....itten (Lyotard, 1975: 115). Lyotard describes the
erection of a disjunctive bar whose function is to draw and to
maintain critical distinctions. This bar at once invokes a dis- and
a con-junction, Lyotard thinks, 'since in order to demarcate this
side from that, one must be on both sides'. One must work the
bar from both sides, the two sides (at least) which hold it up.

Such bawdy talk, in drawing attention to itself, to its mono-
phallo-erotism, has given rise to a power play at which Jane
Gallop has pointed with reference to Jacques Lacan's placement
of the signifier over the signified, the former thus exercising
power over the latter (*avoir sur barre*) (Gallop, 1985: 120). It is,
however, the bar which will concern me here because it is
powerful, a power bar, as Baudrillard has described it in
L'Echange symbolique (1976: 201): 'When one says that power *tient
la barre*, this is not a metaphor: it *is* this bar between life and
death, this decree which interrupts the exchange of life and
death, this tollgate and this control between the two banks'. The
bar represses death. It is invested with the social power to do so;
tenir la barre means to take control, to take the helm. The power
bar between life and death is the archetype, Baudrillard maintains, of all the disjunctions which constitute the code. Life and
death are reunited when there is no bar whose power lies in its
ability to block an ineluctable relation in which there is an
incessant obligation to give, to receive and to return, and thus to
enter into a symbolic communion. Baudrillard too will work
both sides of the bar. But this is not his only bar. In fact,
Baudrillard will work a number of them.

A certain bar will at first prove to be too weak to differentiate the domain of value from the field of non-value; this bar of implication (*la barre d'implication logique formelle*), that is to say, will not suffice. Therefore, Baudrillard will require a second, more solid bar of radical exclusion (*la barre d'exclusion radicale*). Even so, Baudrillard will need to straddle this strong bar so that he may develop critically and theoretically the concepts which it separates. The strong bar is not the power bar, although it is powerful. The strong bar is not an archetype. I am a little further along the bar at 'Archie's Place' than Paul de Man was when he joked about archie debunker's bowling shoes.

The bar games which Baudrillard plays in his essay 'Pour une théorie générale' in *Pour une critique* cannot contribute to a general theory since there is, he admits, 'no organizing theory' behind them. But the use of *pour* marks general theory as a destination, and also indicates that the central issues through which one moves are exchange and equivalence. There is, despite Baudrillard's protests, a general theory of symbolic exchange supported by anti-semiological bar games in his work. The bar in question is the one in semiological and structural analysis which holds basic concepts and relations together and keeps them apart (i.e. the bar between the signifier and the signified, and the slanted bar between this/that). One plays a game with the bar in order to reconfigure the sign and reshape structural relations. The goal of the game is, in general, to destroy the sign, and to pass through 'structure' into a more radical realm. But the important point is that one gets into the game – just as one ultimately puts an end to the game – by hanging around the bar.

'Pour une théorie générale' has been largely ignored by readers of Baudrillard save Jean-Claude Giradin (1974). Giradin responds favourably to Baudrillard's homology between the commodity and the sign and proposes a further homological relation between labour and the signifier and wages and the signified, a relation which, he believes, completes Baudrillard's formulation but in a less abstract way. Although Mark Poster includes this short chapter in his *Jean Baudrillard: Selected Writings* (Baudrillard, 1988a), he mentions only in passing the 'systematicness' of the essays as a whole in *Pour une critique*. Even those critics such as Poster (1981) and Robert D'Amico (1981) who have analyzed with some care Baudrillard's homology between the sign and the commodity share the dual goals of revealing his misunderstandings of Marx's critique of political economy and discrediting semiology. Within this approach to Baudrillard, the charges of semiotic objectivism, idealism, and even fetishism predictably levelled at Baudrillard unfortunately dissuade one from an analysis of his stormy encounters with semiology and structuralism (Kellner, 1989). The refrain that Baudrillard has a 'critical semiology' has not entailed the investigation of the pseudo-algebraic formulations of 'Pour une théorie générale', which are classically structuralist in the sense that they demonstrate formal similarities or homologous relations among different key concepts in the domain of value, *and* explicitly semiological in that they reveal the combinatorial principles which govern this domain as a code. Bar games are central operators in Baudrillard's project. Baudrillard's structuralist and semiological operations articulate the tradition in which he works, while his bar games demonstrate his struggle to free himself from it. Gane (1991: 83–5) devotes several pages to what he calls Baudrillard's 'programme of 1972' and perspicaciously isolates a dilemma in his thinking. The radical bar of exclusion commits Baudrillard to, as Gane puts it, 'an unbridgeable gap between exchange value and symbolic exchange', even though certain practices (i.e. sharing wine) may involve 'a complex interweaving of symbolic exchange and sign consumption' (Gane, 1991: 84). But Baudrillard's commitment to the externality of symbolic exchange does not permit this interweaving, Gane laments, and it requires him to elaborate a theory of the symbolic and to join in the widespread poststructuralist critique of the sign, about which Gane says little. Indeed, the concept of interweaving substitutes Baudrillardian ambivalence for ambiguity and invests symbolic obligation and circulation with the consumption of differences (the range of 1989 Bordeaux). Conviviality is no substitute for agonistic relations.

Pour une critique, Baudrillard's third book, continued his earlier structural analyses of the system of object-signs and the ideological genesis of needs in consumer society, but with a critical turn towards his methods of analysis. Its eleven essays contain key hypotheses on the limits of structuralist method and the metaphysical faults of Marxian political economy, semiology and communication theory. It will be instructive, for my purposes, to review the text as a whole before concentrating on what I call Baudrillard's 'table of conversions'.

Pour une critique is Baudrillard's most systematic book to date because it moves toward a general theory summarized in a table of conversions between Marxian political economy and semiology. Guided by his elaboration of the homological structuration of the commodity and the sign, whose mutation into an 'object form' means ultimately that both are 'abolished as specific determinations' in what he calls *semiurgic* society, the table formalizes conversions and reconversions among four logics of value; each logic has its own operational principle, its own specific determinations, and assumes different forms. The table is interpreted in three clusters: production/consumption, transfiguration and, most importantly, transgression.

The first cluster expresses the mutual dependence of the processes of production and consumption in classical and Marxist political economy. The second group entails the systematic identity of material and sign production in virtue of Baudrillard's equation of the commodity and the sign (the structural relation of implication between economic exchange value over use value equals that of the signifier over the signified, hence economic exchange is to the signifier as use value is to the signified). The determinations and principles of use value and economic exchange value are redefined by the coded differential positions and rules of combination by which object-signs are manipulated for different kinds of profit (social, aesthetic, etc.). The conversions of transgression indicate the passage from the domain of economic and semiological value to the symbolic, while the reconversions describe the reductive revaluing of symbolic exchange through its reinstrumentalization as a commodity or a sign.

Baudrillard includes symbolic exchange among the other theories of value in order to define general political economy, although it stands 'beyond' all value. Symbolic exchange is virulently anti-semiological and in the wake of its violent 'effraction' (break and entry) into the sanctuary of value by means of revolutionary consumptive practices, 'signs must burn'. Baudrillard analyzes the ideological process which defines the contemporary social order in terms of the 'semiological reduction' of symbolic relations based upon a transparent, concrete, agonistic, ambivalent and obligatory pact between persons sealed by an absolutely singular symbol (a wedding ring and other ritual objects). When the symbol is reified as a sign whose value emanates from the system, its ambivalence becomes structural equivalence, rendering social relations of production and consumption abstract and opaque. The symbolic is Baudrillard's revolutionary anthropological antidote to the political economy of the sign, and it challenges signs from the perspective of what they attempt to expel and annihilate.

Central to Baudrillard's critique is his insight into structural form revealed through the homology between the commodity and the sign. Exchange value and the signifier have a 'strategic value' greater than the 'tactical value' of use value and the signified. Binary oppositive structuration is never symmetrical since each antecedent term produces its own 'alibi' as its consequent term. Use value and the signified are 'effects' or 'simulation models' of their antecedent terms. They are produced respectively by Marx's analysis of commodity fetishism in terms of exchange value alone, while semio-linguistics privileges the signifier as its principle of circulation and regulated interplay. If for Marx use values were incomparable and thus not implicated in the abstract logic of equivalence of exchange value, for Baudrillard they have a specific code of their own, especially in relation to symbols. Similarly, Baudrillard's signified–referent lacks the metaphysical status and autonomy afforded to it in the tripartite division of signifier–signified–referent, precisely because it does not exist beyond the shadow of signification.

Baudrillard theorizes that the exclusion of the referent in Saussure's separation of the sign (signifier–signified) from the world entails a 'metaphysical representation of the referent'. Baudrillard demonstrates this by criticizing Emile Benveniste's relocation of the arbitrariness of the signifier–signified relation between that of the sign (signifier–signified) and the referent. This relocation is possible only by reviving the sign's initial separation from the referent and by repairing it with what Baudrillard calls the 'supernatural' provision of motivation (it matters little whether motivation is affirmed or denied). Motivation parallels the concept of need in political economy. Need is a function of the capitalist system, just as motivation is a function of the sign system.

Baudrillard then applies his critique to the Left's faith in revolutionary praxis to effect a critical reversal of the media by liberating its 'fundamentally egalitarian' nature perverted by capitalism. The Left fails to analyze the 'ideological matrix that communication theory embraces' and thus accepts uncritically a theory which simulates a genuine exchange based on personal and mutual responsibility. He further demonstrates these shortcomings by focusing on Roman Jakobson's model of communication.

Baudrillard hypothesizes that agency has passed into the code which terrorizes communication by positioning the sender and receiver in an 'abstract separateness' and privileging the sender. Jakobson's phatic function in his model of communication, for instance, is evidence for Baudrillard of the distance between the poles and a critical fiction akin to motivation. Jakobson's model reproduces social relations based upon the power of the media to give what cannot be returned except by the simulacral detour of a response (a poll or referendum). Under the guise of admitting ambiguity and even polyvocality, the model excludes an ambivalent exchange between persons. Baudrillard claims that it is the code which speaks since it dictates the unidirectional passage of information and guarantees the legibility and univocality of the message. The model is therefore ideological rather than scientific and objective. I will return in detail to these themes in the following chapters.

THE TABLE OF CONVERSIONS

The 'general conversion table' of all values which unfolds in Baudrillard's essay is a 'combinatory exploration' rather than a rigorous arrangement of equivalent values. By the same token, Baudrillard plays on the idea of a conversion table such as weights and measures in which British, American and metric equivalents are given together with the conversion factors and formulae; the table in addition suggests a translation-conversion in computer technology from one code/language to another. The codes in question consist of terms from Marxian political economy and semiology. What is ironic is that this so-called conversion table will also be used to express the limits of convertibility at the horizon of a generalized structural law of value, beyond which lies symbolic exchange. The table of conversions is itself inconvertible. The components of Baudrillard's computation towards a general theory may be expressed in the Table 1, consisting of four columns.

Table 1 Logics of value

Use value (UV)	Economic exchange value (EcEV)	Sign exchange value (SgEV)	Symbolic exchange (SbE)
1. UV–EcEV	4. EcEV–UV	7. SgEV–UV	10. SbE–UV
2. UV–SgEV	5. EcEV–SgEV	8. SgEV–EcEV	11. SbE–EcEV
3. UV–SbE	6. EcEV–SbE	9. SgEV–SbE	12. SbE–SgEV

The horizontal dash is a mark of the transit from one domain to another, as Baudrillard explains (1972: 145). For each of the antecedent terms in the twelve correlations, transit to the consequent term takes the form of a conversion, the reconversion of which is not accomplished along the same line but rather, takes place with respect to a correlation which presents the same terms flanking another dash of transit in reverse order under a different logic. This dash is straight, and thus goes only one way at a given time. The proliferation of dashes and correlations is necessary in order to illustrate the multiple transits between the logics.

The table consists of three clusters of conversions/ reconversions:

Production–Consumption	Transfiguration	Transgression
C1 – R4	C2 – R7	C3 – R10
	C5 – R8	C6 – R11
		C9 – R12

Each of the four columns of the logics of value has an operative principle (utility, equivalence, difference, ambivalence); each has its own determinations (functional, commercial, structural, psychical); and each takes a different object form (instrument, commodity, sign and symbol). The three clusters, about which Baudrillard says surprisingly little, although his interest comes to be focused on transgression, will be distilled into two areas within a single domain through the homology between political economy and semiology. The fourth column represents the exception to the rules of conversion and reconversion.

The first grouping (C1 – R4) expresses the mutual dependency of the processes of production and consumption. The production of consumption (production of EcEV, conversion of

UV–EcEV) and the consumption of a commodity which consummates the process of production (reconversion of EcEV–UV in the purchase of a commodity) are the two non-identical moments of the cycle of political economy (Marx, 1973: 90–4). Production is the dominant moment of the cycle and it is unconsumable; consumption is a moment of production and distribution is a product of production.

There is no strict linguistic equivalent for distribution in this conversion. One can imagine, however, that syntagmatic and associative relations are distributive mechanisms. Both the order of succession and familial clustering, with their respective fixed and unfixed numbers of elements, result from the movement of elements in different kinds of relations along the line of syntagms structured oppositionally with one another within language, and from the concatenation of terms according to memory. Moreover, this transit zone of classical and Marxist political economy does not take into account the political economy of the sign. A political economy of the sign presumes to have analyzed the structural logic of the commodity and to have abolished its specificity as a determinant of social relations in the object form. This so-called political economy is general insofar as: (1) It considers the demonstration of the logical affinity between the commodity form and the sign form to be sufficient to describe an entire domain of value. No attempt is made to express the formal (semiological) equivalents of the definite interrelations of the different moments of production, consumption, distribution and exchange. (2) If the commodity form and the sign form are abolished as specific determinants, the analysis relies on a specific form of sign (Saussurean) with which to generalize monosemiologically about an entire domain; that is to say, this form of sign is always only specific to a particular semiological order and theory. Baudrillard at no point makes this clear.

The second cluster (C2 – R7; C5 – R8) marks the conversion of UV into SgEV and back again, as well as the conversion of EcEV into SgEV and vice versa; at this level of analysis, the 'homological structuration' of the commodity and the Saussurean sign remain implicit. These correlations take place under the principle of transfiguration (Baudrillard, 1972: 146).

Marx's unforgettable phrase 'all that is solid melts into air' describes well, when read against itself, the passage from UV–

SgEV. More precisely, in *Capital I*, one finds that 'the utility of a thing makes it a use-value. But this utility is not a thing of air' (Marx, 1954: 44). Utility is solid; it is definite, physically grounded in a commodity, and it contains useful labour, etc. But in this atmospherics, air is also a use value without value since it contains no human labour. What is air? Strange airs arise from the vaporization of use value and they perfuse the entire range in which utility is destroyed in the name of the consumption of differences (it is not that one consumes a vial of *l'air de la mer*, but that one thereby distinguishes oneself from those who prefer *l'air de la campagne*).

The reconversion of SgEV into UV suggests that one lives and indeed breathes in a system which produces culturally signifi- cant differences. One experiences the consumption of certain of these differences (those which reach one by means of specific targetting practices) both as the satisfaction of a need and as a utility of sorts. This sense of utility, which is marked as meta- functional and metaphysical by Baudrillard, is associated with several practices of consumption by means of which one makes a profit of sorts (i.e. socially, professionally, personally, aesthetically).

Baudrillard describes, in the manner of Thorstein Veblen (1953), several practices of consumption (Baudrillard, 1970: 129–30; 1972: 145–6). To the logic of conspicuous consumption (EcEV–SgEV understood as a process of consumption), Baudrillard adds the practice of inconspicuous consumption, or voluntary deprivation. The obverse of conspicuous consump- tion, then, is underconsumption, a strategy of personalization by indistinction. This practice may be cast in either economic or cultural terms (EcEV–SgEV): one may possess the economic means to consume the trappings of underconsumption, whether these are eco-services or the novelties of downscaling (in some monied circles it is *chic* to appear to be less wealthy); the conspicuous absence of the marked tokens of under- consumption ('organic', 'recycled') as sumptuary value, has its own meanings and privileges (from minimalist to anarchic to the pretension of having no pretensions). The reconversion of these 'have nots' as sign values into EcEV is evident in the capital and cultural monopolies in the area of health food, green products, men's beauty aids – not tested on animals! Here, green purity is an expensive semiotic privilege. Underconsumption is not to be confused with unproductive consumption which is a form of conspicuous idleness.

The three conversions of transgression (UV–SbE; EcEV–SbE; SgEV–SbE) indicate the passage from the domain of value (economic and semiological) to the symbolic. The parallel reconversions (SbE–UV; SbE–EcEV; SbE–SgEV) describe the reductive re-valuation of the symbolic in terms of functional, commercial and structural determinations. In all three reconversions, the symbolic collapses in what is for Baudrillard a single process: its reinstrumentalization as a commodity or a sign.

Symbolic exchange is the other side of political economy. One crosses over to it from use value, exchange value and sign value by means of a symbolic *consumation* which liquidates value (*consumation* is a way through *consumativité*). During this passage, hyperconsumption replaces underconsumption. That is to say, if the hypersimulative conformity and the hyperlogic outlined in *A l'ombre des majorités silencieuses* and *L'Effet Beaubourg* may be situated along the way of Baudrillard's general theory, it is in the transitional zone where structure ends and the so-called potlatch begins.

The masses, Baudrillard argues, 'have turned consumption into a dimension of status and prestige, of useless oneupmanship or simulation, of potlatch which has surpassed use value in every way' (Baudrillard, 1978: 49). The term 'potlatch' designates that the masses have completed the passage from UV–SbE since this term is a marker of the symbolic. The masses do not respect any notion of 'needs'. Yet, if they can be said to 'block the economy', they do so, Baudrillard insists, by setting 'sign value against use value', not to the profit of exchange value as one might think – it is difficult, contrary to Baudrillard, to claim otherwise given the matters of frenzied spending and the (ab)use of services – but in a hypersimulation of sign value, a pathological manipulation which overcomes and upends the differential relations of the sign system.

In his 'Essai sur le don', Marcel Mauss reserved the concept of potlatch for 'total prestations of the agonistic type' in Melanesian and Pacific Northwest American indigenous cultures (Mauss, 1973: 153). By analogy, then, and in a manner which exhausts neither Baudrillard's use of the concept nor Mauss's distinctions between the practices of several tribal societies, the masses consume chaotically and do so presumably without satisfying any individual's needs. This potlatch-like behaviour parallels the sumptuary destruction of riches through the intermediary figure of the chief under the principles of rivalry and antagonism. This kind of behaviour issues a challenge to a rival clan *and* to value. In general, Baudrillard combines concepts borrowed from Mauss with Georges Bataille's (1933) reading of Mauss. Neither Bataille nor Baudrillard are interested in drawing subtle anthropological distinctions. The Baudrillardian potlatch emphasizes even in its most banal adjectival instances the idea of *obligation* (a gift is returned in kind or with interest because of the fear of the loss of mana), thus highlighting Mauss's understanding of the gift as a spiritual mechanism; for his part, Bataille emphasized the power of *loss* in his notion of expenditure or purely sumptuary destruction. Baudrillard in turn treats loss as a particular kind of ceremonial event, namely, death. In fact, the burning of signs may be conceived of in this way as a postmodern ceremony which clears the way for a greater understanding of symbolic exchange and death.

In 'Vers une critique de l'économie politique du signe' in *Pour une critique*, Baudrillard poses the problem of what can be signed (named, inscribed) after one has made an anti-semiological gesture in favour of the symbolic:

> And it is the symbolic which continues to haunt the sign, to dismantle the formal correlation of signifier and signified. But the symbolic, which is in its virtuality of meaning subversive of the sign, cannot be named except by allusion, by *effraction*, because signification, which names everything after itself, only speaks of value, and the symbolic is not value.
>
> (Baudrillard, 1972: 196)

The symbolic is not barred by the Lacanian bar. It does not return, like the repressed, since it has never had a place in the territory of the sign. Signification bars the symbolic. The latter breaks the law of the sign; it loosens the bar and tears the sign apart. The symbolic is an *effractor*, that which breaks through, a burglar if you like. The judicial language of *effraction*, which may be translated as 'break and enter', helps one to understand Baudrillard's reading of the behaviour of the masses at Beaubourg. The masses rifle through the exhibits, finger the cultural merchandise, and spirit away whatever valuables they find; they are 'burglars' who grab, plunder, dismantle and even 'kidnap'. These are the sorts of activities which manifest and enhance their power and prestige in spite of the passivity and stupidity often accorded them.

In the case of Beaubourg, the masses engage in an antagonistic display, neither by burning it down nor by protesting/contesting its existence, but simply by visiting it (Baudrillard, 1977: 34). They bring their weight to bear upon the structure: mass critique is critical mass. The masses enter Beaubourg in the manner of the symbolic, by *effraction*. Baudrillard writes:

> They [organizers, artists, and intellectuals, among whom Baudrillard must be counted] never expected this active, destructive fascination, a brutal and original response to the gift of an incomprehensible culture, an attraction which has all the features of an effraction and the violation of a sanctuary.
> (Baudrillard, 1977: 37)

The masses are the undoing of Beaubourg, in the same way as the symbolic undoes the sign. Like the symbolic, the masses are figured as effractors, even though they do not enter the building after hours (but the street action in the plaza and the parking lot never stops). Baudrillard is not suggesting that the symbolic rips out the *points de capiton* along the bar in order to slip surreptitiously into signification. No, it sticks itself in the face of high culture. The masses, then, use their weight to deliver a symbolic counter-gift to the purveyors of modernist art.

Baudrillard's use of the concepts of the semiotic and the symbolic may be related to Julia Kristeva's analysis of these concepts' interdependence in her theoretical work. In 'From One Identity To An Other', a paper which Kristeva originally presented in a seminar organized by Jean-Marie Benoist in 1975, the semiotic disposition to heterogeneousness 'unsettles' the homogeneous transparency of the symbolic. Benoist has used the word *effraction*, by which he means a 'forcible entry', to render the resurfacing of the semiotic (the instinctual drives of a semiotic body oriented toward the mother; carnivalesque poetic language, etc.) in the symbolic (the paternal, legalistic regime of the transcendental analysis of signifying and predicative operations) (Kristeva, 1980: 146; Benoist, 1978: 167). Kristeva's semiotic resembles Baudrillard's symbolic, while her conception of the symbolic parallels his semiological domain. Indeed, the manner in which the semiotic and the symbolic break through and disrupt their respective repressive and legal dominions puts an emphasis on the break, its disruptive, radical and even 'criminal' nature. This is a crossing far removed from Lacan's stroking of the bar, *le franchissement de la barre*. The fundamental difference between Kristeva and Baudrillard on this point is that with Kristeva the semiotic and the symbolic dispositions are in 'permanent contradiction' and are thus 'inseparable'. For Baudrillard, the goal of the symbolic is to destroy the semiologic and in some sense replace it. Lyotard (1974: 128–32) has criticized Baudrillard on precisely this point.

While Kristeva's semiotic economies are subject to the 'biophysiological and sociohistorical constraints' of individuals and the tendency to establish symbolic-like 'signifiying apparatuses', Baudrillard thinks that his symbolic is not inscribed in or by the semiologic. His so-called radical anthropology has been treated by Robert Hefner as both 'romantic' and 'ethnographically fantastic' (Hefner, 1977: 111). It is, in anti-semiological terms, an asignifying imaginary which rests upon the dichotomy of the ambiguity of semiology and the ambivalence of the symbolic; the latter is the privileged replacement.

The second phase of 'Pour une théorie générale' attempts to demonstrate that SbE is a heterogeneous factor without a place in the homogeneous domain of value. By means of two equations which ultimately prove to be incoherent, Baudrillard 'advances', as he puts it, from the 'mechanical combinatory of values' to the demonstration of homological equivalents, at least to a point. These equations fail the test of logical affinity along their vertical and horizontal axes since SbE and UV are not implicated in a structural 'copulation' given: (i) both bars are *saussurienne*; and (ii) with respect to the consequent of the equation, the non-reconvertibility of the cluster of transgression:

$$\frac{SqEV}{EcEV} = \frac{SbE}{UV}$$

Whereas in this equation

$$\frac{SqEV}{SbE} = \frac{EcEV}{UV}$$

the double vertical implications express a reduction from the concrete: SbE–SgEV; UV–EcEV. SbE≠UV since the former stands alone, incommensurable, and establishes in its singularity, transparency and ambivalence, an ongoing obligation to give, to receive and to return between persons. Although the second phase seems to add little to our understanding of the general theory, it sets the stage for Baudrillard's explicit expression of SgEV, not as a 'global value', but in terms of the relation of its parts to the commodity. Moreover, there is an uncanny resemblance between SbE and UV in the second phase. Both SbE and UV are subject to reductions, but only to terms other than one another. From a semiotic perspective, Baudrillard's much commented upon contentious interpretation of Marx's so-called claim that use values are incomparable produces a mirror effect between UV and SbE. There is, however, only one object in Baudrillard's structural deduction of a universe which is incomparable – and it is not use value. When the mirror of a certain conception of use value is broken, symbolic exchange sparkles in the fragments.

In 'Au-delà de la valeur d'usage' Baudrillard writes: 'Only the objects or categories of goods invested in the singular and personal act of symbolic exchange (the gift, the present) are strictly incomparable. The personal relation (non-economic exchange) renders them absolutely singular' (Baudrillard, 1972: 157). What Baudrillard 'found' in Marx was a complementary effect of a structural deduction which can only admit one unique element which does not acquire value in terms of differential relations in a system. But like the symbolic, use value in its purest conceptual form is 'never truly inscribed' in the domain of value (Baudrillard, 1972: 54–5); they are both said to be 'concrete' and 'particular'.

I am not claiming that this is Marx's conception of use value. It is, on the contrary, a notion which Baudrillard takes in the opposite direction from the charge that Marx naturalized needs: the imaginary of use value is SbE. Both UV and SbE contain the same promise of singularity, a promise which only SbE is permitted to keep: 'And it [UV] holds . . . the promise of a reappearance beyond the market economy, money and exchange value, in the glorious autonomy of man's simple relation to his work and to his products' (Baudrillard, 1972: 155).

Since UV is implicated in the domain of value, only SbE stands beyond the bar of radical exclusion, beyond semiology. Indeed, according to the structural logic to which I will turn in the following pages, the negation of UV leads one into a theory of SbE. A reflection on this odd couple suggests that an irony dwells at the heart of ambivalence, a concept which is also, given its relation to the symbolic, incomparable. The origins of ambivalence in *ambo* (both, pair) and *valens* (*valere*: to be strong, stout, powerful) suggest that even beyond the semiologic, through the mirror of use value, one finds a strong pair, a trace of the binary logic of the code. Burnt signs leave ashes.

The domain of general political economy (value) is expressed by the coherent (vertically and horizontally) equation:

$$\frac{EcEV}{UV} = \frac{Sr}{Sd}$$

Both bars maintain their respective terms in a structural relation. Baudrillard refers to this kind of relation as 'positive' since he claims that the bar separates such terms into a distinctive structure and 'eternalizes their [structural] separation'. While the bar guarantees the structural copulation of terms, it also conjures a phantasm of the unity of signification. It reduces and excludes ambivalence, understood as that which is irreducible to binary logic (even though, as I have shown above, there is such a logic in its Latin origin), and expels the idea of the *consumation* of meaning from the well-proportioned, well-appointed body of the Saussurean sign. If *la barre saussurienne* bars ambivalence, it is really *une barre lacanienne*: 'It [the structural/inclusive/ copulative bar] becomes the bar of repression itself, no longer that which articulates, but that which censors, and thus the place of transgression' (Baudrillard, 1972: 197, n. 1).

Even if, Baudrillard adds ironically, the bar found its 'true meaning' in the work of Lacan, he does not accede to the semio-psychoanalytic scheme of meaning. The bar may bar the symbolic, just as it barred the repressed, even though the symbolic bears no relation to the repressed and does not occupy the place of *le signifié lacanien*. Transgression should not be confused with the Lacanian crossing of the bar and the emergence of signification by means of metaphor.

In a qualifying paragraph to the same note, which did not find its way into the English translation, Baudrillard writes:

The operation of meaning and the psychoanalytic signifier have so little to do with the linguistic signifier and the operation of the sign that the use of the same terms creates insoluble misunderstandings. It is necessary to leave once and for all the terms of the signifier and signified (and others still) to their linguistic pertinence and to return, from a radical critical perspective on the linguistic economy of value, all of its antagonistic value to the symbolic as the non-place of value, the non-place of signification.

(Baudrillard, 1972: 198, n. 1)

Baudrillard's appeals to 'non-places' raise the question of his theory's collapse into a 'mystical nothingness' (the danger of which he is well aware). Until I take up this issue in greater detail in chapter 3, suffice it to say that his anti-semiological gaming is also directed at Lacan's algorithm of the sign. In *L'Echange symbolique*, Baudrillard attacks the psychoanalytic bar through the work of Octave Mannoni (1969).

The psychoanalytic conception of the sign renders equivalence problematic, but not for the benefit of ambivalence. As an ellipse, Mannoni thinks, the sign has an ellipsis of sorts in the place where Saussure found the signified. This 'empty' space comes to be filled by certain signifiers which are subject to primary processes. While Baudrillard appreciates critically the subtleties of Mannoni's work on the sign, he argues that even though the sign has been put on the couch (bar games terminable and interminable) and the meaning of the bar has changed, the architecture of the sign remains intact. According to Baudrillard, Lacanian psychoanalytic insight was restricted because it relied on the concept of the sign. One may recall a similar remark of Jacques Derrida in an interview with Kristeva: Saussure did resist the signifier/signified–body/soul analogy and even went so far as to de-substantialize phonic substance, but he still reconfirmed the metaphysical tradition by his use of the sign (*signans/signatum*) (Derrida, 1981: 18).

Baudrillard (1972: 151) displaces the bar of structural implication and simultaneously redefines it as the strong bar of radical exclusion between the domain of value and symbolic exchange:

$$\frac{EcEC}{UV} = \frac{Sr}{Sd} \, / \, SbE$$

General Political Economy / SbE

This bar flips and settles in between the antecedent of critique and the consequent of theory. Baudrillard continues: 'A critique of general political economy (or a critical theory of value) and a theory of symbolic exchange are one and the same thing. It is the basis of a revolutionary *anthropology*' (1972: 151). As I indicated at the beginning of this section, this anthropology plays a bar game with the foundational power bar. But like the power bar, the strong bar too must be lifted so that symbolic exchange may assume its place, having overwhelmed political economy and signs.

Since the power bar is the archetype of all the disjunctions which found the simulative structure of the real, it is the work of the symbolic to disbar it; to erase the bar is to end, at least in the asemiotic imaginary towards which the anti-semiological gaming points, the disjunctive code, revealing that the real was only an effect of multiple disjuncts (the referential/real is an effect of the sign just as UV is said to be an effect of EcEV). In any structural and arbitrary separation of two terms, the consequent term serves to found the principle of reality, even though it is for Baudrillard only the imaginary of the antecedent and vice versa (Baudrillard, 1976: 205–6). The strong bar is lifted so as to reveal the unity of critique and theory in the development of an anthropology which is built upon elementary bar games.

BAR GAINS: NEITHER SAUSSURE NOR LACAN

Poststructuralist bar games renovate the bar of the Saussurean sign and any bar of difference by weakening and/or enhancing or at least tinkering with its form and function: the bar spins, splits, turns, drifts, flies away; it is crossed, cut, stroked, etc. These games are standard exercises, compulsory figures really, in poststructuralist critical routines. The most well-known bar game is the critique of the signifier. It is important to note that this critique does not always take an anti-semiotic form; that is, the critique of the semiological sign may not include Peircean signs.

The first requirement of a Baudrillardian theory of bar games is a visit to Saussure's bar. For *la barre* in question is first and foremost the one found inside of the Saussurean sign between the signifier and the signifed. Of course, during the gaming I also come across little rods (virgules, slashes, slants) and separatrices such as dashes (swung and straight). This is not a typology so much as a preliminary indication of the kinds of objects upon which poststructuralist thinkers perform their *exercises à la barre*.

To be sure, the two-sided sign may be the bar's keeper, but not all bars belong to the sign, even though they do articulate at least two sides. The sign is a symbol of a certain kind of target: a theoretical edifice which is built out of the mortar of value, that is, of linguistic difference, and the bricks of signification, two-sided signs, among other salient dichotomous ingredients; this edifice houses both semiology and structuralism. Structural systems are said to be under the 'hold' of the empire of the sign. They are plied with bar games in the names of deconstruction, symbolic exchange, anti-psychiatry and libidinal economics; they are tampered with under the banners of a return to Freud, translinguistics, and a-signifying semiotics. Women, Hélène Cixous and Catherine Clément tell us (1986: 96–7), have to mock their way around bars of separation and to uproot posts and punch holes in the fences drawn around them.

Everyone may have learned the formula 'value precedes signification', but the focus on value has served to shift attention away from its poorer partner, signification. To focus on signification is not to seek to dis- or re-place value or to repeat the same kind of misemphasis, but rather, to create a interpretive foil against those who have subsumed signification under value. If I have surmised correctly, I, too, must in the end take the stand (*venir à la barre*). In the domain of Saussure scholarship, Robert Godel in his important work *Les Sources manuscrites du Cours de linguistique générale de F. de Saussure* treats signification as a secondary fact, a derivative of value, from the point of view of the system. Godel does not, for this reason, neglect signification since in his work on the MSS out of which the *Cours* appeared as an edited object, he recognized the wide range of definitions of signification recorded by Saussure's students. Godel duly notes, for instance, that certain MSS lend themselves to the explanation given by Albert Sechehaye, one of the original editors of the *Cours*:

> In the system, the relation a'/a" is only a secondary effect of the relation A/B. On the other hand, the relation A/B has

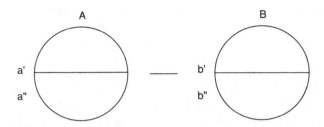

meaning, a raison d'être, only because A contains a'/a" and B b'/b". This, in fact, is a linguistic relation.

(Godel, 1957: 247, n. 379)

From this point of view, value also depends upon signification because the system requires both horizontal and vertical relations. I argue against those who not only consider the system to be hierarchical in that the relation between value and signification involves a unidirectional dependence of the latter on the former, but make the system monotonous in the tone of value. Baudrillard's criticism of the positive structuration of the linguistic sign hints at an often overlooked dimension of Saussure's *Cours*. It is for this reason that I want to revisit the well-trodden perimeter of the figure of the two-sided psychical sign because Baudrillard's anti-semiology is directed at the sign's so-called positiveness.

Upon revisiting the sign, then, one first notices traces of the ongoing search for a third term whose absence has driven readers of Saussure off the track and into extra-linguistic reality. The claim that Saussure did not consider the referent in his *Cours* is a common feature of meta-semiological reflection. The absence of an extensional entity has led some to reject Saussure's linguistic definition of the sign (Barnouw, 1981). For Derrida, on the other hand, it is an occasion to deconstruct the sign in all of its ideality. That is to say, what we call the third position is empty, exterior space into which Saussure banished all that was sensible, graphic and physical under the sway of oppositional–metaphysical suppositions the demonstration of which reveals for the grammatologist not only how the very constitution of the sign depends upon them, but the very impossibility of the sign's full self-presence in virtue of them.

From a vantage point on the edge of the sign, the very place where one may best experience the emptiness into which one stares as itself a sign, one need only remark that the search for a third term has been characterized by forays to the 'outside' as much as by prohibitions limiting one's ability to exit a given text or system, except by moving intertextually within a systemic trans-text. These 'quandaries of the referent' are 'semiology's delirium', Vincent Descombes thinks, for which there can be no treatment until one recognizes the paradoxes generated by the poverty of one's options. It is from the sign's circle that one may see how the quandaries of the referent may be outflanked (Descombes, 1989: 67).

I will not attempt to resolve such quandaries. My quest for 'thirdness' – in a non-Peircean sense at this juncture – is a flanking manoeuvre since I am not concerned with the referent just yet. Rather, there is a third way at the very centre of the sign which is not an aside in the debate on the status of the referent. Since this third term is the bar, there is no need to launch a search for it; yet, having 'found' it, one may ask: What is it? How does it work?

Godel has insisted on the purity and completeness of the sign within its circular enclosure (keep in mind that the bar in his illustration is not continuous with the sign's body):

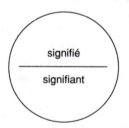

However, the circle that encloses the signifier and signified must above all mark their necessary union: a series of sounds or syllables devoid of sense would not be a signifier, nor would an idea without verbal support be a signified. *But nothing from the exterior, nothing material, for example, enters into the constitution of the sign: it exists only by this union of two psychical elements.*

(Godel, 1966: 54; my emphasis; Godel's figure)

The circle (or oval) delimits the sign in a rigorous way. It is the border across which no foreign (material) element shall be allowed to pass. Since the bar already lies within the circle, I will smuggle no foreign agents into the country of the sign. Moreover, one must revise the supposedly exhaustive inventories of the sign's contents given by the descriptions two-sided, dual, two-faced, etc., since the bar is literally third (this does not mean that the circle is literally fourth).

The bar is a line which keeps the signifier and the signified together, and necessarily so, Godel says, even in their difference. The bar, then, is diacritical, although Merleau-Ponty, in noting that 'the sign is diacritical from the outset', focused on the circle, the 'skin' (Merleau-Ponty, 1964: 41). The bar also appears to be the sort of hinge (*la brisure*) which Derrida found at work in Saussure's linguistics. The simple infrastructure of the sign, articulated by a bar-hinge, Derrida suggests, 'marks the impossibility that a sign, the unity of a signifier and a signified, be produced with the plenitude of a present and an absolute presence' (Derrida, 1974: 69). There can be no positive plenitude because the vertical relation of signification requires the doubly horizontal relation of value. The latter is defined negatively along the conceptual (signified) and 'material' yet incorporeal (signifier) axes of interdependent relations between the parts of signs. Thus, it seems as if the vertical, differential relation of signification is also defined in negative terms.

In 'Différance', one cannot help but notice how Derrida carefully constructs his argument by overemphasizing and overextending the linguistic concept of difference without positive terms. In other words, Derrida thinks that this sort of difference is *the* difference in Saussure's *Cours*, whereas I think that Saussure had a further difference at work in his linguistics. By invoking Saussure's conception of positive difference, I admit to taking advantage of a puzzle often overlooked by readers of Saussure. But I am in good company. For positive difference was a notion with which Barthes flirted by introducing non-differential elements, that is, non-negative elements, as support structures (i.e. *dress* supports the distinction between long/short) into his semio-linguistics. The support has a positive value which gives substance or body to oppositional values (Barthes, 1964: III, 3, 1).[1]

Derrida explains that 'this principle of difference affects the *whole sign* . . . in both the signified and the signifying parts. The signified aspect is the concept, the ideal sense. The signifying aspect is what Saussure calls the material or physical . . . "image". We do not here have to enter into all the problems these descriptions pose. Let us only cite Saussure where it interests us' (Derrida, 1973: 139–40). And he does just that, in his own interest, producing two effects: (i) by quoting Saussure to the effect that *dans la langue il n'y a que des différences* (in language there are only differences) – these differences, although they seem to imply positive terms, are for Saussure *at first glance* without them – we are led along with Derrida to read this as a general principle which obtains in the differential unity of the sign; but this is only a first reading; (ii) *différance* is not a concept and hardly a word but it is said to be, in a moment which turns the tables on Saussurean difference, the very possibility of the first effect. Further, 'it is not what we represent to ourselves as the calm and present self-referential unity of a concept and sound' (Derrida, 1973: 140). This fanciful representation belongs to an unknown, non-Saussurean and non-Derridean 'we'. Regardless of Derrida's claims for his neologism it, too, like any other sign, is played by the negative and differential relations of language and thus is never 'full and present'. Yet, what if it also has a positive element, a positively metaphysical body?

Derrida omits mention of the qualifying paragraph following the one which contains Saussure's idea of difference *sans termes positifs* and this is, of course, consistent with his *modus operandi*. I am not, to be sure, seeking a *modus vivendi*. My argument does not occlude recognition that one is always 'reading Saussure' (Harris, 1987). It would be more accurate to say that one is always reading readings which have been read and edited and presented as the *Cours* before one reads the sorts of pronouncements which pass as the so-called 'lessons' of Saussure, who is really 'two', etc. Baudrillard has, for one, two Saussures to handle.

The paragraph that Derrida could not help but ignore begins in this way: 'But to say that everything is negative in language is true only of the signified and signifier taken separately: when we consider the sign in its totality, we find ourselves in the presence of a positive thing in its own order' (Saussure, 1985: 166). There is good reason for Derrida not to take up the problems posed by the signifier and signified since when one does the play of *différance* must be checked. The 'play' in Saussure's presentation was itself curbed by this specification. It's true that the pieces of the whole are structured differentially and negatively when they are considered separately and horizontally, but the sign in its wholeness is quite otherwise. Positive difference is still structured horizontally in the system, but neither in pieces nor in the monotone of value. The sign's own 'order', then, is positive. Signification is positive because it has not been invaded by negative difference, which is to say that the parts of the sign's body are positively separate. Still, a single horizontal line which bears an arrow on each of its ends marks the bidirectional way between one positive whole and another. The positiveness of the sign helps one to understand why the attacks on it have been so virulent; it is no easy nut to crack! And this is the insight to which Baudrillard has led us.

I do not mean to suggest that Derrida believes there is nothing radical in Saussure's thought. Still, Derrida never tires of pointing out how semiology accedes to the onto-theo-teleology, although Jakobson, for his part, makes it explicit that Saussure's general orientation was anti-teleological (Jakobson, 1985: 126). In Derrida's estimation, semiology has the necessity of a transcendental signified imposed upon it (all the weight of the tradition as Derrida represents it shifts to the side of the *signatum*). This signified is not a trace for any *signans* because it is 'unthinkable' outside of such mediating terms. The signifier, on the other hand, is a trace since it *is* in relation to the signified. This sort of unevenness, as I have argued, results from Derrida's exclusive use of negative difference and thus relies upon the subsumptive asymmetry of the signification–value relation.

Saussure continues:

> Although both the signified and the signifier are, taken separately, purely differential and negative, their combination is a positive fact; it is even the sole type of fact that language possesses, since the function of the linguistic institution is precisely to maintain the parallelism between these two orders of differences.
>
> (Saussure, 1985: 166–7)

The two orders in question are positive (signification) and negative (value) and they are often confused given 'the delicacy of the distinction that they mark'. Derrida allows this delicate distinction to collapse so that he may confound the 'linguistic institution' that seeks to uphold it. Indeed, when one compares positive wholes as wholes, 'difference' itself becomes an inappropriate term which must be replaced by 'opposition'. What does this tell us about the bar?

If the bar is a Derridean hinge and it articulates the two sides of the sign, the sign cannot be a positive fact since the other side of articulation is a negative split. Rather, the sign hinges on the bar as its central rule. The bar is the articulator of an *articulus* (sign) inasmuch as it upholds the sign; the bar is not the removable pin of a hinge.

The bar is the bond (*le lien*) that ties together the signifier and the signified and it should at first be considered by analogy in terms of a chemical compound such as water (Saussure, 1985: 145). It is the attraction of the bar which draws the signifier and signified together like the atoms of a molecule. In this sense, the bar is to signification what the circle is to value; or, what positive difference is to negative opposition. In a further respect, linguistics is drawn to the bar since this 'science' works 'on the border-line [*le terrain limitrophe*] where the elements of the two orders combine' (Saussure 1985: 157).

Saussure then shifts his choice of analogy from water to paper: 'Language is also comparable to a sheet of paper: thought is the front and sound is the back; one cannot cut the front without at the same time cutting the back' (Saussure, 1985: 157). The relation between the domains of thought and sound, especially the contiguous slices of language, which divide into signifier and signified, unites the sheet of paper and the bar in kind in a radical way. One cannot cut the front of a sheet of paper without at the same time cutting the back and, as far as the sign is concerned, one cannot cut along the bar as one would cut along a dotted line and thus cleanly sever the concept from the sound image. This is not at all evident from the figure that represents the sign since its two sides appear as if they might fall away from the bar if it were to be cut, although Saussure did emphasize the intimacy and bi-directionality of the sign's internal relations (Figure 1).

The indissociability of two sides and a bar enclosed by an oval does not threaten the arbitrariness of the sign. To claim that this bond is positive is not to call it natural or motivated. Recall that Godel omitted the arrows outside of the sign's circle and

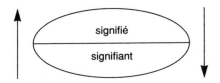

Figure 1 Two-sided physical sign, *after Saussure*

shortened the horizontal reach of the bar (given his exacting research, these oversights are perhaps surprising; still, Godel was, after all, much more interested in the concept of linguistic value). Godel's sign incorrectly suggests that the circle is the fourth piece of the puzzle of the sign. The arrows express the mutual belonging, a kind of calling (*s'appellent l'un l'autre*) of the signifier and signified. Although the bar gathers the parts of the sign and holds them together, such gathering is not always successful, which is to say that bodies are imperfect.

The vertical arrows which flank the sign's body point the way to the problematic status of what has been called an 'inversion' in Lacan's presentation of Saussure's sign. Unlike Saussure, Lacan put the signifier, the capital S above the bar, below which one finds the signified, an italicized small *s*. While this 'algorithm' differs from the diagrams of the *Cours* as we know it, the sign's arrows indicate that Lacan may have been justified in turning the sign on its head. The mutual calling of the signifier and the signified is not prima facie violated or indeed inverted by Lacan as far as his positioning of the terms is concerned since the arrows point in both directions. Lacan took advantage of the leeway given by the arrows even though he did not reproduce them. Recall that Barthes, too, noted the clumsiness of representing signification and that he placed the signifier above the bar. Having noted such clumsiness, however, Barthes criticized Lacan's spatialized writing of the algorithm of the sign because he gave *la barre* between S/s its own value.

It is the spirit of the arrows which Lacan and Barthes capture. The sign's body may be willing but the spirit is, perhaps unfortunately, weak. As long as one considers Lacan's inversion with respect to a pair of double-pointed arrows which mark a reciprocal relation, the spirit is willing. As soon as one notices that without explanation Saussure's pair of arrows give way in the manuscript sources of the *Cours* to a single arrow on the left side of the sign with a single direction from signifier to signified, one may begin to speak of the withdrawal of this spirit. The representation by means of arrows of the reciprocal relation of the sign's body was not always foremost in Saussure's mind. The claim that the arrows were added by the editors does little to clarify the issue (Harris, 1987: 59). A reader of the manuscript sources cannot help but notice that changes occur. Lacan proceeds from the 'upper nave' on the basis of certain elements of Saussure's thought captured by some of his students.

The opening move in Lacan's bar game is, however, modified by his understanding of the strength of the bar. The signifier and signified are 'of distinct orders and separated initially by a barrier resisting signification' (Lacan, 1966: 254). Since *la barre lacanienne* bars (*barrer*) signification and expresses a subject for whom desire is barred, signification in Lacan's sense not only bars Saussure's notions of intimacy, mutuality, and attraction, but pans out onto the axis of value and in so doing takes the signifier and signified separately and differentially. Lacan bars the positive wholeness of the sign (he 'skins' the sign of its circle, capitalizes on the signifier, etc.).

Imagine, however, the following operation. This is a bar game designed to reveal what Saussure may have meant by the positiveness of signification. There is a sheet of paper whose front and back correspond to the signified and signifier respectively. Pick it up with both of your hands, as you have done with similar sheets of paper many times before, and look at it as if to read what is on the front. Be sure to place your hands in such a way that they are in the same position across the width of the sheet, and more or less in the centre of its respective vertical sides. Now, using the position of your hands as an imaginary horizontal axis which cuts across the width of the sheet, turn the top of the sheet away from you until both the top and the bottom are aligned with the aforementioned axis. You should be looking at what was the bottom edge of the sheet. You will notice that what was the front is now the top, and what was the back is now the bottom. The edge that faces you is the bar of the sign; what is on top of the bar is the signified and below it is the signifier. This is how Saussure's figure of the sign must be handled if one is to grasp the fact that the signifier and the signified are cut simultaneously. In order to sever them cleanly, one would have to make a cut which is, while in principle not impossible, difficult to make with a pair of scissors. One would have to cut the sheet by aligning the blades of the scissors with the horizontal axis of the edge of the sheet, and then cut through the edge so as to separate the top from the bottom. In order to dispel any disbelief, confusion, or objections concerning the specificity of certain moves in my description, note that this bar game may be played in a variety of ways (i.e. by tipping the top of the sheet in the initial instance towards oneself).

A point of clarification is in order. My emphasis on the analogy of the sheet of paper should be read as an attempt to restore signification without exaggerating its significance. The figure of the sign symbolizes signification and I would need several sheets of paper to symbolize value. The idea of restoration is à propos here since one way of reading the overvaluation of value is to imagine a vertical bar of signification buried within a rectangular and horizontal block of value. As one removes the theoretical accretions, one rediscovers signification.

Now, if all value emanates from the system, the system (figured as the semiocracy by Baudrillard) must be smashed. On the one hand, this cry is a false alarm: signification disappears from view because it impedes the marshalling of forces against value; and value, one might suppose, is rather threatening since it has been inflated. On the other hand, the rally cry preferred by Baudrillard, 'signs must burn' (!) alerts us to the unity of the sign's body and stability of the metaphysics of the signifier–signified relation which grounds the structural revolution of value against which the forces of the symbolic struggle. The rally cry is, of course, a string of signs. Despite this fact, Baudrillard thinks that the sign's bar must be broken and its body burned. He has led us to reconsider both that signification is positive and that this feature makes the work of burning signs so difficult. This brief overview of the essentials of Saussure's and Lacan's bars will enable us to understand better what is at stake in Baudrillard's critique as he developed it with respect to Jakobson's model of communication and the power bar.

Chapter 2

Simulation and semiosis

The concept of the simulacrum does not originate with Baudrillard, even though he has played a significant role in putting it into circulation in contemporary social and political theory. It is best understood in relation to several ancient (Egyptian and Greek) and modern (French) religious, metaphysical and aesthetic traditions. Most important, however, is that in Western metaphysics the simulacrum has always stood at some distance from 'the real' in a position of weakness, having been banished ontologically to the margins.

In the *Sophist* (236–7), Plato draws a distinction in the realm of image-making between an iconic likeness and a semblance. To the extent that the former image 'participates' in the Idea of the thing of which it is an icon or a copy, it is endowed with 'resemblance'. The latter image does not resemble the Idea of the thing of which it is a semblance or a simulacrum because it does not participate in the Idea. A simulacrum only seems to be a likeness. Gilles Deleuze explains that the Platonic simulacrum produces 'an *effect* of resemblance' (Deleuze, 1983: 49). This effect is the result of: (i) the point of view of the spectator being included in the simulacrum; (ii) or, as is often the case, the sheer size of the simulacrum does not enable a spectator to take a point of view from which one could control the effects of resemblance and thereby determine that the work does not really resemble the original.

Deleuze asks: How does one overthrow Platonism? By means of the simulacrum, of course. In a Nietzschean reverie on the power of *Pseudos*, the original and the copy crumble under the assertion of the rights and the powers of the hitherto degraded simulacrum. Baudrillard will advance a 'heretical' version of this assertion.

The art of the imitator is thrice removed from true knowledge. In his study of Bataille, Baudrillard and Lyotard, *Heterology and the Postmodern*, Julian Pefanis uses Plato's argument of *Republic* X concerning the progressively unreal and therefore inferior arts of the user, the maker, and the imitator to situate Baudrillard's 'theory of the third order'. Pefanis contends that 'the thought of Jean Baudrillard comes closest to operating within, and on, the epistemological framework of this Platonic discourse' (Pefanis, 1991: 60). While a reading of the *Republic* would seem to be a prerequisite for a critical contextualization of Baudrillard's model of simulation – with the addition of a fourth stage, Baudrillard effectively confounds any Platonic expectations – this is not a 'great books' argument. Like Deleuze, Pefanis's reading is Nietzschean. One might even say, to quote Nietzsche from *The Twilight of the Idols*, that with Baudrillard 'Plato blushes for shame' (Nietzsche, 1968: 41). But Baudrillard is also interested in the Persian prophet Manes, the founder of Manicheism, and displays no strong need to turn Platonism on its head, although he would surely enjoy the acrobatics.

In *Republic* X 603b, one reads: 'Mimetic art, then, is an inferior thing cohabiting with an inferior and engendering inferior offspring'. Recall that 'imitators' such as poets and Sophists would not be allowed into the ideal Platonic state. Plato argues that the imitator produces a semblance distant from the truth and inferior to it, and this kind of practice appeals to the 'part in us that is remote from intelligence'. Unreason and simulation belong together. Today, as Pefanis claims, Reason leads a phantom existence in the ruins of the Platonic hierarchy of representation.

Baudrillard's claims for simulation have led cultural conservatives to retreat into a Platonic elitism, what may be called a eugenics of representation, and to charge Baudrillard with irrationalism. Baudrillard himself is suspect because of his interest in metaphysically and ethically inferior phenomena. On this view, Baudrillard, like Socrates, is guilty of corrupting the youth – not of Athens, but of America (Vine, 1989).

The investigation of simulacra has never been a wholly technical affair. On the contrary, the hierarchical division of representation has been accomplished with respect to a moral order which must be either maintained or destroyed (to cite two extreme positions), even though neither the Platonic nor Nietzschean options may suit everyone. There is, however, a third option.

In contemporary French letters, the concept of the simulacrum is associated as much with Baudrillard as it is with Pierre Klossowski. Indeed, in an essay on Klossowski originally published in 1964, 'The Prose of Actaeon', Michel Foucault (1988) reads the problem of the vertigo of the Same through the troubling resemblance between the simulacrum of God (Satan) and the simulacrum of Satan (God). Since Descartes addressed 'this great peril of Identities' in his 'Third Meditation', Foucault thinks 'the concern over simulacra has fallen into silence'. Foucault in a sense opens a space for the Baudrillardian project, without neglecting Klossowski's contributions to 'the game of the simulacrum'.

Anne-Marie Lugan-Dardignan (1986) alerts us to Klossowski's interest in the Carthaginian theologian Tertullian's *De Spectaculis*, a moral treatise on spectacles such as the theatre and chariot races. One need only recall two of the Deuterocanonicals, *Bel and the Dragon* and *The Letter of Jeremiah* – both found in the Septuagint Greek text among the books of the Old Testament – in order to situate historically and theologically this critique of the worship of idols, while maintaining a keen sense of the irony of culling lessons on simulacra from second order apocrypha. In the story of Bel – the Babylonian idol – Daniel refutes King Cyrus's claims regarding Bel's appetite and in so doing reveals the game of this simulacrum. Daniel proves by means of indexical signs (footprints) that the priests and their families have entered surreptitiously the chamber in which Bel and the food and drink provided to appease his hunger were sealed by Royal decree and consumed all of the offerings. In *The Letter of Jeremiah*, Jeremiah's critique of Babylonian idols including Bel takes on a mocking tone when he relates them to perches for bats, swallows and even cats – they are useless scarecrows as it were. No matter how richly appointed an idol may be, it cannot itself produce any signs of life.

Klossowski understands Tertullian's charge of idolatry against spectacles in terms of a 'gathering of the ungodly'. The evil demon and the work of the simulator occupy the same position in Klossowski's universe: 'To succumb to the Devil is to succumb to the imposter'. The title of one of Baudrillard's essays on film, *The Evil Demon of Images* (1984b), states the irrevocability of the bond between the principle of evil, an evil demon, and the image, an irreal, irrational and immoral spectacle.

Ulysses Santamaria (1979: 82) has astutely observed that 'one can situate Baudrillard's work within the long tradition of gnostic Manicheism', a matter upon which Baudrillard commented in an interview in the *Evil Demon*. Baudrillard's thought is Manichean in the explicit dualities it engages. The symbolic and death stood against everything which was touched in some manner by the orders of the sign and the real. A Manichee thinks in radically dualistic terms and posits the co-existence of two irreconcilable principles (Good and Evil; the symbolic and the semiological–real). The source of Evil is not the Good, but rather, a Demon. Baudrillard remarks: 'What the heretics posited was that the very creation of the world, hence the reality of the world, was the result of the existence of the evil demon. The function of God . . . was really to try to repudiate this evil phantom' (Baudrillard, 1984b: 41). The semiological order is, like the order of the Good, impinged upon by the symbolic principle of Evil. The active force in Manicheism is Evil, a seductive Thanatos, while the Good is relatively passive because it is under assault. While the principle of Good must try to repudiate Evil, it may be subtly transformed (weakened) in the process. It is at this point that the parallel demonologies of Baudrillard and Klossowski begin to diverge.

The demon invoked by Klossowski (1985) serves as the artist's model for the production of a simulacrum. This 'demon' does not have a transcendental origin. It is an obsessional force hypostatized by the artist, who attempts to 'seduce' it by resemblance in working on a simulacrum (a work of art). The artist's so-called seduction of the demon by means of the simulacrum is a self-seduction since the artist hypostatizes the demon in question. Klossowski understands this seduction contrastively through the hermetic tradition. His reference to Hermes Trismegistus, the 'thrice greatest Hermes', or as Tertullian called him, *magister omnium physicorum*, the 'author' of the *Corpus Hermeticum*, throws into contrast Klossowski's own subjectivistic and psychologistic view of the artist's creation of a soul to inhabit a simulacrum with Hermes Trismegistus's refusal to grant such a power.

The 'magic of the statues' practices by the fathers of the

Egyptian religion – a practice with which Augustine associated
Hermes in *The City of God* (viii. 23–6; xviii. 39), and which
involved the worship of simulacra, a practice tantamount to the
worship of the Devil in the Christian tradition – has been described by the Florentine neo-Platonist Marsile Ficin and may be
described in terms of seduction (Allen, 1988). The statues contained specific materials and had certain forms in virtue of a
sympathetic relation of harmony: like attracts like. Only a likeness (material and formal) could attract a demon, an angel, the
soul of the deceased, or a divinity of some sort. The demon,
then, would occupy a simulacrum and speak through it. With
respect to Greek mythology, in *De la séduction* Baudrillard employs the concept of seduction to describe the relations between
Gods and mortals. Since the simulacrum always seduces, all
meta-human entities must beware of its power (Baudrillard,
1979: 143).

The artist gives a sensible, visible form to the invisible demonic force in order to exorcise it. The only thing which stands
between Klossowski and the cliché of the artist who 'exorcises
his demons' is his peculiar appropriation of ancient tradition.
This exorcism is also described as a means of 'communication'
since the simulacrum is said to act upon those who view it in the
same way that the demonic model acted upon the artist. There
are limits to this sameness since the simulacrum cannot deliver
the intensity and fullness of the artist's phantasm. Art is still a
sympathetic contagion of psychoneurosis, yet the simulacrum
signifies only by means of the traces of the artist's largely
incommunicable experience (Klossowski and Monnoyer, 1985).
If these simulacra communicate anything, it may be the
Klossowskian communion of lascivious gay and heterosexual
fantasies which the viewer, who must also be male, must inevi-
tably strive to reproduce, to commune with as it were. As Gallop
has established in her study of Klossowski's critique of his
colleague Bataille, sodomy is understood as a simulacrum which
in the Sadean character assumed by Bataille furthers neither
communication nor community. Rather, it is a 'rite of complicity' (Gallop, 1981). This key simulacrum, in other words,
produces nothing but remains (*les déchets*); Baudrillard's concept
of *le reste* (remains) is understood as value, that is, as simular,
which is another kind of leftover opposed to a remainderless
symbolic equilibrium. *Le reste, c'est valeur* (Baudrillard, 1976:

292). The residuum is not subject to the sumptuary destruction and agonistic prestations of the potlatch. The remains may be, on the contrary, accumulated, reconstituted.

Klossowski's Sadean vision in *La monnaie vivante* (1970; there are no page numbers in this edition) presents his obsession with a form of exchange in an 'apparently impossible regression' to an industrial phase which 'exists in fact': producers demand from consumers payment in objects of sensation, in living money – men are paid *en femmes*, and women are paid *en garçons* (the imaginary in this case is straight). This 'money' is drawn from collections of 'persons supposedly destined to pleasure, to emotion, to sensation'. What Klossowski reads as fact is the seduction and the expression of a demon of exchange in a perverse numismatics: without recourse to a literal exchange (*un troc*), all modern industry rests on an exchange mediatized by the sign of inert money, neutralizing the nature of the objects exchanged, that is to say on a simulacrum of exchange . . . *Un troc* can mean barter and exchange, throwing a confusing light on the emergence of money from barter.

Klossowski is playing upon and indeed parodying an ambivalence in symbolic economies. In the *Grundrisse*, Marx observes parenthetically that although money has taken many different material forms, its materiality is 'by no means a matter of indifference' (Marx, 1973: 145). In Jean-Joseph Goux's (1990) structuralist reading of the Marxo-Freudo symbolic economy, this is a challenge to the arbitrariness of the body of money. The question of value throws into relief Klossowski's play on money's body: the value of Klossowski's living money is strictly symbolic, which is to say that it is relatively worthless in itself since it can be cashed in for its 'face value' even if it, like a coin, wears away; but, as the source of sensation, its value resides in its 'corporeal presence', and thus money's body is a matter of great, even grave concern. What is not ambivalent in Klossowski's work is the equation of exploitative mercantilism and the instinctual life. The lesson of Sadean 'libertinage' is that living beings are possessed as objects when the rules of capital are applied to affective relations (Guillaume, 1989: 201).

The concept of 'living money' wreaks havoc with the arbitariness of the sign's body and the logic of its replacement by another body whose identity as an equivalent value is irreducible to its corporeality and qualitative attributes. The concept requires that the quality of the sign is already merchandise, richness itself, even money, inseparable from the emotions, desires, and merchandise its bodily presence yields. This is not, then, a marginalist economics in which what Klossowski calls the 'industrial slave' (model, star; Klossowski mentions Sharon Tate in particular) produces desire and its lack and provokes consumable emotions as the semiotic spin-offs of films and magazines.

From the Deuterocanonicals and Tertullian, through the Hermetic writings and Plato to Klossowski and Baudrillard, the simulator has played a game of seduction. Although the metaphysical and ethical status of this game has been viewed in radically different ways over time and put to work for quite different regimes, the simulacrum has not ceased to exert a significative but troubling influence as a diversionary force. While this is the explicit message of the simulacrum for Plato and Tertullian, Hermes and Klossowski emphasize its power to capture and to contain, whereas Baudrillard treats it as a principle of evil with the strength to issue a challenge to Goodness and Truth in the context of his Manicheism. In the end, however, it needs to be emphasized that the historical alignment of simulacra–seduction–Evil does not fully serve Baudrillard's theoretical purposes. Since simulacra are produced semiologically and Baudrillard theorizes from the perspective of the anti-semiological principle of the symbolic, simulacra, like certain kinds of signs, must perish in the violent *effraction* of the symbolic in all of its manifestations (including that of the principle of Evil) into the simulational world of Saussurean signs and abstract codes. Still, this little survey of simulacra gives one a sense of the seductive games played around and with simulacra as well as the ethico-metaphysical stakes of these games.

THE METAPHYSICS OF THE REFERENT

In theorizations of referentiality, some of the most hotly contested ground may be found between the sign and the real. The positions taken with respect to this relation are influenced by one's conception of both the sign and the real. The difference between Umberto Eco and Baudrillard on these matters is not merely attitudinal. Their differences revive the metaphysical issues which have arisen historically and continue to haunt signification and simulation, and they complicate the investigation of the structure of the sign form by discrediting particular 'metaphysical' conceptions of it.

Eco and Baudrillard disagree on the matter of the place of the referent in determining the elementary features of signification. The disagreement revolves around their competing claims regarding the metaphysical implications of the referent. In *A Theory of Semiotics* (1976) Eco maintains that if the referent is *included* in a theory of codes, then the theory will be contaminated with the 'metaphysics of the referent'. On the other hand, in 'Vers une critique de l'économie du signe' in *Pour une critique*, Baudrillard thinks that the *exclusion* of the referent which occurs in the separation of the sign (signifier–signified) from the world involves a 'metaphysical representation of the referent'. The referent carries metaphysical implications because it is a first semiotic principle, the very sort with which metaphysics deals. Suffice it to say that 'metaphysics' is a term with a rich array of negative connotations, only some of which I will consider.

Eco distinguishes between the place of the referent in Saussure's linguistics and Peirce's semiotic in this way: 'objects are not considered within Saussure's linguistics and are considered within Peirce's theoretical framework only when discussing particular types of signs such as icons and indices' (Eco, 1976: 68). Although the object in Peirce's complex senses of it is irreducible to the referent understood as a real thing (extralinguistic in the Saussurean tradition) upon which a sign depends for its meaning, it is not even Peirce's dynamic (real) or immediate, and certainly not the final object which interests Eco. In fact, he asserts that some of Peirce's definitions of the sign (i.e. CP 1: 339)[1] 'leave too important a place for the object' (Eco, 1976: 76). If Eco is neo-Peircean, his debt to Peirce must be expressed in another fashion.

As far as Eco is concerned, the abstract cultural aspects of the processes of signification are obscured if one clings to the Fregean *Bedeutung* or any denotation: 'from the point of view of the functioning of a code (or many codes), the referent must be excluded as an intrusive and jeopardizing presence which compromises the theory's theoretical purity'. This is the sort of 'purification' which Baudrillard treats as a 'fiction' of the idealistic semio-linguistics initiated by Saussure and later 'analyzed' by Benveniste (Baudrillard, 1972: 182ff; Benveniste, 1966).

What interests Eco is a 'cultural unit', an abstract entity whose meaning is a convention which is not determined in relation to a referent. A cultural unit is 'the meaning to which the code makes the system of sign-vehicles correspond' (Eco, 1976: 67). 'The code makes . . .': this phrase bears a close resemblance to Baudrillard's claim that it is only the code which speaks. Baudrillard's aims are different from those of Eco. Baudrillard's critique of Jakobson's (1960) model of communication in 'Requiem pour les media' in *Pour une critique* is based on the idea that the code has an *agency* and is an intermedium which determines the controlled circulation of semantic contents (Baudrillard, 1972: 220ff). The code *terrorizes* the process of communication by fixing the two poles of sender and receiver and by privileging the sender. Further, the code: (i) reduces communication to 'munication (the receiver may become in turn a sender, but the active–passive split is repeated); (ii) ensures the non-ambivalence (the assumption of univocality which may be transmuted into polyvocality but only under the rational dictates of the code) of the message; (iii) excludes the ambivalence (not to be confused with the ambiguity, for instance, of the poetic function, as some of Baudrillard's readers have suggested; Racevskis, 1979) of a constant symbolic exchange unmediated by the code. The code lines up the sign-vehicle and the cultural unit, the sender and the receiver, and the signifier and the signified. This 'positioning' (a holding pattern) is metaphysical. The code appoints the terms of these dichotomous entities in an abstract separateness and itself articulates their intimate non-reciprocal (in symbolic terms) relation. Baudrillard does not and cannot explain how communication could take place if encoding and decoding did not occur between persons. Instead, what he focuses on is the obligation (which replaces the code understood as a cold, remote and digital structure) to give and receive *between* persons in the absence of their abstract separation and togetherness (by virtue of the bar of implication).

The code in its most general sense is a system of rules for the combination of stable sets of terms into messages; the logic of the code is disjunctive. Baudrillard reduces Jakobson's model to the simulation of communication by discovering its unidirectionality, the assumptions of legibility and univocality (of the message) and an agency (of the code). Indeed, as a controlling schema, the code does entail a certain instrumental influence.

Eco's programmatic distinction between an s-code (a finite set of elements structured oppositionally according to combinatorial rules by which values are established in relation to the respective positions of the elements in the system) and a code (which must include elements ruled by internal combinatorial laws, contents conveyed by the elements and some kind of proof that the message has been correctly received) includes many of the aspects which are normally found under the semiotic definition of code (Eco, 1976: 36ff; Greimas and Courtés, 1979). Of the three Cs of communication (code, contact, context), Baudrillard seizes upon the power and the irreducibility (if there is signification, then there is a code) of the first and elevates it to the status of an overwhelming context (the code becomes *modernité*) whose 'extras flee the stage' (all of Jakobson's functions) when (and if) its dictatorship crumbles. Contact fares no better.

The phatic function, Jakobson writes, is 'a physical channel and psychological connection between the addresser and the addressee, enabling both of them to enter and stay in communication' (Jakobson, 1960: 353). In *De la séduction* Baudrillard returns to his assault on Jakobson's work and charges that the need to isolate the phatic function is evidence of our progessive loss of contact. Contact is empty in the era of telephatics (*le téléphatique*) since it is suspended electronically in the 'teledimension' between the purely operational switching stations of a network (Baudrillard, 1979: 224).

Baudrillard's critique of Jakobson is based on several of the principles about which Jakobson has himself raised objections. It is especially important to note Jakobson's belief that it is a 'delusional fiction' of Saussureanism to posit a uniform code for all the members of a speech community, thereby initially diffusing Baudrillard's charges of univocality and legibility (Jakobson, 1971: 719). By the same token, Baudrillard's remarks directed against Eco make it clear that he is not merely advocating the complication and reproduction of the code (Baudrillard, 1972: 227). Eco suggests that it is not enough to change the content of a message because a truly subversive gesture must engender a new code. Jakobson suggests something similar to Eco when he notes that the code is multiplex and consists of a hierarchy of sub-codes, many of which a single person (who belongs simultaneously to several code-using communities) will draw upon. Yet, by isolating and hypostatizing the code, Baudrillard partakes in what Jakobson calls the Saussurean propensity to confine analysis to the code in spite of the dialectical unity of the code/message and competence/performance. In Baudrillard's estimation the code is ubiquitous, and it has become so, he will argue, with the assistance of cyber-semioticians.

Eco's cultural unit is modelled on Peirce's interpretant, understood minimally as the significance or meaning of a sign (CP 8: 179); the cultural unit is itself a sign, which explains why it too can have interpretants. Eco specifies that 'the idea of the interpretant makes a theory of signification a rigorous science of cultural phenomena, while detaching it from the metaphysics of the referent' (Eco, 1976: 70). The interpretant enables one to avoid both the referential fallacy and the extensional fallacy (whereby the truth value of a sentence supplants its meaning). By considering the referent, one lapses into an invalid theory of meaning which severely restricts the scope of one's investigation given the need to find an empirical object to which a given sign corresponds. Eco argues that if one identifies the meaning of a term with a referent, then one must exclude from consideration all of the terms (syncategorematic) which do not have referents. Every term has at least a cultural unit which stands in an interrelationship of opposition (pure difference) with the other units in a system. Eco does not deny the existence of terms (categorematic) with referents; it is just that their meaning is dissociable from their referents. The referent stains the purity which comes with a principle of value which issues from the system, a classically Saussurean notion (Eco, 1976: 73).

'In so far as it immediately establishes a distinctive opposition between signifier and signified and between sign and referent, etc., from the very first point of departure what semiology tries to do is to *domesticate* the sign', Baudrillard has claimed (1984b: 44). The sign is a product of the domestication of meaning. This domestication takes place under the 'empty and magical' concept of *motivation*. Baudrillard targets Benveniste's relocation of the arbitrariness of the sign in his *Problèmes de linguistique générale* in order to elicit its metaphysical operationality. Metaphysics is a means of domestication and obfuscation.

It is only possible, thinks Baudrillard, for Benveniste to re-situate arbitrariness outside of the signifier–signified relation between the sign and the referent in virtue of their initial metaphysical separation. Benveniste, then, 'strongly risks reviving the eternal metaphysical solution of the problem' (Baudrillard, 1972: 183) by flooding the gap between the sign and the world with an unmotivated relationship, that is to say, by working under the metaphysical provision of motivation. It matters little for Baudrillard whether one affirms or denies arbitrariness, or even, like Saussure, whether one uncovers shades of motivation (since no language is either completely unmotivated or motivated), since the operational principle obtains in every case.

Baudrillard attacks Benveniste's repair of the sign–referent relation by first stating that 'things are just not cut out according to [his and others'] idealist scheme'. If there is a *coupure*, it occurs between the signifier (form) and the signified/referent (content) or, between thought and the perceptible world. The referent, Baudrillard argues, is not beyond the sign's shadow. The sign cannot 'jump outside of its shadow'. In one respect, Baudrillard suggests that the referent is a phenomenological halo of the sign, which is to say that there is no noetic moment without a noematic correlate or object pole at which stands the perceived signified/referent, the 'phenomenal referent'. In the introductory remarks to his English translation of *For A Critique of the Political Economy of the Sign* (1981a: 11), Charles Levin remarks on Baudrillard's complex relation with semio-linguistics: Baudrillard 'is proposing a phenomenology, if it is a phenomenology, of structuralism itself, in the form of the social world already analyzed structurally'. While Levin does not develop this insight, and even though his language here is far from convincing ('if it is . . . '), phenomenology does serve Baudrillard's critical reading of structural linguistics. But this service is shortlived.

If the separation of the sign and the referent is a 'fiction', then their reunion is a 'science fiction'. Baudrillard isolates a comment of Benveniste's to the effect that 'for the speaking subject, there is complete adequation between language and reality: the sign recovers and commands reality; even better, it *is* this reality (*nomen omen* . . . magical power of the verb)' (Benveniste, 1966: 52). The speaking subject has no interest in the sign–referent distinction. Elsewhere, Baudrillard argues that although Benveniste is more interested in a 'linguistic subject' of knowledge than a 'speaking subject' of everyday linguistic practice – Benveniste is surely also the latter when he is not serving the cause of his science – he does not and cannot refute the claims of the latter (Baudrillard, 1976: 320–1). Baudrillard takes up the cause of the 'speaking subject' by advocating a curious 'marxism': 'When Harpo Marx brandished a real sturgeon in place of pronouncing the word 'sturgeon', well, then, in substituting the referent for the term, in abolishing their separation, he truly destroys arbitrariness' (Baudrillard, 1976: 311). Although the writing was already on the wall in 1968 with *Je suis un marxist (Groucho)*, one nonetheless signed Harpo non-linguistically.

While Benveniste was busy filling the non-existent gap between the sign and the referent, a 'speaking subject' like Harpo was destroying the metaphysical sign upon which such gaps were manufactured and repaired. Baudrillard's example is bizarre, not to mention anachronistic, because Harpo was a subject who did not speak! Nevertheless, he was a 'signing' subject who traded in non-verbal signs, the very kind of sign by which one can establish an intimate bond with a referent, since the sign in question is also the referent.

Baudrillard's position on the status of the referent rests on his reversal of the ontological and chronological priority usually afforded to a field of referents anterior to the signs which signify them. If this order collapses, one may claim that signs become the means of presenting and representing referents; the referent is an effect of a creative sign. What is important in this reversal is that the referent is signified or described *as if* it were external and anterior to the sign system from which it has issued (Rotman, 1987: 27). For Baudrillard, *as if* is simulacral. The sign gives itself a referential alibi, as Baudrillard puts it. In this respect, *motivation* is an empty concept which 'analyzes nothing at all'.

Baudrillard does not merely recognize, as Eco does, that every time there is a lie, there is signification, and every time there is signification, there is the possibility of lying. By lying Eco means the signification of 'something to which no real state of things corresponds'. In Baudrillard's terms, every time there is signification, there is lying, for the reason that what is real is an effect of the sign, and thus, every referent is an alibi: signification simulates reference to a real state because no real states correspond to the sign.

THE MODEL OF SIMULATION AS A CONDENSED HISTORY OF MODERN SEMIOTIC DEBATE ON THE REFERENT

In this section I will be concerned with the semiotic aspects of Baudrillard's model of the orders of simulacra and the stages of the mutation of the law of value. His model condenses the history of the question of the inclusion or exclusion of the referent. The question has been primarily debated in the tradition of European semiology, in and against which Baudrillard works. I will recontextualize semiotically several stages of the model on Peircean grounds so as to enrich and further problematize the otherwise totalizing and reductive claims made for the monosemiological simulacrum. There are, I contend, semiotic processes at work in the constitution of the four stages of simulacra which may be reconstructed in Peircean terms.

My reading of the model in terms of the status of the referent provides a further context in which to consider some of the elements of the stand-off between Eco and Baudrillard. I do not intend to resolve their differences. Peirce does not give us access to some sort of noumenal reality, nor does his complex conception of the object deliver us a lost but nonetheless real referent; nor does the interpretant alone suffice to obviate the need for an object, given the violence done by this interpretation to the Peircean categories in the name of a theory of codes.

I also want to upset the prevailing idea that the orders of simulacra describe in some straightforward way successive historical stages. In *L'Echange symbolique*, Baudrillard states explicitly that the orders parallel the mutation of the law of value which have followed one another since the Renaissance (Baudrillard, 1976: 77). Baudrillard's idea of 'stages' is rather crude since he first divides the post-Renaissance world into three (Renaissance to the Industrial Revolution; Industrial Era; post-Industrial Era) and subsequently adds a fourth order to a poorly differentiated third order. He does this, however, without designating that the fourth order might be postmodern as opposed to modern, or a mature postmodernity (post-historical or transhistorical) as opposed to an earlier postmodernity. The model is only vaguely historical and does not participate in the naming and dating games which are so often played over the transition from modernity to postmodernity.

The model constitutes a historical relevancy for itself but only as a broad context for the critical analysis of the mutation of the law of value through the conceptual achievements of Marx and Saussure (stages two and three), and the metaphorical extension of Mandelbrot's geometry of fractals (stage four). Here, history is histrionic.

My focus on the referent is a way to position Baudrillard in a milieu of debates concerning the relationship between a signifying order and the real. It is precisely this relation which the model theorizes through the progressive satellization of the referent. Consider Baudrillard's model in Table 2.

Table 2 The orders of simulacra

Law/value	Dominant form	Semiotic features	Sign form
natural	counterfeit	arbitrary, neutral	corrupt symbol
market	production	serial	icon
structural	simulation	reign of the code	Saussurean sign
fractal	proliferation	metonymic	index

Although the model (at least the first three stages) is now a familiar feature of the socio-political theoretical landscape, it still requires comment. What does the model model? Kellner, for instance, thinks 'Baudrillard presents a theory of how simulacra came to dominate social life, both historically and phenomenologically' (1989: 78). Accordingly, the orders of simulacra should be read as a 'historical sketch', a description of the phenomena (empirical and perceptual, Kellner suggests) which define 'a long historical process of simulation'. I will tell a different story. In passing, let's note once more the suspicion of phenomenology cast upon Baudrillard, this time by Kellner, since it is supposed to be the very thing which makes his semiology 'critical'.

In *Amérique*, Baudrillard writes:

What is new in America is the clash of the first level (primitive and wild) and the third stage (the absolute simulacrum). There is no second level. This is a situation difficult for us to understand since we have always privileged the second level, the reflexive, split personality, the unhappy consciousness.

(Baudrillard, 1986: 208)

Prior to *Amérique*, one could say that the third stage repeats (by simulating) the second stage in the same way that the second stage repeats the first stage at a higher level. A change occurs when the model is adjusted so that the stages are no longer related intransitively (this is a relation in which a first stage is related to a second, and the second is related to a third, but the first is not related to the third; thus, according to the orders, the third never precedes the first, the second never precedes the first). Rather, they are related transitively. That is to say, the first stage is immediately succeeded by the third, and their relation is a clash. In Baudrillard's America, the second stage is absent. There are no historical grounds for the claim that the law of the market and forms specific to capitalist production did not come to America. This is one instance where the model may be said to possess a limited descriptive valency. The model does, however, enable one to produce suggestive combinations of images, metaphors and 'mythical operators' with respect to the idea that America is in some sense a 'real fiction'.

In making this kind of claim about America, Baudrillard takes a page out of McLuhan. In the 1960s, McLuhan explained French Canadian nationalism in terms of the features of the age of electricity. Cultural decentralization was, McLuhan believed, a normal consequence of the general decentralization engendered by electric instantaneity and global awareness. In Québec this took the form of a linguistic nationalism and separatist politics. McLuhan specified, however, that *les Québécois* were people of the seventeenth century, and therefore tribal and feudal. Unlike their Anglo-Canadian counterparts, French Canadians did not experience the eighteenth and nineteenth centuries. English and French Canadians have difficulty communicating with one another because the nineteenth-century mind of the Anglophone makes no sense to a seventeenth-century Québecker. It was by McLuhan's example that Baudrillard was able to find a 'black hole' in history between the seventeenth and twentieth centuries of francophone experience. His claim is just as suspect as was McLuhan's before him. In the end, McLuhan's attempt to show that De Gaulle misunderstood

French Canadian aspirations and that his famous phrase 'Vive le Québec libre' was misguided, led to his own downfall in Québec after a meteoric rise at Expo 1967.

In an interview in *Magazine littéraire*, Baudrillard refers to his model with a hedge against his own formal requirements: 'In a manner a little formal, one can distinguish four stages of value' (Baudrillard, 1989d: 22). The following year in an essay entitled 'Après l'orgie' in *La Transparence du Mal*, Baudrillard returned to the same matter but in more explicit terms:

> I had previously, in an obscure design of classification, invoked a trilogy of value. . . . These distinctions are certainly formal, but it is a little like the situation among physicists who each month invent a new particle. One does not dispel the other: they succeed one another and increase in number in a hypothetical trajectory. Thus, I will add here a new particle to the microphysics of simulacra.
>
> (Baudrillard, 1990: 13)

Baudrillard rejects a strictly phasal and subsumptive reading of the orders in favour of a more ambiguous 'hypothetical trajectory'. Along this trajectory one may plot the particles of value without having the other, earlier points subsumed by them. Instead of using the work of physicists to legitimate his enterprise, Baudrillard takes the opposite tack of further dehistoricizing and metaphorizing the orders so as to reduce them to an abstract problematic. The orders appear to accumulate and to coexist as an informal assortment subject to the whims and the rhetorical goals of their inventor.

In 'Stucco Angel', the first section of 'The Orders of Simulacra' in *L'Echange symblique*, Baudrillard posits the existence of what he calls the sure signs (*signes sûrs*) of a symbolic order (1976: 78ff). This is a period before the orders and the birth of the 'modern sign' in the Renaissance. Prior to the emergence of the counterfeit and the first stage of simulation, then, in the order of premodern and non-arbitrary signs, a sign established a bond of 'unbreakable reciprocity' between persons and groups. The 'obliged sign' of Baudrillard's cruel societies (feudal, caste, archaic) is arbitrary only in the sense that it can take the form of anything which is 'inseparable from the concrete relation in which it is exchanged' (Baudrillard, 1972: 64). This sign is also non-arbitrary in the linguistic sense since it is motivated by its referent.

The sure sign is a symbol which guarantees a bond with the world. While Gail Faurschou (1990) has described in some detail the death of the symbol and its rebirth as a sign-commodity, what is remarkable about Baudrillard's description in 'Stucco Angel' is that he uses the word 'sign' (obliged and sure) in a positive way together with symbolic exchange. This is the only place in his *oeuvre* where such a relation is allowed to stand, since for Baudrillard the symbolic is usually and radically opposed to the order of signs. What wins out here, however, is Baudrillard's romantic conception of a pre-simulacral era perfused with sign-symbols and the surity of reference, albeit in cruel, hierarchical societies (Baudrillard does not reveal which societies he has in mind).

One enters the world of simulation and the counterfeit at the semiological moment when the symbol is emancipated from its referential obligation (motivated by status, for example) and multiplies on demand. Baudrillard uses the endo/exo distinction to mark the sign's movement from the endogamous symbolic system of strictly limited relations to an exogamous signifying order of 'democratic' and 'free' relations. The referential obligation is perpetuated by its simulation. Reference comes to require a reason, while the sign dreams of a 'lost' bond with a referent outside of the system in which it is embedded, and to whose other signs it now refers (Baudrillard, 1976: 79). Benveniste's efforts were, in a manner of speaking, mere stucco work.

In a pamphlet entitled *Le Trompe-l'oeil*, Baudrillard (1977b) aligns stucco with *le trompe-l'oeil* and together they constitute a metaphysical category in virtue of their respective abilities to imitate and parody most things. Baudrillard has no interest in the technical applications of stucco, Benvenuto Cellini's *pece greca* in the art of enamelling, for instance. Stucco (and later plastic) is the principal 'substance' of the order of the counterfeit. But stucco is not matter. It is a category, a 'mental substance', even though Baudrillard is fascinated by those 'angels of baroque stucco whose extremities meet in a curved mirror' (Baudrillard, 1976: 81). The same image (without the mirror) introduces Baudrillard's book *L'Ange de stuc* (1978b). The curve symbolizes a closed mental substance. This is the world of the linguistic sign, a psychical entity enclosed by an ellipse like the conjoined wings of a stucco angel. In

Deleuze's *Le Pli* (1988), Baudrillard's angels resemble Leibniz's monads. For Deleuze, the operational principle of the Baroque is *le pli* (the fold); that is, to make folds, to bend and to curve them fold upon fold to infinity. Baudrillard thinks, however, that operationality is always metaphysical. Like the sign in the hands of Benveniste, the stucco sign bears a relation to a 'natural referent' in virtue of a referential reason which operates under the metaphysical principle of (un)motivation. As a 'mental substance', an actual stucco angel is put 'in brackets', and may yield – *if* this were a phenomenology – a general principle by an eidetic reduction, and by an *epochè* hyletic stucco, mental stuff. But there are no signs of these operations.

In 'Automaton and Robot' and 'The Industrial Simulacrum', Baudrillard (1976: 82–8) moves into a discussion of the second order of simulation. The corrupt symbol totters in a machinic operationalization: 'only the extinction of the original reference allows for the generalized law of equivalence, that is, for the *very possibility of production*' (1976: 85). Not only does the scale of this simulation increase, although it is temporally shorter than the previous stage, but the logic of equivalence destroys and re-places the problematic trade in appearances between a counter-feit and an original.

The 'serial repetition of the same' in the form of a 'pure series' whose objects 'become the undefined simulacra of one another' (Baudrillard, 1976: 85), may be read in Peircean terms. The logic of the second order is immanent, although this does not tell us very much about the relations implied by the phrase 'undefined simulacra of one another'. A sign in a series is, first of all, iconic. The icons of a series may have one another for their objects. An icon, Peirce wrote (CP 2: 247), 'is a sign which refers to the Object that it denotes merely by virtue of characters of its own, and which it possesses, just the same, whether any such Object actually exists or not. It is true that unless there really is such an Object, the Icon does not act as a sign; but this has nothing to do with its character as a sign'. An iconic sign does not lead one away from itself to an object because the latter is what it exhibits 'by virtue of characters of its own'. The muteness of the icon helps us to understand why Baudrillard refers to the relation-ship between simulacra as undefined, or as he also puts it, indifferent. In a series of iconic signs, any sign which has another member of the series as its object may be said to be indifferent to its actual existence.

A further element of the internal relations of the members of a series appears in Thomas Sebeok's (1975) idea of symmetry or backwards iconicity. Although we normally think that the sign–object relation implies both the anteriority of the object and the irreversibility of the signifying relation (from sign to object), there is nothing in Peirce's presentation of the icon which precludes the idea that the object is also an icon of the sign it exhibits, giving rise to a kind of bi-directional iconicity (i.e. Baudrillard is an icon of a photograph of him). In a series consisting of iconic simulacra, there are neither privileged uni-directional signifying relations, nor an original or more primary sign pole. There is a kind of rampant iconicity, or undefined iconic relations within the logic immanent to the series.

In the second order all simulacra are iconic and all icons are qualisigns. When a sign is 'of the nature of an appearance' (CP 8: 334), or considered only in terms of the appearances it presents, it is a qualisign. All icons are embodied by sinisigns, such as the individual members of a series. The qualisigns of an iconic sinisign are not absolutely idenitical with those of an(other) object in the series since they will differ in virtue of being embodied in different sinisigns. But since each member is mechanically reproduced, they will not differ in significant ways and therefore they will exhibit a rather uniform set of appearances. The signs of this second order are for this reason 'crude, dull, industrial, repetitive, without reverberations, operational and efficacious' (Baudrillard, 1976: 90).

The following section of *L'Echange symbolique*, 'The Metaphysic of the Code', brings us into the third order. While the waning of the first order revealed in a condensed form the 'ambition of a universal semiotic', and the second order realized this ambition in part through its technical accomplishments, the third order transcends mechanical reproduction to the extent that 'forms are no longer mechanically reproduced but *conceived henceforth in terms of their very reproducibility*' (Baudrillard, 1976: 87). In this order, the so-called 'universal semiotic' operates according to the 'metaphysic of the code'.

As we have seen, Baudrillard focused on the code as the key concept of the communication ensemble. In the third order, the code has an 'anterior finality' as a model of models, a first semiotic principle of principles which determines everything in advance. Baudrillard finds evidence of the 'reign of the code' in Sebeok's work on semiotics and genetics (Baudrillard, 1976: 90–2). In spite of Sebeok's purpose, and indeed in light of it, Baudrillard reads Sebeok against himself by identifying DNA with operational simulation. For Baudrillard, Sebeok's cybernetic vision is the 'metaphysical sanctuary' of the single postulate which explains both bio- and socio-logics. In short, the genetic code fuels Sebeok's pursuit of a unified semiotic field and this pursuit is representative of 'the structural revolution'. The rampant iconicity of the second order is reduced to a single 'resemblance': everything is affiliated with the fundamental invariant of the genetic code. While Baudrillard is quick to point out that theorists like Sebeok have raised the code to metaphysical heights, Baudrillard himself makes use of this elevation since it helps to explain the third order of simulation. Baudrillard seems content, then, to exploit the excesses of what he calls 'molecular idealism' by both using them to lend a uniform character to a particular stage of simulation, and to push them over the edge, thus necessitating the invention of a new stage, in whose description a reference to molecular particles appears (unwittingly) as a leading analogy.

The essay which introduces the third order is in large measure an excursus on Jacques Monod's *Le Hasard et la nécessité* (1970). In particular, Baudrillard is concerned with Monod's statement of the scientific *a priori* of objectivity, which is set against all of the *a prioris* of the Western philosophical tradition (the latter were really only *a posteriori* constructions and justifications of certain social theories). Baudrillard (1976: 94) quotes Monod to this effect, although Monod (1970: 65–6) takes the idea from Karl Popper. As a discourse, Baudrillard contends, science produces and sanctions from within itself certain postulates and thus also has its own ideological dimension. Indeed, scientific discourse demands for its justification 'a real "objective" reference' because only this will satisfy its postulate of objectivity! The genetic code is a product of the circularity of a discourse which is set up as the model discourse in bio- and socio-semiotics. Surely, if we follow Baudrillard's argumentation, the code's significance is as much a result of his focus on it as an objective manifestation of something called the third order of simulacra.

Monod may be a 'theologian of molecular transcendence', but his natural philosophy is only an initial step in Baudrillard's sense of the code's influence. But Monod's work on the genetic code clarifies for Baudrillard the idea of the agency of the code. If everything in the third order proceeds from the code, and the code is genetic, then the code is a machine, to use Monod's metaphor, which reproduces itself invariantly and carries out a teleonomic project, the transmission of the invariant character-istics of the species (and the species are signs). The genetic code is a reproduction machine. The code is both universal in the biosphere and chemically arbitrary (Monod, 1970: 123). If a kind of 'social genetic code' is proposed beyond the biosphere, one may speak of a universal semiotic based upon a hierarchy of 'integrons': 'the genetic conception of integron – called "shred out" in general systems theory . . . is equivalent to the semiotic notion of "radius of communication", the progressive widening of which mirrors the history of civilization' (Sebeok, 1979: 42–3). Both Sebeok and Baudrillard draw upon François Jacob's *The Logic of Life* for their respective visions: the former finds a hierarchy of codes (from the molecular to the verbal) which confirms the science of semiotics as the trans-disciplinary bond of contemporary knowledge, while the latter simply finds the science of signs to be evangelical since it saves meaning but only by (re)producing it. Baudrillard contends that Sebeok, Monod and Jacob are all 'technocrats of biological science' who hide their social programmes behind molecular biology. As this science 'shreds out' into everyday life, it becomes a system of domination based upon the irreversible logic of the regulation of distinctive oppositions all along the 'great semiotic chain of being':

> What is hypostatized in bio-chemistry is the ideal of a social order ruled by a sort of genetic code of macromolecular calculation, of P.P.B.S. (Planned Programming Budgeting System), irradiating the social body with its operational circuits.
>
> (Baudrillard, 1976: 92)

Baudrillard borrows from Monod the notion of a 'stereospecific complex' which may be defined as the rigorous positioning of molecules in relation to one another, and the role this complex takes in orienting and specifying an enzymic reaction.

Baudrillard suggests that molecular communication may be 'reinjected' into 'cyberneticized social exchange' at any point since the latter is no more than a series of coded similarities and dissimilarities, no different in structural terms from covalent bonds at the atomic level or the digitial logic of the referendum. Recall that it was the rigorous positioning of the poles of the sign and the communication dyad which made them both metaphysical and idealistic.

Baudrillard's sardonic use of the acronym borrowed from economics (P.P.B.S.) continues his tendency in *La Société de consommation* (1970) to acronymize in what has been called a *langage baudrillardien* which 'integrates to perfection the pseudoscholarly discourse that the mass media convey in the richness of their function of *distanciation* with respect to the real' (Ballion, 1971: 568). From mathematics Baudrillard acquired P.P.C.M. (*Les Plus Petites Communs Multiples*) to designate that the 'multiple' is a democratic and homogenizing notion (1970: 158ff). P.P.C.C. (*La Plus Petite Commune Culture*) marked the transition from symbolic communion to communication by means of technical support systems in a culture of the common denominator (1970: 154–5). P.P.D.M. (*La Plus Petite Différence Marginale*) captured how the semiological means with which to differentiate oneself from others at the same time abolished any real differences between people (1970: 135).

The cybernetic model which brought the concepts of information and communication to bear upon the processes of the genetic code's replication, translation and expression, is evident in Edgar Morin's *La Vie de la vie, La méthode* (1988). Especially significant is Morin's claim that '*all* life, from the cellular up to the anthropo-social domain', falls within the province of (Morin's 'incompressible paradigm') the auto-(geno-pheno-ego)-eco-reorganization (computational, informational, communicational), which encompasses molecular and cellular biology (auto), genetics (geno), ethology (pheno-ego) and ecology (oikos) (Morin, 1988: 352–3). This 'organizational paradigm' not only incorporates cybernetics, but may be adjusted so as to take into account the angle from which one approaches 'the question of life' (i.e. from the angle of eco-organization: eco [auto-geno-pheno-ego)]-reorganization (computational, informational, communicational)). Morin is a thinker whom Baudrillard holds in derision, but of whose work he says nothing concrete

(Baudrillard, 1976: 92–3). Morin's idea of adjusting and fine tuning the paradigm, however, does express Baudrillard's idea of an operational and simulative 'dashboard' which programmes rather than guides understanding. For Baudrillard, Morin, too, is a semiocrat.

The 'structural revolution of value' has brought about the complete emancipation of the sign from the referent. The third stage of value is populated with Saussurean signs. In the *Cours*, Saussure paid virtually no attention to the status of the referent since it was an extra-linguistic entity. His interest lay with the oppositions between signs and the differences within signs and, in general, with the internal relations of a closed system. The scientificity of a linguistics of the system from which value emanates rests upon the principle of internal coherence. As A.J. Greimas (1987: 193) explains, unlike structural linguists, neo-positivist logicians, whose discourse required both internal logical coherence and relations with things in the world, issued a challenge to the concept of a closed system. The central issue became, then, how to account for linguistic entities which did not have actual referents, entities that had undefined referents, and those that seemed to have referents. Greimas's solution, which is quite different from Eco's, is 'to consider the extra-linguistic world as no longer being the *absolute* referent, but as the place where what is manifested through the senses can become the *manifestation* of human meaning, that is to say, of signification'. The referent is a 'set of more or less implicit semiotic systems'.

Baudrillard has capitalized on Euro-semiology's point of departure: values issue from the system and the referent is impertinent to this brand of analysis. If by 'referential fallacy' one means the erroneous attitude that a sign necessarily requires a real referent, then Baudrillard commits what one may call a 'non-referential fallacy'. The third stage of simulation requires that the impertinence of the referent in Euro-semiology and the structural law of value always entail some form of internal, intra-systemic opposition or difference (the structural play of difference orchestrated by the code); it therefore precludes, as anything other than simulacral, an extra-systemic anchor. Baudrillard is at his most seductive when he generalizes from Euro-semiology, hiding the specificity of this conception of the sign, in such a way that one no longer equates either the real or a referent with signs because all signs seem to be Saussurean and thus have no connection with an extra-semio-linguistic order.

Beyond the structural law of value which characterized the third order, Baudrillard introduces a fourth stage in 'Après l'orgie'. Readers of his work will recognize the question: *Que faire après l'orgie?* What are you doing after the orgy? The orgy has with some consistency signified all the explosive forms of liberation which have characterized modernity: political, sexual, etc. After this explosion of availability and the realization of what were formerly utopias, 'it remains for us only to hyper-realize them in an indeterminate simulation' (Baudrillard, 1990: 12). Such revolutions are no longer revolutionary, although they still occur with frequency and with complete disregard for their former content.

In an interview Baudrillard described the fourth fractal stage as 'a sort of proliferation of value, a species of an epidemic of value, but in which value has been completely fractalized and can no longer be located' (Baudrillard, 1989d: 22). The fourth stage is fractal, viral, 'the irradiated stage of value', in which 'there is no longer reference at all'. A law of value gives way to a 'cancerous proliferation' which cannot be brought under control by the agency of the code. When Baudrillard 'refers' – if such an idea is still intelligible – to the irradiation of value in all directions, to aleatory dispersion, and to chain reactions, he attempts to erase the problem of the status of the referent once and for all. At this (final?) stage, the flotsam and jetsam of value 'refer' only accidentally and exceptionally.

Baudrillard's reading of Mandelbrot's *Les Objets fractals* (1975) consists primarily in the metaphorical extension of the neologism 'fractal' (*objet fractal* or *fractum*). This concept had already appeared, however, in *Amérique* in the following adjectival form: 'American culture is a seismic form: a fractal, interstitial culture born from a rift with the Old World, a tactile, fragile, mobile, superficial culture' (Baudrillard, 1986: 127). Although the rhyme and rhythm of this citation expresses even in translation the notion of a runaway fissure, and to some degree illustrates Baudrillard's strictly formal interest in the concept, he might have added, for either formal or substantive reasons, the adjective *brownien(ienne)* since Brownian motion was the first fractal object.[2]

The processes by which things become indistinct (confusion and contagion) exhibit several semiotically relevant and relatively constant characteristics. I interpret these characteristics through the Peircean index, and thus attempt to reorient semiotically what otherwise purports to figure a complete collapse of *difference* in the lubricious instability of all discourses, objects and signs. Peirce's remarks on the index have heuristic and critical value.

The 'total and viral metonymy' leaves no field or object distinct from another. While the second stage involved relations which were symmetrical and similar, those of the fourth stage are metonymic and contagious. Metonymy is the trope of combination, while metaphor is the trope of selection, at least linguistically. Similarity and contiguity, like metaphor and metonymy, are characteristics of icons and indices respectively (although Peirce specified that metaphors were hypoicons (CP 2: 277)). Baudrillard remarks that 'metonymy . . . establishes itself on the disillusionment of metaphor' (1990: 16). The predominant sign of the fourth order is an index, which is not to exclude iconicity since every index has a certain character, a firstness (CP 2: 283), although generally speaking indices 'have no significant resemblance to their objects' (CP 2: 306). When there is a dyadic relationship of secondariness between a sign and an object, this sign is an index. Secondariness is an existential relation of 'brute force'.

Sebeok defines an index in terms of its contiguity with an object, although physical proximity (neither adjoining nor adjacent) is not a central concern. Rather, in a structuralist fashion, contiguity is considered in juxtaposition with similarity. While this relation cannot stand on strictly Peircean grounds, Sebeok's definition will help us to understand the nature of contiguity.

Contiguity is the means by which the reduction of significant differences proceeds, and the pure form in virtue of which value irradiates in all directions. Indices direct one's attention to their objects by 'blind compulsion' (CP 2: 306; 2: 286). They exercise a certain *force*. One of Peirce's examples of an index is a symptom of a disease (CP 8: 835): the symptom is really connected with its object.

Baudrillard's rhetorical effort is to convince us that today things are condemned to a delirious proliferation and they proceed in this manner with a compulsive virulence. Moreover, this indexical theme is worked through by means of the 'virus'; in fact, Baudrillard understands metonymy on the model of infection. Baudrillard's indexical signs are events – the AIDS epidemic, the stock market crash of 1987, terrorism, computer viruses, the telematics revolution. These events are the indexical signs of a viral culture, a disease ridden social body.

Each stage of the model requires a monosemiological and/or semiotic perspective built upon a particular kind of sign. But my interest in the index is not merely descriptive since Baudrillard's index-like language and tropes betray themselves with regard to the status of the referent. Reference does not disappear in the fractal order. The index forces us to think through a Peircean referential logic. Baudrillard evokes a world which is a dense mass, and a confusing mess, of indexical collisions and so-called infections.

The index does not 'furnish positive assurance' of a real referent, although it does assure 'the reality and nearness' (CP 4: 531) of a dynamic object. That is, a dynamic object is not real as opposed to simulacral. A third order simulacrum such as Disneyland is a dynamic object which 'by some means contrives' to determine signs of itself, such as those found in the writings of Baudrillard, Eco, Louis Marin, etc., which in turn generate interpretants such as my understanding of the immediate object as it is in fact represented by Baudrillard, for example. An index is, according to Peirce (CP 8: 335), 'a sign determined by its dynamic object by virtue of being in a real relation to it'. The being of the dynamic object is independent of the sign's representation of it, although it is representable in principle while remaining indifferent to how it is represented; unlike an immediate referent, whose being is dependent upon the sign's representation of it (CP 4: 536). An index tells one nothing about the nature of its dynamic object. It is simply connected with it or focuses attention on it. In short, Baudrillard's indexical events do not tell us anything about the nature of the culture of the fourth order. Such signs draw our attention to the social body without confirming or for that matter disproving its cancerous nature and its indistinctness. It is sufficient for Baudrillard's purposes to use indices to create the effect that contemporary events are really viral. The brute force of the metonymic bombardment described by Baudrillard veils his generalization of the image of the virus. In Baudrillard's hands, indexicality is a license to generalize on a pathological model, despite his complaints about molecular idealists.

A PEIRCEAN TURN

In the first order of the corrupt symbol, we found ourselves in the presence of an arbitrary, unmotivated sign which directed us forward to the third order, at which we may as well have already arrived in some semiological terms. For instance, Saussure considered that 'entirely arbitrary signs realize better than the others the ideal of the semiological process' (Saussure, 1985: 101). These 'others' are symbols or motivated signs such as onomatopoeic words and interjections, even though Saussure will ultimately dispute their symbolic origins. By the time we reached the third order proper, such origins had vanished completely. Tzvetan Todorov (1982: 259) relates anecdotally that Saussure's aversion to the symbolic, his almost complete neglect of it throughout his career, was prefigured by his attitude toward the strange case of Mlle Smith's glossolalic productions. It seemed that Saussure was 'more willing to acknowledge the supernatural (transmigration of Mlle Smith's soul) than to modify his method of investigation' and place more emphasis on the symbolic aspects of glossolalia.

A point of terminological clarity is in order. We should not confuse Peirce's symbol with Saussure's sign by subsuming them under the rubric of unmotivated, conventional signs. A Peircean symbol is not the sign of an object because of its agreement with a 'convention' which exists in virtue of having been posited by an individual or a group. A symbol is a rule (CP 2: 292) which will 'determine its Interpretant' that it is one; an interpretant is not an interpreter, although the latter grasps the former. In addition, a Peircean symbol is a sign that is a law, while a 'legisign is a law that is a sign' (CP 2: 246). Every symbol is a legisign but not every legisign is a symbol. The object of a symbol is not an existent individual, a particular thing: it is of a general nature, a kind, which has instances (CP 2: 301) since that which is general has instances (CP 4: 551).

Since Baudrillard's corrupt symbol is similar to Saussure's sign, the differences between them and Peirce's symbol must be respected. But Baudrillard's symbolic order also has the flavour of the Peircean symbol. The fact that Peirce's symbol is unmotivated is a nightmare of sorts for Baudrillard since his symbolic is always motivated. But consider Baudrillard's example of the caste system (for example, in Hinduism) as a set of symbolic relations, but in a Peircean sense. To be an Untouchable is a symbol of a certain kind of person who has a lowly station in life. This symbol determines interpretants of itself such that it is a sign of a certain person without giving any other or further indication about that person. This is the symbol's and the symbolic's cruelty. Now, this feature is accented if one takes into account Mohandas Ghandi's intervention (or any other such as that of the government of the state of Kerala) into the caste system. By calling the Untouchables 'Harijan' (children of God), Ghandi sought to give to them a spiritual aspect normally applied to the upper castes, especially the Brahmin caste. Ghandi's intervention did not stop the symbol from generating interpretants of itself as a sign of a certain person and nothing more, especially for those who wanted to uphold the existing social order. In order to weaken the symbolic's presentation of itself as a law, Ghandi had to emphasize a hitherto suppressed semiotic relation: although all Untouchables sprang from Vishnu's FEET – hence their lowly status – the term Harijan emphasized the indexicality of this relation. The Untouchables sprang from VISHNU'S feet, and therefore they deserved, as children of God, like any other children of God – and here Ghandi introduces the iconic dimension of offspring – a fairer place in the social structure.

Baudrillard's belief that signs evolve and produce themselves with no basic reference standard is not entirely at odds with the Peircean view even though Baudrillard's aims are rather different from those of Peirce. Baudrillard thinks that the (re)productivity of signs issues a challenge to the semiological effort to divide and conquer meaning. On the other hand, Peirce (CP 2: 302) wrote that 'symbols grow' out of other signs. In general terms, signs have power, semiosis, since they generate their interpretants, which are themselves signs in an infinite progress of signs. Signs are by no means passive and Peirce noted this feature by treating the symbol as a living thing, just as much alive as a human being, who is also a mixed sign. The production of signs by other signs is not a feature peculiar to simulation, nor does this feature warrant the claim that signs are somehow less real than things. Reality is incessantly produced and reproduced through signs for both Baudrillard and Peirce. But Peirce's lesson is that semiosis is not ineluctably bound to simulation; the sign is in itself multiform in that it is at once engaged in several kinds of signifying, and therefore irreducible to a dominant type across a given order. On a sympathetic reading of Baudrillard, a given order may be reducible to a dominant sign form for the purposes of theoretical clarity and simplicity, without for this reason excluding or subsuming the lingering influence, albeit in a marginalized way, of earlier semiotic forms. Baudrillard does not strongly suggest, however, that his vision of the world is polysemiotic.

DELEUZE AND GUATTARI IN THE POLYSEMIOTIC FIELD

If one wanted to explore the possibilities afforded by a polyse-miotic perspective in the context of poststructuralism, one would have to turn to the work of Félix Guattari. For Guattari is a bar gamer, although his theoretical and practical interests are in many ways quite different from those of Baudrillard. Despite these differences, Guattari's critique of the signifier explicitly valorizes Peircean semiotic relations; whereas in Baudrillard's work, Peircean semiotic relations are evident but unacknow-ledged as such. Guattari's contributions to anti-semiology and anti-linguistics (structural and generative) have involved attempts to theorize radical modes of passage from one sign to another in view of a semiotic heterogeneity in the midst of which language has no unified, autonomous domain of its own.

Guattari reads the Danish linguist Louis Hjelmslev's work in glossematics micropolitically, pragmatically, and schizoanalyti-cally – schizoanalysis is a micropolitical pragmatics of the uncon-scious – in the context of attacking the binarism of structuralism, the universals of linguistics, the instrumental pertinences and competences which block recognition of language's fluidity and the multiple non-linguistic encodings which traverse it. He opens up the semiotic field to passionate and political clustering with reference to Peircean semiotic concepts (principally indexi-cal and iconic, although even these may be overcoded and become rigid), describing little packets of signs forming around points of subjectivization irreducible to transcendent, enunciat-ing subjects. The bars of language are perforated by multiple crossings like the passage of hands, glances, money, leftovers, sandwiches, salads, cutlery, over and along a snack bar.

Recall that it was Barthes in his 'Eléments de sémiologie' (1964) who popularized Hjelmslevian terminology by developing a connotative semiotic whose staggered systems were modelled on Hjelmslev's distinction between connotation and metasemiotic (metalanguage); Barthes acronymized the relation of the former semiotic of the expression plane with the latter metasemiotic of the content plane as ERC. The acronym for Expression–Relation–Content in turn was caught in the critical anti-structuralist sweep conducted in the early 1970s by Baudrillard among other poststructuralist thinkers for whom this 'post' (structuralism) was 'anti' (structuralist) since signifying relations were homologous with repressive and reductive social systems.

In a milieu characterized by a variety of creative departures from structuralism and semiology, Deleuze and Guattari's *Anti-Oedipus* found a place in the widespread critique of the signifier and the prevailing anti-Saussureanism of the period but with one important exception. Unlike Baudrillard, for instance, who saw in the linguistic theories of Hjelmslev and Barthes further examples of the ideology of signification, Deleuze and Guattari combined a critique of a linguistics of the signifier with praise for Hjelmslev: 'We believe that, from all points of view and despite certain appearances, Hjelmslev's linguistics stands in profound opposition to the Saussurean and post-Saussurean undertaking' (Deleuze and Guattari, 1977: 242). Neither Deleuze nor Guattari have followed Barthes's translinguistic approach to semiology.[3] To do so would have brought them into step with the practices of specialists who exercise control over diverse signifying phenomena by making them dependent upon language. To claim, for instance, that translinguistics is imperialistic is to recognize that signification is a power relation, one of whose effects has been the colonization of signification. What is most disturbing in the tag of 'linguistic imperialism' is that Hjelmslev has long been recognized as one of its agents, even though his sense of language – as I will explain momentarily – is not, strictly speaking, reducible to actual languages. While linguistics ordinarily concerns itself with particular languages, Hjelmslev's algebra aims to calculate the general system of language in relation to which particular languages would reveal their specific characteristics. The calculation of theoretically possible formal relations at the level of the general system includes non-materialized elements, that is, those not found in any existing languages.

Deleuze and Guattari have, in a sense, fulfilled Hjelmslev's own wish since he had specified as early as 1948 that, despite his debt to Saussure, 'glossematic theory must not be confused with Saussurean theory' (Hjelmslev, 1971: 39). The specific object of Hjelmslevian structural linguistics is *la langue* – an essentially autonomous entity consisting of internal dependencies among categories. Glossematics studies neither *le langage* nor *la parole*, as Saussure employed them. Hjelmslev's purely structural type of linguistic research which conceives of *la langue* as form independent of substance, takes off from the final sentence of Saussure's *Cours*: 'the true and unique object of linguistics is language [*la langue*] studied in itself and for itself'. Hjelmslev's immanent linguistics cannot be counted among any of the post-Saussurean projects such as that of the Prague school in which language is not independent of substance but dependent upon usage and *la parole*. While Hjelmslev generously admitted that one could read the *Cours* in this way owing to certain ambiguities in the text, glossematics would neverthless pursue the ideal of studying *la langue* 'in itself and for itself'. Moreover, Hjelmslev's divergence from Saussure may be explained in large measure by his, as one reviewer of the *Prolegomena To A Theory of Language* (1969) put it, 'one-sided interpretation of the Saussurean concept of langue' as form and not substance, emphasizing Saussure's theory of value and the opposition between distinctive elements and non-distinctive variants (Garvin, 1954: 90).

For Deleuze and Guattari the work of Hjelmslev is 'profoundly opposed' to Saussurean and post-Saussurean 'isms' inasmuch as it takes the high road of form by not only studying *la langue*, but rather, *la langue* – *la langue* is a manifestation of a typological class to which it belongs, and the type is a manifestation of and thus subordinate to the class of classes, *la langue* or species-language. Deleuze and Guattari do not complain that Hjelmlsev's theory is not abstract enough. This high level of abstraction is precisely one of its virtues, and they rejoice in the irreducibility of the planes of expression and content to the signifier and signified. Deleuze and Guattari believe that glossematics 'is the only linguistics adapted to the nature of *both* the capitalist *and* the schizophrenic flows: until now, the only modern (and not archaic) theory of language' (Deleuze and Guattari, 1977: 243; modified translation according to 1975: 288–9). This kind of linguistics treats language as an inclusive and intensive continuum whose variations conform neither to linguistic constants nor to variables, but are on the contrary open to continuous and hitherto unrealized conjunctions.

Glossematics is 'schizo' because it offers a rarely permitted (grammatically, that is) freedom to connect and combine phonemes into possible morphemes; to pursue, in other words, unusual if not unnatural connective syntheses, generalizable in structural terms as unrestricted and unpoliced passages, meetings and alliances at all levels and places. Glossematics starts to 'schizz' in the *Prolegomena* as Hjelmslev 'feel[s] the desire to invert the sign-orientation' of traditional linguistics. For Hjelmslev, a sign is a two-sided entity whose expression and content planes are understood as functives which contract their sign-function. These functives are present simultaneously since they are mutually presupposing. Glossematics becomes modern at the moment when Hjelmslev, reflecting on the fact that a sign is a sign of something, maintains that this entity can no longer be conceived of as only a sign of content-substance (a content-substance is ordered to and arranged under a content-form). A sign is equally a sign of an expression-substance (subsumed by an expression-form which it manifests). Hjelmslev attempts to destroy the hierarchy and directionality of signification which was hitherto based upon the definition of the sign as that of an expression-substance for a content-substance by carrying to its radical end the mutual solidarity and equality of linguistic expression and content. It should be possible, Hjelmslev believed, to devise a grammatical method for the study of linguistic expression by 'start[ing] from the content and proceed[ing] from the content to the expression' (Hjelmslev, 1969: 75); a method contrary, in fact, to his own earlier grammar. This claim has led some of Hjelmslev's readers to charge him with idealism since it is only possible to study content by proceeding from linguistic expression. Hjelmslev's inversion implies that an analysis might begin with a concept (content-substance) ordered to its form by the sign in a way which forgoes words or the means to identify the content in question without first expressing it in some manner. Glossematics may be 'schizo', but was Hjelmslev schizophrenic? That is, did he not only think like a Deleuzoguattarian schizoanalyst and theorize the schizoprocess in order to free the flows of language, but also suffer from something called schizophrenia? Was he another Artaud, Van Gogh, Mary Barnes – a Judge Schreber whose breakthroughs enlightened us all? On the floors of conferences, in obituaries, in diagnostic speculations, Hjelmslev's 'depression', his 'long and tragic illness', and 'withdrawal' are made reference to not as breakthroughs, but as breakdowns. For all of the care Deleuze and Guattari take in recognizing the dangers of turning clinical issues into metaphors, and to the extent that Guattari based his extrapolations on clinical experience, they have said nothing about the 'case' of Hjelmslev.

Although Hjelmslev may have pursued a rarefied vision of linguistic form, this venture does not entail for Deleuze and Guattari an 'overdetermination of structuralism'. In *Anti-Oedipus* and *A Thousand Plateaus* they explicitly reject Nicolas Ruwet's critique of the combinatory freedom permitted by Hjelmslev's generative grammar. Oft-quoted by French readers of Hjelmslev, Ruwet's work stands alongside the pioneering studies of Hjelmslev by André Martinet (1942–45; 1970) in French linguistics. This makes Deleuze and Guattari's resistance to Ruwet a radical gesture. Deleuze and Guattari aim to recoup Lewis Carroll's 'Jabberwocky' and James Joyce's *Finnegans Wake* – the two texts which Ruwet uses as examples of a 'type of creativity . . . [with] only extremely distant connections with the creativity which operates in the ordinary use of language' (Ruwet, 1973: 30). Joyce's phonemes can be monstrous, exploiting phonologically grammatical possibilities (and otherwise!) and raising the stakes of semantic content. Deleuze and Guattari refigure Ruwet's appeal to the proximity of ordinary language and rule-based creativity, but not in order to valorize an unbounded creativity well beyond the demands of a grammatical model to account for competence and the subtleties of degrees of acceptable usage. Linguistic competence is not, however, a concept Deleuze and Guattari embrace. Still, the authors they recover (Carroll, Joyce, e.e. cummings) are not marginal figures, and these choices reveal that agrammaticality is not produced by and reducible to correct grammar. This sets Deleuze and Guattari against Ruwet for whom agrammatical writing does not force language to face its limitations.

Although they are at odds with Ruwet on this point and others, Deleuze and Guattari embrace his observation that the order of the elements is not relevant in glossematic syntax. This is one of the reasons why Hjelmslev's linguistics is 'profoundly opposed' to Saussureanism: 'the order of the elements is secondary in relation to the axiomatic of flows and figures' (Deleuze and Guattari, 1977: 242–3). Ruwet points out that Hjelmslev has a set-syntax rather than a concatenation or string syntax. The order of elements in the set is not relevant at the level of content-form (what would correspond in transformative grammar to deep structure) and contains less information than the string. This differs from Saussure's syntagmatic perspective in which the value of a syntagm is tied to linearity and the order of succession of the elements. What is axiomatic (assumed for the sake of the study of its consequences), here, for Deleuze and Guattari and Hjelmslev is that a set is a more productive flow-machine than a string. The creative aspects of language are at the outset marginalized and trapped by the dominant grammatical and syntactical machines, as Guattari has argued in *La Révolution moléculaire*, yet there are experimenters boring through the walls of dominant encodings (Guattari, 1977: 307).

Guattari's brand of anti-structuralism hinges on a definition of signification which is itself based upon Hjelmslev's rethinking of *la barre saussurienne* between the signifier and the signified as a semiological function rather than an association. Saussure's definition allowed structuralists to separate the signifier from the signified (i.e. this is how *la barre lacanienne* works) in the name of the signifier (i.e. a postmodern metonymic slide and all other reductions of content to formal signifying chains). Guattari adopted Hjelmslev's position on the mutually presupposing solidarity of expression and content in order to ensure that neither term would become as a matter of course independent of or more dependent on the other. This was a prophylaxis against signifier fetishism. Guattari interrogated the aforementioned solidarity in 'search for the points of articulation, the points of micropolitical antagonism at all levels' (Guattari, 1977: 242).

Guattari defines signification as an encounter between diverse semiotic systems of formalization (asignifying and signifying) on the planes of expression and content imposed by relations of power. The encounters between formalizations of expression and content require that the semiological function is read micropolitically because the mutual presupposition of the planes exhibits a variety of shifting power relations. Guattari sought to reveal the social and political determinations of signifying phenomena through the use of modified versions of Hjelmslev's categories. More than Deleuze, then, for whom linguistics is less important than music, for instance, in the elaboration of key concepts, Guattari showed that signification is a struggle of liberation against any system of signs, any universal code operating in a given domain such as psychoanalysis. For the analyst brings the analysand into line with a restricted regime of meaning. The analysand's significations are not permitted to produce their own meanings independently of the points of reference and dominant values of the analytic code.

By the time Guattari published *L'Inconscient machinique* (1979), his reasons for turning to Hjelmslev had become more explicit. Guattari's opening salvos were directed against linguistic imperialists because they attempted to annex both semiotics and pragmatics and used structural analysis to depoliticize their domains of inquiry; these salvos lead at once to the choice of Hjelmslev as an alternative while running against the grain of glossematics. For if there is no language in itself (unified and autonomous), and if, on the contrary, language 'always remains open to other modes of semioticization' as Guattari thinks (1979: 25), then Hjelmslev's efforts to establish the 'truth' of Saussure's linguistics must be counterbalanced (to say the least) in some manner. Guattari writes that his return to Hjelmslev is really a detour since he does not continue the Hjelmslevian project; instead, he takes up certain categories because they 'appear to be the only ones resulting from a truly rigorous examination of the whole of the semiotic problematic, by drawing out, in particular, all of the consequences of calling into question the status of content and expression' (Guattari, 1979: 40). Guattari had, however, two regrets about glossematics: (i) 'le bi-face hjelmslevien' of expression and content coincided with the two-sided Saussurean sign and other 'binarist reductions'; (ii) Hjelmslev seemed to participate willingly in the sovereign overcoding of language when he wrote 'in practice, a language is a semiotic into which all other semiotics may be translated' (Hjelmslev, 1969: 109), thus leaving ample room for the Barthesean reversal of Saussure's statement concerning the place of linguistics in semiology. Guattari wanted nothing to do with this dogma cherished by linguistics and Barthesean (glottocentric) semiologists.

Guattari delivers the aforementioned counterbalance by making a double detour around the pure formalism of glossematics and the privilege and superiority afforded to language in general semiotics. Although expression and content are first and foremost considered as form, they are manifested in particular substances; therefore, Guattari thinks, form should be considered in terms of the substances in which it is manifested. Such substances are produced, he argues, by non-linguistic (and non-signifying) agencies before privilege can be conferred upon language as the primary agency in the formation of substances.

Of course, Hjelmslev sought to banish substance from the glossematic paradise of form, whereas Guattari wants to bring about the fall of form from this paradise. As I noted earlier with regard to Hjelmslev's definition of the sign, he included expression-substance and content-substance as significant parts of his treatment of expression-form and content-form, even though substance is said to exist in virtue of form and, indeed, 'lives exclusively by its favor and can in no sense be said to have independent existence' (Hjelmslev, 1969: 50). The word 'hat', for instance, is a sign of a thing on one's head – a thing exterior to the sign itself. A hat is referent-like at the physical level. A hat-thing is a content-substance which, through the word-sign, is ordered to a content-form and arranged together with other entities of content-substance (things on one's head such as scarves, lampshades and, to be sure, different kinds of hats, etc). On the expression plane 'hat' is a sound, and on the content plane 'hat' may be a physical entity or a conception of a physical entity, or something in between. The important theoretical point is that the linguistic system is independent of the particular substance in which it is manifested.

Guattari's 'counterbalance' is the implicit admission of substance into the paradise of form already present in the *Prolegomena*. Glossematics cannot do without at least the relation of the constant of form to the so-called variable of substance despite its claims for pure formalism (Siertsema, 1965: 127ff). It needs to be kept in mind that glossematics is neither a phonetics nor a semantics since it claims to be independent of physical, physiological and non-linguistic substance. Moreover, Hjelmslev writes that 'substance is thus not a necessary presupposition for linguistic form, but linguistic form is a necessary presupposition for substance' (Hjelmslev, 1969: 106). For Guattari the manifestation of form need not be bound to linguistic usage. Having dethroned the linguistic formation of matter into substance, Guattari makes two claims: (i) not all substances are linguistically formed; (ii) matter may be formed without passing through the category of substance.

Guattari's attention to the semiotic formation of substances on the planes of expression and content is nevertheless modelled on Hjelmslev's interpretation of the formation of linguistically unformed matter (purport) into substance. A language casts a shadow like a 'net' over the amorphous thought-mass of purport and lays down boundaries in this 'sand'; purport is continually reworked in different ways by different languages. The French word *car* (for, because) and the English word *car* (automobile) have the same expression purport but different content purport; the French *dix* (10) and the English *ten* (10) have the same content purport but a different expression purport. Guattari makes light of Hjelmslev's metaphors of the 'net' and of 'sand' by arguing that there are not, on the one side, 'little building blocks of semiological construction and, on the other side, the amorphous mass of possibility' (Guattari, 1979: 205). For Guattari, the Hjelmslevian sand is already 'as differentiated as the most material of matters'.

Guattari further resists a purely formalistic and translinguistic encoding of the formation of substances by, for example, establishing a category of asemiotic encoding including those natural codes which do not have the forms of writing and speech projected upon them. These categories engage non-linguistic encodings which enrich the monosemiological landscape of linguistic significations. There are, then, several species of signs and semiotic connections involved in the formation of matter and the conjugations of unformed material fluxes, and many of these are borrowed from the work of Peirce. Consider Guattari's classification of semiotically formed substance and unformed matter in Figure 2 (Guattari, 1977: 279).

In Guattari's hands, 'algebraic immanence' descends from its

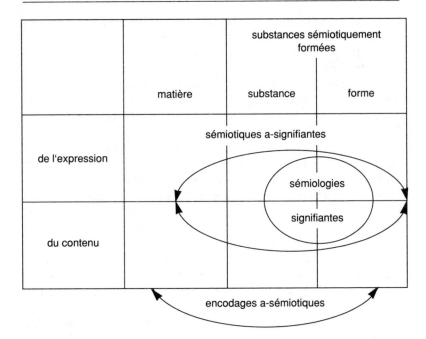

Figure 2 Hjelmslev in the polysemiotic field, *after Guattari*

immaterial paradise to the semiotic formation of substances *and* non-semiotically formed matter. Beyond Hjelmslev, asemiotic encodings do not enter the column of substance since they 'function independently of the constitution of a semiotic substance' (Guattari, 1977: 279). They are formalized but remain in flux. Guattari's example of this kind of encoding is the genetic code 'or any type of encoding said to be natural'. Material intensities are formalized without recourse to the projection of the shadow of writing onto the natural field, which is to say that 'there is no genetic writing'. Asemiotic encodings are not haunted by the 'shadows' of linguistic reason which inform *sens* (matter) in the Hjelmslevian system. Thus, Guattari provides an alternative vision of the genetic code diametrically opposed to the understanding of DNA as the single principle by means of which the molecular idealists named by Baudrillard control biological and social bodies. Guattari contrasts Jakobson's comparison of genetic and linguistic codes with Jacob's emphasis on their differences, and adopts what he takes to be the latter's position by pointing out that in the case of the genetic code there is neither an addresser nor an addressee; neither a subject nor an interpreter (Guattari, 1977: 302–3).

There are two types of signifying semiologies. First, semiotically formed substances such as gestures, postures, rituals and archaic practices are formalized but always incompletely. These so-called multiple substances of symbolic semiologies retain a *jouissance* specific to them and therefore a certain amount of autonomy. They cannot be translated into 'a system of universal signification'. The vicious semiotic circles which seek to contain them cannot be, in the end, sealed. By contrast, Baudrillard's conception of the symbolic does not keep the sign-circles sealed but unseals them with an autonomous and irreconcilable anti-semiological violence. Second, semiologies of signification are all centred on a single semiotic substance of expression (sonorous, visual, etc.) which can be extended as a kind of non-Derridean *'archi-écriture'*. This 'writing' is an instrument of domination. Polysemiotic events become dependent upon a signifier, a permanent post (*le Dieu-signe*) to which all paths from one sign to another are forced to return. This is a monosemiotic culture not unlike one of Baudrillard's unmixed orders of simulacra.

Finally, asignifying semiotics or postsignifying semiotics are 'revolutionary' inasmuch as they produce significations without the authority of a signifying semiology. Although asignifying semiotics support themselves on signifying semiologies, they do not serve them. Rather, they establish connections between material fluxes and function independently of 'the fact that they signify or fail to signify something for someone' (Guattari, 1977: 281). Although they have meaning for me, most of my scribbles concerning this notion did not make it into this book because they could not be 'translated' into a communicable semiology. Still, such scribbles signify even if they cannot be properly encoded, which is only to say that they do not behave like well-formed signs in a universal system of signification and fail to pass smoothly through the simulacral dialogism of ideal models of communication. Asignifying semiotics break the rigorous determinations, the simulacral dialogism of models of communication, in ways which Baudrillard, as we have seen, has theorized; in addition, these semiotics defy the standard definitions of the sign.

It would be a gross oversimplification to oppose signifying semiologies to asignifying semiotics since there are only mixed semiotic relations in Guattari's work. Polysemiosis, however, is always political. Despotic semiological formalism aims to crush asignifying polyvocity and polycentricity by putting everything 'poly-' on the binary rack and 'writing' over it. Structuralism was an interpretive undertaking driven by vested political interests which expressed themselves in a kind of tortuous isomorphism. Guattari plays bar games with expression and content by identifying multiple micropolitical antagonisms between the planes. In this politics of signification, antagonistic crossings abound between those semiocrats who perform an interpretive violence in the name of the control of intensive multiplicities by structuring new semiotic alliances and experiments, and those who put together such clusters and participate in unauthorized, non-hierarchical, independent and oppositional – one wants to say 'pirate' – constellations of forces. I will call such groupings 'weak'.

Guattari advocates a wild polysemiotics irreducible to an anti-semiology like that of Baudrillard since he wants to bring asignifying semiotics out of the shadows of the repressive semiologies superimposed on micropolitical resistances. An anti-semiology based upon a concept like Baudrillard's symbolic cannot hope to generalize the weak points or 'schizzes' of dominant significations because in the place of forming new alliances, hammering out new rhythms and excavating semiotic strata it wants to destroy signs and move beyond them. This is not to say that there is no ideal in Guattari's work. It is just that the ideal of a pure a-signifying semiotics, an absolutely deterritorialized semiotic field is too simple, non-conjunctive, consistent, and blind to the provisional measures and tactical necessities of polysemiosis.

A PEIRCEAN RETURN

Although some semionauts hold that semiology lifted off under Hjelmslev from the Saussurean launching pad, it is Peirce, as Deleuze and Guattari (1987: 531, n. 41) write, who 'is the true inventor of semiotics. That is why we can borrow his terms, even while changing their connotations'. Deleuze and Guattari regret that Peircean icons, indexes and symbols 'are based on signifier–signified relations (contiguity for the index, similitude for the icon, conventional rule for the symbol); this leads him to make the "diagram" a special case of the icon (the icon of relation)' (ibid.). In order to liberate the diagram from the supposed yoke of the Saussureanism which infects icons, for example, Guattari in particular has developed the semiotic category of diagrammatism through the division of icon and diagrams along the lines of signifying semiotics and asignifying semiotics, the latter involving signs which are more deterritorialized than icons.

Diagrammatic machines of signs elude the territorializing systems of symbolic and signifying semiotics by displaying a kind of reserve in relation to their referents, forgoing polysemy and eschewing lateral signifying effects (Guattari, 1977: 310–11). For Peirce, diagrammatic reasoning is iconic: 'A Diagram is mainly an Icon, and an icon of intelligible relations . . . in the constitution of its Object' (CP 4: 531). In Guattari's terminology, a diagram connects deterritorialized material fluxes without the authority of a signifying semiology. Returning to Peirce, a diagram is mainly but not exclusively an icon. It incorporates certain habits involved in the creation of graphic abstractions (in geometry and syllogistics); it also has the indexical feature of pointing 'There!' (CP 3: 361) without, however, describing or providing any insight into its object. Since a diagram displays in itself the formal features of its object, it may be said to take the place of its object: 'the distinction of the real and the copy disappears, and it is for the moment a pure dream' (CP 3: 362). This simulation defies, Guattari specifies, the territorializing effects of representation and denotation. In Peirce's work, too, diagrams can be deterritorializing because they are iconic – icons do not lead one away from themselves to their objects, rather, they exhibit their object's characteristics in themselves. Icons can be indifferent to the demands of dominant semiotic formalizations. In fine, even though Deleuze and Guattari effect a 'schizz' in the species of Peircean iconic phenomena, they do so along what is, on my reading, a line consistent with certain Peircean principles. A Peircean would undoubtedly claim that Deleuze and Guattari have engaged in acts of interpretive violence by playing favourites with iconic phenomena.

In their reading of this 'American master', Deleuze and Guattari adopt an uncannily Peircean attitude toward Peirce.

They read him against himself by extending interpretation beyond his conventional definitions. This is precisely the approach which Guattari adopted in his use of Hjelmslevian categories, and it is what Peirce called critical–philosophical thinking since it requires that one observe an author's line of thought, from which one then extrapolates imaginatively. Take, for example, Deleuze and Guattari's phrase: 'Look at mathematics: it's not a science, it's a monster slang, it's nomadic' (Deleuze and Guattari, 1987: 24). This glance at mathematics is Peircean. An active mathematical mind is, according to Peirce, necessary for interpreting signs. The ability of mathematics to travel is part of its dynamic character. Peirce held that mathematical practice or what he called theorematic reasoning bears little relation to the semimechanical deductive inferences and demonstrations of logical calculus. A monster slang is not limited to a class or profession or generation. It is a playful practice which involves active and creative experimentation. In his discussion of theorematic reasoning (CP 4: 233), Peirce wrote: 'It is necessary that something be DONE.' An asignifying abstract machine is diagrammatic. So too is theorematic reasoning. Points are made and stretched. Hypotheses are advanced. Algebraic relations pour forth. Pins are stuck in maps. Pages are covered in scribbles. 'Living' mathematical thought involves the construction of diagrams and experiments with points, surfaces, lines, etc. Deleuze and Guattari's diagram is also constructive. It 'conjugates' physically and semiotically unformed matter; in Hjelmslev's linguistics, functives 'contract' (draw together) their function. A diagram is a pure Matter–Function machine which joins together and changes the shape of semio-chips – edges, points, particles, degrees of intensity, etc. In short, the diagram facilitates connections between the most deterritorialized particles of expression and content. Diagrams are irreducible to icons, Guattari contends, because icons remain encysted (*enkystés*) in pre-established semiotic coordinates (Guattari, 1979: 224; Deleuze and Guattari, 1987: 141). Guattari adds that semiotically formed substances may be diagrammaticized by being 'emptied' as if pieces of them were flung centrifugally along certain vectors toward new spaces to which they cling.

It would be necessary to examine the schizoanalytic cartographies of Guattari (by which I mean literally his map and diagram making) in order to trace the subtleties of his brand of political polysemiotics. Hjelmslev puts the linguist on guard against substance and warns of the non-linguistic seductions of purport. Guattari puts the glossematician on guard against substance as a category between form and matter with the diagram. Hjelmslev's 'sand' (his purport was Saussure's substance) was substance for new linguistic forms, to which substance was inferior and upon which it depended. But Guattari thought that this kind of study of substance occluded the mapping of purport (unformed matter) about which linguistics, Hjelmslev believed, would not concern itself and, even if it did, could only come to know purport to the extent that it was formed. Guattari deviates from Hjelmslev on this point by deviating from Peirce and opening up the category of asignifying semiotics. By reading Deleuze and Guattari, although primarily the latter, through the problems inherent in glossematics, in the broad context of an inquiry into the refiguring of the Saussurean bar by Hjelmslev as a function, I have sought to indicate some of the possibilities afforded by polysemiosis in the expanded field of an anti-semiology which does not forgo every kind of sign. In placing Baudrillard's theorizing in the larger context of the critique of signs, his arguments may be measured against the approaches of his contemporaries. In this way, his focus on simulation and signs appears as a unique contribution to the problems addressed by several key European intellectuals during a period in which signification and its vicissitudes were matters of general theoretical debate.

Chapter 3

Varieties of symbolic exchange

AFFIRMATIVE WEAKNESSES

The publication of Vattimo and Rovatti's *Il pensiero debole* (1983) put one idea of 'weakness' into circulation. This so-called Italian response to French poststructuralism (Borradori, 1987–88) arose in large measure due to the latter's exclusive emphasis on beings in virtue of Being's so-called dissolution in the generalization of exchange value.

What I call an *affirmative weakness* reflects the paradoxical character typical of Vattimo's thought, a further example of which is his exploration of the opportunities (performative, political, historical) presented by the accomplishment of nihilism (Vattimo, 1988). But the phrase reflects no more than this. In general, as strong, normative foundations and transhistorical values begin to weaken and, for some, to sink below the horizon, thought is rendered weak, but in a positive way.

The concept of weakness is not exclusive to Vattimo. In poststructuralism it appeared as the condition of thought for those such as Lyotard and Baudrillard who proclaimed the death of depth models and *les grands Récits*. Unlike Vattimo, however, for whom this death warrant was itself *un grand Récit*, these thinkers sought to break with and to break the master narratives of modernism and bid them *bon débarras!* (good riddance!), so as to embrace a resplendent weakness, non-recuperable by systems of value.

In this first section on the varieties of symbolic exchange, I will explore the limits of the strength of the weak. I begin by describing the weak tools of Michel de Certeau and Lyotard. Such tools or devices may be considered in the context of their relation to the strong sites against which they are said to operate deconstructively and critically. I argue, first of all, that in the work of Certeau and Lyotard, a normative ground for this weakness appears in the primacy afforded to competition (*agon*) and to agonistic relations; Baudrillard, too, reads the potlatch in this way. The conflict between protagonists both underwrites and undermines weakness. Moreover, a tradition of the weak reveals itself through the numerous references these authors make to the Sophists of ancient Greece.

I will use my critique of 'weak ideas' in poststructuralism to put into context Baudrillard's own *affirmative weakness*. I read his concepts of seduction, wit and the anagram as strokes of weakness directed against the edifices of semiology and psychoanalysis. While a general agonistics also plays the role of a constant for Baudrillard, he struggles to maintain an affirmative weakness against a complete fall into nothingness, on the one hand and, on the other hand, he unsuccessfully attempts to resist the seductions of a strong theory which establishes itself by occupying the place of the opposing theory it has sought to vanquish. Baudrillard's strokes of weakness are played on diacritical slashes (/). It is a mistake, then, to uncritically valorize one of the weak devices of poststructuralism. In *Cool Memories II*, Baudrillard even jokes that just as 'Bad Painting is *truly* bad; in philosophy, weak thought is a *truly* weak thought' (1990a: 61). I will show, then, how he unintentionally falls prey to his own ruses.

Baudrillard's 'strokes of weakness' are the means by which he enacts his brand of nihilism. Nihilistic 'theoretical violence . . . is the only resource which remains for us', the only way to challenge 'the other nihilism' of the hegemonic system which attempts to neutralize everything, even Baudrillard's own challenges (Baudrillard, 1981: 235). This theoretical violence is pataphysical and symbolic, and even childlike, since Baudrillard likens his sense of violence to that of a child who tears apart a doll or dismantles a mechanical toy in order to see what is inside (Baudrillard, 1975: 37).

Certeau and Lyotard are fascinated by the famous conceptual couple of military science, strategy and tactics. Both thinkers wage criticism for the sake of tactics over strategy and advance alongside the weak against the strong. This preference for what they call 'tactics' is a symptom of the privilege which the part has over the whole in poststructuralist discourse. The choice of the strategy/tactics couple, however, is not innocent, although it sits comfortably in a field of argumentation littered with root metaphors of war. The most obvious example is Lyotard's *La Condition postmoderne* (1979), a work which relies heavily upon metaphors of fighting (war, agonistics, battle, balance of power) in order to advance and affirm various heteromorphisms.

In *The Practice of Everyday Life* (1984), Certeau employs the concept of 'strategy' to refer to a circumscribed territory (under the control of a system) which serves as the site from which relations with forces exterior to itself may be launched (a business enterprise may mount a campaign against one or more of its strategic competitors, thus initiating a coca-cola or a computer war). The important point is that tactics operates on the site of strategy. Tactical actions avail themselves of certain aspects of strategic wholes in order to turn them to ends other than those which they normally serve. There are numerous ways in which one may put this relation to work. For example, Constance Penley uses Certeau's understanding of tactics as *bricolage* to augment her analysis of the phenomenon of 'slash zines' (1991: 139–40). That is, in amateur Star Trek fanzines, the slash between K/S, Kirk-slash-Spock, signals that this 'zine' contains creative recombinations of elements derived from the television and film series. Such bar games 'mimic and mock those of the industry they are "borrowing" from while offering pleasure found lacking in the original products'.

Since a tactic does not have a space of its own at its disposal, it must depend primarily upon time for its activities. But time must be retaken in a surreptitious manner given the demands, for instance, of the work schedule and the surveillance systems of capital. The polemology of the weak is an art of time, of the timely moment. It is in the shadow of management that a worker diverts company time into a personal project. Every tactical manoeuvre on the strategic site of the workplace may be seen as an attempt to reclaim one's labour. To 'rip-off' is to humanize the conditions of employment so that work becomes more bearable. The very presupposition that there can be 'ripping-off' at this level already speaks to the opportunities unintentionally afforded by strategy.

While Certeau holds that tactics makes use of strategy as it seizes occasions on the wing in a wide variety of non-verbal acts, tactics operates in discourse in similar ways. Lyotard favours the tactics of the rhetor. Armed with spurious syllogisms and sham enthymemes, this exemplary figure attacks the strategic discourses of syllogistics and dialectics. Like Certeau, Lyotard thinks that one must attack such discourses from the inside. The seeds of deconstruction are, after all, found in place, on site, as it were.

Weak weapons are used to upset rather than to overthrow magisterial discourses. The goal of the tactician is not to assume the place of strategy. Instead, one takes pleasure in the sort of creative moves which turn situations to one's advantage. Tactics is not revolutionary, although it might be seen to have been so retrospectively, nor is it reducible to an accommodation to the status quo.

Both Certeau and Lyotard refer to an argument of the rhetor–lawyer Corax, related by Aristotle in his *Rhetoric* (ii. 24. 1402a, 3ff) as a special case of an attack by a weak force on a normative system (Aristotelian syllogistics). Corax's lost book, *Art of Rhetoric* (we know of Corax and his pupil Tisias only through references to them; in Radermacher, 1951) contained, according to Aristotle, the following spurious argument. Corax has a client who has been accused of violent assault. If the client is not open to the charge – if he is a weakling – then the defence is that since he is a weakling, the accused was not likely to have commited the offence. As Aristotle puts it elsewhere in the *Rhetoric*, 'a weakling is unlikely to be charged with violent assault, or a poor and ugly man with adultery' (i. 11. 1372a, 21ff). But if the client is open to the charge – if he is strong and vigorous – the defence will take the same form: he was unlikely to have done such a thing because he knew that his strength alone would lead people to suspect him. So, given his knowledge of the likelihood of being convicted, he did not commit the assault, and is thus innocent. Aristotle objects (and rightly so) to this defence on the grounds that it is based on specious probability; Corax passes off a specific probability for an absolute probability (for Aristotle there is no specific probability which is universal) or, as Lyotard has phrased it, 'verisimilitude is used in a verisimilar way' (Lyotard, 1978: 204). One might also want to hear some facts, see some evidence, and establish the motive for the crime, so as to rely less upon a characterological analysis.

For Aristotle, Corax makes the weaker argument seem the

stronger. Recall that in Plato's *Apology* Socrates was charged with 'making the weaker argument defeat the stronger' (18d, 19b–c, 23d), a stock charge against all philosophers to be sure, but one which must still be feared (Lyotard, 1983: 38ff). The wily art of Corax the Syracusan reverses logic and therein lies its sophistry and cunning. Corax was the author of one of the earliest works on rhetoric and is reputed to have been the one who taught the division of the speech into introduction, presentation, argument and epilogue, to his students-at-law, among whom one counts his most famous pupil Tisias.

Now, as the story goes, Corax launched a suit against Tisias in order to recover unpaid fees. Tisias maintained that if he lost the case he should not have to pay since this would be evidence of the inadequacy of Corax's teaching. Tisias, then, sought to be rewarded for the weakness of his position, even though this weakness could obviously become a strength. Corax argued on the contrary that even if Tisias won he should be obliged to pay since this would be evidence of his good teaching: 'the judge is reported to have dismissed the case with the proverbial remark: a bad egg from a bad crow (*korax*)' (Moss, 1982: 209).

A dextrous enemy like Tisias, armed with the cunning of rhetoric, like any of the ancient misologists (haters of the *logos*) gives one a sense of the way in which a strong discourse may be upset, if only for the time it takes to hit and run, by a tactical blow. Plato and Aristotle may have held persuasive speaking of the sort taught by Corax, Gorgias and Protagoras (the first professors *au large*) in disrepute, but such speaking held their attention because it challenged truth by advocating appearance: 'In the law courts nobody gives a rap for the truth about these matters [what is good or just conduct], but only about what is plausible' (Plato, *Phaedrus*, 272d–e). Lyotard and Certeau are defenders of a kind of *metis* (cunning intelligence; craft) which is as deceitful as it is fluid, protean, and seductive. These are the highly prized characteristics of a robust weakness in thought.

What is the relationship between the part and the whole? The part does not stand alone in a space exterior to the whole. Rather, the part poaches on the whole and siphons off what it needs from inside of the whole; it performs inside jobs which, as Certeau understands them, may be penalized in some way but often go unreported. The strategic whole, it seems, is not tolerant out of good will (every employee should realize this). It is perhaps overextended, incapable of not tolerating the 'guests' it hosts or dealing with the multiplication of microtactics in the interstices of its own wings. There is, of course, a certain textual *jouissance* in ransacking a received intellectual tradition for morsels of wisdom and figures with which to constitute discourses built of parody, pastiche and travesty, even though one may be policed by the granting agencies, journals, university programmes and one's teachers in doing so.

What, then, is the effect of landing a few blows on a strategic opponent? These blows do not accumulate, as both Certeau and Lyotard note, and therefore by definition they are deemed not to become strategic. Do tactics proliferate and collide with strategy like moths against a light? The opportunity for punning on 'Corax' was taken by Cicero: *quare Coracem istum vestrum patiamur nos quidem pullos suos excludere in nido, qui evolent clamatores odiosi ac molesti;* 'thus, let us for our part suffer your dear Crow to hatch his own chicks in the nest who will fly forth as annoying and molestful bawlers' (*De orat.*, 3. 21 (81); in Radermacher, 1951). Corax hatches his chicks or teaches his students and sends them out of the nest so that they may bawl their wares or caw in the courts. The weak collide with strategy not like moths – true, they are drawn to strategic sites as moths are attracted by light, but they must find those places which are poorly illuminated – but like birds against a pane of glass, causing a momentary crash and explosion which startles the unaware. Each blow can have the effect of reinforcing the impossibility of a breakthrough. The weak are strong as long as they remain weak. On the other hand, the weakness of the strong reveals itself when the crowing of the weak becomes an exotic, addictive object of interest, a pleasing diversion for the masters of the language mart and captains of the marketplace. Still, how weak must one be so as to remain strong in one's weakness?

Lyotard believes that his writing is tactical. He is a case worker who makes judgements according to local conditions and spins little narratives, like a rhapsode, as the circumstances dictate. As Samuel Weber, Richard Rorty and others have argued, Lyotard seems to 'totalize multiplicities' or to treat tactics as a strategic principle (Weber in Lyotard and Thébaud, 1985; Rorty, 1985).

Lyotard insists that tactics is 'pagan' and the pagan is postmodern. That which is pagan does not aim to conquer but is satisfied with having an opponent acknowledge its subtlety. Paganism, in Lyotard's usage, is an imaginative way of playing in existing games. The weak pagan does not learn the lessons of the strong strategist in order to be able to repeat them correctly when one is permitted to do so (Lyotard, 1977: 41). A brilliant riposte or witty aside opens up the game by breaking the monopoly over speech and the conditions of its employment held by any strong narrative canon or formula.

A brief look at Lyotard's concept of *le différend* will go some way in explaining how difficult it can be to speak and why one might want to 'go pagan'. There is a *différend* when a conflict between two parties cannot be judged equitably due to the lack of a rule of judgement which would apply to both parties. A victim of a *différend* is one who has suffered a wrong and lacks the means with which to prove it. For example, Lyotard found that the *différend* with his friend and comrade Pierre Souyri over the ability of Marxism to provide a revolutionary critique of the contemporary world and to direct intervention in that world forced him into a 'sentence universe' (every sentence presents four poles of sender, receiver, referent and meaning) in which he could only give up his position: '[Marxism] thus presented itself not as one party in a suit, but as the judge, as the science in possession of objectivity, thereby placing the other in the position of stupor or stupidity in which I found myself . . . a point of view . . . incapable of making itself understood, unless it borrowed the dominant idiom – that is, unless it betrayed itself' (Lyotard, 1988: 61). It is out of such cruel silence that new idioms must emerge, those which enable *différends* to be expressed. It is the task of philosophy and politics to find these idioms. In other words, this is a project which has thus far worked itself out through the concepts of paganism, weakness and tactics.

Most naturalists and conservationists understand Lyotard's point. Imagine that a stretch of wilderness is being defended by a nature group against a developer. The plaintiff, presenting the case for preservation, appears before a panel of scientists, lawyers, civil servants, etc. During the presentation of the case it becomes clear that the plaintiff cannot provide the sort of evidence which the panellists wish to hear. Why is this so? The argument for preservation is based on regard for natural beauty, the wonder of the forest, perhaps even the spiritual power of the land and the injurious effects of having non-human beings such as trees with which one strongly identifies razed by a logging company. The panellists press for hard data: evidence of the negative impact of development on certain habitats, the costs of such losses, tangible benefits of non-development, etc. The plaintiff cannot adopt the language of the panel without adopting the very terms of reference against which the case was launched; yet, in not adopting this language, the panel may treat the case as mere poetry, noble sentiment, mysticism or worse. The plaintiff has no way to state the case and express the fact that a wrong has been suffered. The plaintiff has lost the means to prove the damage since any attempt to explain to the panel that a wrong has been suffered meets with the response: what you have suffered was not a wrong because you bear witness to it before us; there is no evidence or only poor evidence of this so-called wrong.

The arguments of Certeau and Lyotard are set upon a field which is taken to be one of conflict. With Lyotard, it may be the case that social bonds are composed of 'moves' in language games, but such gaming falls under the rubric of a general agonistics: a battle fought with the weapons and ammunition of the weak. In Certeau's writing, the ordinary hero is a kind of guerrilla of the workplace and the marketplace, fixed in a series of adversarial relationships with the strategic wholes in which one is trapped. Language is a war game and *bricolage* is a form of fighting: cooperative, playful and peaceful exchanges may break out now and again one might hope, even though Certeau and Lyotard might show little interest in them.

The use of strategy and tactics seems particularly appropriate in a generalized field of battle; that is to say, inasmuch as the couple is isomorphic with the features of discourse and everyday life. The war mould, as Lyotard demonstrates in *La Condition postmoderne*, consists of many dimensions. He alludes to Heraclitus's quarrel with the Pythagoreans (and others) concerning the latter's peaceful and harmonious view of the world and takes the *logos* to be warlike; Lyotard's reading of Wittgenstein's idea of language games overemphasizes the dissimilarities between games to the detriment of family resemblances, leading to the 'isling' of games and the forced elevation of incommensurability.

Given Certeau's and Lyotard's supposition of conflict or

textual and extra-textual skirmishes – what are called *combats minoritaires* – one may assume that conflict is basic, universal and not so much a grand or strategic narrative but a substratum in the sense of what is a ground or fundamental. The thinkers of the tactical part have retained precisely what they challenge as the sub-stance of their attempts to redress the power of the weak. The battles of the weak fall prey to the whole inasmuch as they are conflictual and the sort of engagements which are victimized by their own ruses. The pagan cuts a Heraclitean figure with a Gorgian penchant for paradox. The weak weaken themselves by becoming too much like their strong, strategic adversaries. Their attempt to express the *différend* they have suffered inadvertently reaffirms a way of being which is all too familiar to their oppressors: war. Very few strategic wholes will have their Dien Bien Phu.

Seduction plays a game with weakness. Baudrillard writes: 'To seduce is to appear weak [*fragiliser*]. To seduce is to weaken [*défaillir*]. We seduce with our weakness, never with strong signs or powers. In seduction we put this weakness into play, and this is what gives seduction its strength' (1979: 115). The seducer eschews the kind of strength which belongs to the challenge in favour of the *strokes* of seduction. A challenge is a game of strength, of setting one's strong points to work on the other's areas of strength. While seduction is structurally similar to the challenge, in seduction one's weak points are exposed to the weaknesses of the other, or one seduces by drawing and being drawn into an arena of mutual vulnerability. This sort of weakness is said to be 'calculated', since the goal is to lift and/or install the stroke that divides this and not-this.

At the same time, seduction functions as a 'root' element of Baudrillard's universe in the manner of an Empedoclean cosmic principle. Baudrillard remarks: 'a stroke [*un trait*] has to bring disconnected things together, as if in a dream, or suddenly disconnect undivided things' (1979: 142). Like Empedocles' powers of Love and Strife – the former brings things together, while the latter separates them – seduction is a two-sided force (thereby collapsing the Empedoclean principles) that regulates both coupling and uncoupling. A single stroke has the power to erase and to mark.

With respect to pre-Socratic cosmogony, Baudrillard offers the following speculative variation: 'The elements of the ancient cosmogony . . . did not at all enter into structural relations of classification (water/fire, air/earth, etc.): they were not distinctive elements, but attractive elements that seduced each other: water seduces fire, water seduced by fire' (1979: 144). On this reading of the elementary substances, Baudrillard reinforces the position which he expressed in *L'Echange symbolique*: the elements are 'neither values nor positive elements . . . they are a metaphor of the continual dissolution of value, of the symbolic exchange of the world' (1976: 340). The cosmic principle of Love, like one side of seduction, works through the principle of attraction, and in the Empedoclean poem of nature creates combinations of the root elements according to its prerogative. For some, Love in the end controls the cosmic sphere, although this is still subject to learned debate. Baudrillard's lack of scholarly interest in such matters should not deter us. He wants to avoid a straightforward alignment of seduction with a version of universal attraction. It is mere mysticism to fuse the elements by lifting the bar between them in the absence of a theory of symbolic exchange. Baudrillard does admit, however, that the effects of some of these strokes of weakness are difficult to calculate. Just as he sought to avoid the charge of mysticism in a footnote in 'Vers une critique de l'économie politique du signe' with regard to the 'resolution of the sign' into 'some mystical nothingness' beyond signification (1972: 182, n. 1), the virgules between structural oppositions may melt under the strokes of seduction, but they do so in a field of *duel and agonistic* relations (1979: 145). This is a high intensity seduction, Baudrillard stipulates. To the extent that Baudrillard's work may be included in Lyotard's and Certeau's general agonistics, it is also subject to the same critique. Like other varieties of symbolic exchange, seduction, too, is agonistic.

The elements of the ancient cosmogony were involved, for Baudrillard at least, in an incessant symbolic exchange among themselves. When the bar is lifted, symbolic exchange can take place. This formula of replacement reappears again and again throughout Baudrillard's work, and I will treat it in terms of the question of the weakness of the symbolic and its manifestations.

JUSTE POUR RIRE

The presentation of Freud's 'joke book' in Baudrillard's *L'Echange symbolique* does not so much appear in a stroke of genius, but in virtue of a stroke of wit, *le Witz, un mot d'esprit*. Baudrillard contends in this book that Freud's account of the source of the pleasure of jokes in *Jokes And Their Relation To The Unconscious* is inadequate. This critique helps to ground his later claims in *De la séduction* that the manifest/latent depth model of psychoanalysis is no longer relevant. That is, this critique gives his more recent claim some interpretive depth.

In his discussion of the technique of jokes, Baudrillard argues, Freud reduced technique to a means or medium of expression in the service of an economy of expenditure (savings as opposed to excess) for overcoming inhibitions. Baudrillard charges that 'every interpretation of the *Witz* . . . in terms of the "liberation" of phantasms or of psychic energy is false' (1976: 334). In the 'joke book', Freud presents wit as a means of undoing the work of the censor, skirting inhibitions and evading restrictions. Although wit also has tactical relevance for Baudrillard, he claims that Freud recognized but failed to act on the idea that the techniques of the *Witz* were by themselves sources of pleasure. Weber's argument that Freud put into question his insight that the pure formal play of joking, independent of meaning, in itself enabled one to recapture childish pleasures, serves as an explanatory footnote to Baudrillard's claims (Weber, 1977). In Freud's terms, such techniques have a sense only in relation to an 'original' source. The medium is never, for Baudrillard's Freud, the message: 'In the *Witz*, or in the dream, the play of signifiers is never in itself the articulation of *jouissance*: It clears the way for phantasmatic or repressed contents. It is a "medium" which is never itself the "message" ' (1976: 324). Baudrillard's McLuhanism is at its most explicit here since he maintains that the medium (technique) is not subordinate to anything that has yet to be resolved from the depths of the unconscious. The medium is the message. But what is this message?

This message has several components which circle around Baudrillard's concept of the symbolic and the degree to which one may attribute anything to it. Given this problematic of restriction, I will need to descend into the lower reaches of weakness toward 'nothingness', a mystical, unfortunate state which Baudrillard, as I have explained, wants to avoid. It is not a matter of *hyper*weakness. We are now in the register of *hypo*weakness.

The idea that the consequences of the intermingling of terms in a 'non-diacritical semiology' are difficult to determine does little to break the fall toward nothingness which results from the positive annulment of the Saussurean semiologic and structural digitality (Baudrillard, 1979: 225). To erase or to lift the bar of structural implication between the signifier and the signified and any digital structure (0/1) is a radical gesture of symbolic importance.

The *Witz* mocks its way through or around the bar. It evokes the reciprocal relations of the symbolic by calling forth a 'veritable potlatch of successive stories' (Baudrillard, 1976: 334); Certeau concurs in regarding the potlatch as a subversive tactic (1980: 3).[1] In this potlatch, it makes no sense to keep a funny story to oneself. One is obliged to make a comic offering; to fail to do so is to risk becoming the brunt of a joke! The stakes here are rather low, as low as the sort of humour which they suggest.

The pleasure produced by the techniques of wit does not belong in the domain of the economic, of value, but rather, arises from the symbolic annulment of value: '*Jouissance* is the hemorrhage of value, the disintegration of the code and the repressive logos' (Baudrillard, 1976: 330). There is total *jouissance*, Baudrillard insists, in the erasure of any bar which is not for anything, but which is a non-place of non-value; with this erasure there is no liberation of repressed psychic energy. The symbolic must remain as weak as possible in the face of those who wish to find a place and a function for it in a system.

In his treatment of the arts of the weak, Certeau appeals to Freud's ideas on wit: 'The art of gamesmanship, of "scoring" on your adversary is at one with a sense of timing. Its techniques – and Freud gives us a whole inventory of them in his book on wit – boldly restructure the initial data in order to transfigure the normal language of a given space with an alien flash' (1980: 6). A lively retort can take on the colour of invective by surmounting certain external obstacles to the rebellion against authority. As Freud explains, a joke is a means to turn an affront or insult back against the aggressor. Baudrillard calls this 'subversion by reversion' and takes it to be one of the key processes of the symbolic (alongside anagrammatic dispersion and reciprocity). The use of invective requires a particular skill at enlisting a third person who takes pleasure in one's jokes so that one may score points against a second person in an aggressive manner. The techniques of *le Witz*, as well as Baudrillard's other symbolic processes, serve to shortcircuit all messages. In some instances, a bad joke results, since a joke is bad because of the lack of an anticipated link between two sets of ideas.

At its weakest, the symbolic is ambivalent since it totters between nothing and naming. At its strongest, it occupies the place vacated by the bar and the semiologic. If Weber (1977: 17) is correct in arguing that the 'bad joke is the essence of the *Witz*' because of its use of meaningless word play, I find further confirmation that the symbolic *Witz* is a contentless bar game, at its weakest, of course; the potlatch-like circulation of jokes might also degenerate into male bonding since in this case dirty jokes circulate as smoothly as bad ones.

ANAGRAMMATIC DISPERSION

Both Freud and Saussure, Baudrillard has argued in *De la séduction*, abandoned hypotheses that threatened the stability and expansion of the theoretical edifices which had begun to surround and rewrite them. Freud's theory of seduction and Saussure's anagrammatic research were 'dangerous' because they compromised the unfolding of their respective sciences of interpretation, psychoanalysis (in particular the Oedipus complex) and structural linguistics.

Edited versions of *les anagrammes* began to appear in the second half of the 1960s through the efforts of Jean Starobinski (1979). Baudrillard devotes a section of *L'Echange symbolique* to the anagram and aligns it with a symbolic operation which destroys the linguistic theory of value (1976: 285–308). The anagram is presented by Baudrillard as a fundamentally anti-semiological concept since it subverts the unity of the sign's body and compromises the linearity of the signifier.

Despite this subversive force and, indeed, in virtue of it, the anagram has been subject to the rehabilitative measures of structural linguists who have sought to annex its positive power, thereby enriching their positions. Baudrillard thinks that these attempts at a structural recuperation are hopeless since rather than accumulating and distributing language as value, the anagram annihilates value. What is at stake is a manifestation of the anti-semiological force of poetics: 'Poetics is the insurrection of language against its own laws. Saussure himself never formulated this subversive consequence. But others have recognized what was dangerous in the simple formulation of another possible operation of language' (Baudrillard, 1976: 289).

Baudrillard counts Starobinski among those who have sought to integrate Saussure's anagrams into the structural linguistic study of poetry (1976: 288). Jakobson is also caught in what Baudrillard refers to as the 'untenable paradox' of recognizing just how subversive the anagram is, only still to model it on a signifier which splits its signifieds into two, latent and manifest.

Saussure's conception of the theme-word – to which I turn shortly – is 'rechristened' ironically by Baudrillard as *anathema* (1976: 287). It is the (ac)cursed principle of language which has the potential to kill the sign. According to Baudrillard in his short essay 'Le Théorème de la part maudite' in *La Transparence du Mal*, 'everything which expurgates its *part maudite* signs its own death' (1990: 11). Since the goal of the semiocrats of structural linguistics is to reduce the anagram to the 'combinatory abstraction of a code', they 'sign' – again the irony is obvious – the death of their enterprise by interring language and expurgating its symbolic principle.

Baudrillard identifies the examples of the law of alliteration to which the syllables and consonants of Saturnian lines of verse conform as the tripartite *loi de la couplaison*. Saussure's initial concern with repetition through alliteration led him to formulate the following rules:

1 A vowel can take its place in a Saturnian line if there is also a *counter vowel* somewhere in the line. . . . if the line does not have an *odd* number of syllables and one must count *every* syllable . . . the vowels pair exactly and must leave, as a remainder, zero. . . .

2 The law of consonants . . . is identical to the law of vowels and no less strict. . . .

3 If there is an irreducible residue . . . as can easily happen with *groups of consonants* irrespective of the number of syllables . . . this residue is not illegitimate. But the poet notes this . . . and one finds it reappearing in *the next line*, as a residuum, corresponding to the overflow of the

preceding line. And it is in such cases that one finds the most entertaining confirmation of this rule.

(Starobinski, 1979: 10–11)

It is important to keep in mind that Baudrillard is not only reading *the* Saussure of the anagrams against *the* Saussure of the *Cours*. His goal is to read the former Saussure against himself, that is, 'against his own restricted hypotheses on the Anagrams'. The rigorous attention to the principle of the counter vowel and consonants outlined by Saussure does not in Baudrillard's reading remain confined to a concern for repetition reducible to the accumulation of alliterative terms in certain lines of verse. Baudrillard makes critical use of the annulment/accumulation pair by emphasizing that the cycle of pairing leaves no remainder. In Baudrillard's estimation, this cycle of redoubling resolves itself completely, without remainder, or value.

The second law of the theme-word contains eight clauses the first of which will suffice for my purposes:

1 . . . This theme, chosen either by the poet or by the person who is paying for the inscription [an elogium] is composed of only a few words, either entirely of proper names or of one or two words added to the inherent function of proper names.

Thus, in this first operation the poet must have before him, with a view to forming his lines, the greatest number of potential *phonic fragments* he can draw from the theme.

(Starobinski, 1979: 11–12)

The theme-word, Baudrillard argues, is diffracted through the text of the poem and along certain of its lines. Just as the counter vowel was for Baudrillard an annihilative *anti-vowel* rather than an additive double, the theme-word explodes into irreclaimable fragments. Of course, one may still rearticulate the name but without reconstituting it, without, in short, 'resurrecting the signifier'.

Baudrillard thinks that Starobinski wrongly favours reconstitution over rearticulation. He does not appreciate that 'the symbolic act is never . . . this resurrection of an identity, it is always on the contrary in this volatilization of the name, of the signifier, in this *extermination of the term*, in this dispersion without return'

(1976: 219). The fragments of the theme-word circulate intensely through the poem – 'as in the primitive group on the occasion of the feast or sacrifice' – under the conditions of hypoweakness. As a symbolic act in the register of hypoweakness, Baudrillard's theme-word is said to leave neither remains nor results.

Le reste, c'est valeur. If the residuum is not subject to the sumptuary destruction and agonistic prestations of the potlatch, it may be accumulated, reconstituted and situated in a system of value (econo- and semio-linguistic). *Le reste* is quickly escorted to the bar, the place where insoluble residues gather.

It is in the following section in his reading of the anagram, 'The End of the Anathema', that Baudrillard reflects on his method. Up to this point, the anathema served as Baudrillard's means to radicalize Saussure's hypothesis. The anathema, how-ever, must end or be pushed to its end, because it presupposes a surface/manifest model. Starobinski's interpretation along these lines 'seems, however, to fall into the trap of presupposing a generative formula whose scattered presence in the poem would be in some sense only the second state, but whose identity it would always be possible to situate' (1976: 301). Reading is not a game of identification for Baudrillard: poetic effect is reduced to a key game played around the repetition of a latent identity. Poetics is on the other hand a bar game which destroys identity. Anagrammatic revolution is always symbolic and never psychoanalytic! The ana-theme is resolved in the poetic *jouissance* of symbolic exchange: '*jouissance* is directly a function of this resolution of all positive reference [of the final term, every reference, every key]' (1976: 302). *Jouissance* dimi-nishes as the sign's body reveals more and more of itself in a game of 'hide-and-seek with the signified'.

Baudrillard's main target here is Freud. In particular, he cites as instances of the traditional anagram or *texte à clef* the puzzles in the pages of *Fliegende Blätter* (*Drifting Leaves*) to which Freud turned in his analysis of secondary revision in *The Interpretation of Dreams* and, I note in passing, whose funnies provided Judge Schreber with material for enjoyable hallucinations. It is Lyotard's (1971) analysis of these cartoon-anagrams that Baudrillard explicitly mentions.

Consider this inscription (which appeared underneath a drawing of a motley band and their leader):

NOVAS PLASMA NUM EROS EX HEBE DA

The manifest text resembles a Latin inscription. A Latin word does in fact appear as the adverb NUM, but DA is a German adverb. In order to reach the latent text, one must not only study the arrangement of the terms but pronounce them while considering the narrative of the drawing: No, was blas' ma? – Numero Sechs – Hebet a'! (*Qu'est-ce qu'on joue, maintenant? – Le numéro six – En route!*; What shall we play next? – Number six – One, two . . . !) (Lyotard, 1971: 264). The difference between such a 'simple cryptogrammatic pleasure . . . and the symbolic irradiation of the poem' is that in the latter case 'the key is definitely lost' (Baudrillard, 1976: 303). It is only when the sign is truly broken, when there is nothing at all but an intense circulation in which the signifier bears no residual signifying bond with, for instance, any and every signified as in automatic writing, that the body of the sign may be said to have been sacrificed in a celebration of the resolution of language itself in the poetic (Baudrillard, 1976: 303, n. 1).

LYOTARD AND THE PRIMITIVE HIPPIES

The most perspicacious treatment of Baudrillard's struggle for an affirmative weakness is found in Lyotard's *Economie libidinale* (1974). In a long convoluted 'run' around Marx which is designed to avoid the trap set by rationality of producing a critique (showing that Marx was still alienated, religious, an economist; that he had forgotten something, etc.), Lyotard writes: 'The quite simple trap consists in *responding to the demand of the vanquished theory*, and this demand is: put something in my place. What is important is the place, not the content of the theory. It is the place of the theory which must be overcome. And this can be done only by displacement and flight' (1974: 129). On this view, one remains soundly weak by resisting the seductive request to occupy the space of theory with one's own strong hypotheses. Baudrillard could not resist: he does not know his own strength! Flight is a strength of the weak, even though certain rhetorical birds may try to fly through plateglass windows.

Although Lyotard notes that there is a *movement* in Baudrillard's work (a libidinal conception of exchange) with which he is sympathetic, Baudrillard installs a so-called non-place of non-value in the place of theory. Lyotard writes: 'the *truth* of the social relation is symbolic exchange in its ambivalence' (1974: 129). Further, in methodological terms, Baudrillard is said to produce through his reading of Mauss a lost referent, a 'fantasy of a non-alienated region' which is not only subversive but is 'present *positively* in modern society, not *negatively*, as Marx imagined it for the proletariat' (1974: 132). The idea of replacing production with seduction or mercantile exchange with symbolic exchange does not amount to a radical displacement in Lyotard's assessment of Baudrillard's hippie anthropology.

Lyotard goes so far as to claim that symbolic exchange seems to obey a semio-logic: the gift which is given, received and returned in the primitive form of exchange is an object charged with affect (i.e. it is the sign-vehicle of one's *mana*; the gift-sign is not inert, it has a soul; Mauss, 1973: 59–60). The gift, Lyotard argues, is a sign of something for someone; it takes the place of something, revealing what has been hitherto absent or hidden in a way which is entirely antithetical to Baudrillard's critique of a depth model of non-immediate, yet forthcoming, truth.

In short, the bar is still at work, it has not become even a silent comma (,), nor has it been 'crossed' successfully. I cannot pursue the extent to which Lyotard's project to show 'how political economy is libidinal economy' has its own ground where desire *is*, even where it is not supposed to be – in the most alienated places (Bennington, 1988: 35–9). Lyotard is at least as nostalgic for a hippie anti-economy as Baudrillard. This is also a battle to achieve a non-recuperable status, to not become something in particular. Lyotard's affirmative rather than critical weakness is a drift that seeks to work around the bar outside of critique (Lyotard, 1973: 15). As I have shown, the textual device of drifting as a tactical mode is the place of war.

According to his own criteria, Baudrillard cannot say very much about the symbolic without engaging the mechanisms of value, yet he must at least get off a few jokes as examples of the flash which decouples the sign. Lyotard's libidinal radicalism of the *Economie libidinale* contains its share of anti-semiological gestures. But in a passing remark in his treatment of the anagram, Baudrillard explains that it is useless to search for the *jouissance* which is symbolic exchange 'in an energetics, in an *économie libidinale* . . . : *jouissance* is not bound to the effectuation of a force, but to the actualization of an exchange' (1976: 289). Even here, though, the symbolic expresses an irreducible exchangeability in place of what had previously barred such pleasure.

The weak must play games of avoidance, especially since their work often demands their hasty flight. To turn on one's heels and to show them in flight is not to say that there is a place of one's own toward which one flees. If the symbolic, in spite of itself, stays in place after wreaking its damage, one must also attend to Baudrillard's observation that the symbolic is still *un terme simulateur* (1976: 13). Perhaps it was retired and assumed new forms because it violated his own criteria for its use. This does not explain why the symbolic was *replaced* by seduction.

THE WEAK AND THE DEAD

In my studies of Certeau, Lyotard and Baudrillard, I found that one could not maintain an affirmative weakness without building up a strong base, a place of one's own. Although one might also risk and win the game of balancing on the edge of a mystical nothingness for a time, this small victory may be spoiled either by emplacing one's theory where and from which a tactician must flee, or by slipping into nothingness in a speculation without value, without remains, without results, etc. Weakness, I argued, situated itself contradictorily on an interpretive and historical foundation of conflictual relations of pre-Socratic origin (which Baudrillard augmented with an anthropology derived from Mauss and Bataille) while borrowing liberally from the Greek rhetorical tradition.

An affirmative weakness must not displace in order to emplace itself; yet, it seems that it cannot help but do the latter. It must try not to mistake its continual trespasses for a kind of proprietory right. In principle, it is this resistance to placement that distinguishes poststructuralist or hypoweakness from Vattimo's Heideggerian sense of weakness; the latter occupies the clearing, the *Da* which understanding must continue to hold open so as to maintain a place for movement, even though some of the long-standing signposts have been defaced by the challenges issued by poststructuralism.

The failures of an affirmative weakness only mistakenly lend themselves to the reassertion of the non-local and non-specific hallmarks of what is called modernism. Why is this so? The struggle to maintain an affirmative weakness against all odds requires a certain kind of strength. A strength, that is, which cannot be consolidated and must be abandoned along the way. This strength will be inoperable and largely incomprehensible in the hands of the enemies of weakness. Hypoweakness is for this reason an effervescence which cannot be stabilized. It is no less genuine for this reason, and it remains irreducible to a passing trend, given its rhetorical lineage.

The capacity to recognize an opportune moment and to execute a timely strike were two closely related aspects of an affirmative weakness. It was equally important to avoid a complete fall into nothingness, even though Baudrillard has invented several ways in which to stumble: by means of his asemiological imaginary and onto the ground of agonistic relations, and by emplacing symbolic exchange and subsequently replacing it as well. Any vanishing act must provide as little evidence as possible of the prospect of a repeat performance, and as little evidence as possible of any of its activities. Baudrillard has paid a heavy price in order to advance his claims for a resolution without remainder. But in order to confound and to elude the system of representations of a dominant order, a weak force must produce more and more irregularly its already sly motions and movements. A temporal practice, for instance, cannot be so easily divided and conquered as if it were a territory. Baudrillard and his colleagues in weakness have had long intellectual careers in which to develop their elusive notions, and I do not want to leave the impression that I believe I have defeated them in one stroke.

From a temporal perspective, autodestruction may be a strength of the weak since it need not necessitate a definitive breakdown. Nothingness is not the equivalent of silence, nor is this silence more than a temporary condition, although it is certainly stronger than nothing at all; neither does it exclude a cagey or Cagean infiltration of a dominant discourse. Although one might not be able to say anything at all about the symbolic, it is not always necessary to speak in order to express oneself in this mode.

In *L'Echange symbolique*, silence equals death. But death is the most radical form of hypoweakness. For Baudrillard death is a *form* in two senses. First, it takes the dynamic form of symbolic reversibility and, second, in a Marxian sense which Baudrillard only suggests in passing (1976: 202), it is a social form as mysterious as a commodity. The fetishism of commodities presents a universe in which things have come alive. The products of labour are shown to their producers as if social relations existed among the former in an object universe which also enters into social relations with the mundane world of the latter. Death, then, appears to living human beings as a 'social exile' strictly separated from life. Under the repressive sway of the power bar, the imaginary and fetishistic disjunction of life/death is held in place. Power, understood as social control, separates each of us from our own death. This power bar is the source *par excellence* of alienation. Baudrillard attempts to decipher the hieroglyphic of death in order to reclaim it as a non-alienated region. Death, he thinks, may in this manner be articulated socially. It is not the death of a subject or a body that is at issue here. This is not a suicide pact.

Kellner has sought to come to terms with Baudrillard's notion of death. He refers to it as 'the ultimate signified in the Baudrillardian universe' (1987: 119), although Baudrillard takes great pains to destroy the logic of finality and irreversibility normally afforded to death. It is not, moreover, that death triumphs over life. In a culture which dreams of defeating death, even beyond its explicit domestication in the 'abstract digitality' put into place by means of bars, death itself is the only thing which can challenge this culture. To articulate death socially constitutes a mortal danger, Baudrillard claims, to the dominant system because it reveals the degree to which death is administered and programmed by the system's Thanatos Centres (funeral home, hospital, highway). Death must be played against death. Death becomes radical when it is resocialized and stripped of its individual fatality; when it becomes, in other words, a condition of social being.

Baudrillard refers to certain initiation rites in the 'primitive order' as privileged instances of the symbolic reciprocity between the living and the dead. The symbolic death of the initiates 'becomes the stake of a reciprocal/antagonistic exchange between the ancestors and the living and, in place of a break, a social relation between partners is instituted, a circulation of gifts and counter-gifts as intense as the circulation of precious goods and women – a play of incessant responses in which death can no longer be set up as an end or instance' (Baudrillard, 1976: 203). Hefner has praised Baudrillard's 'perhaps admirable notion of reciprocity' even though it 'never operated anywhere simply for the sake of its own poetry' (1977: 113). This notion, Hefner concludes, offers little consolation today. As we have seen, Lyotard for his part chides Baudrillard for his hippie dream.

Baudrillard attempts to meet this kind of objection in the following manner. The only thing the weak can retake is their death, not as an individual sacrifice, but as a symbolic relation whose intensity produces pleasure. Today, we are reduced to bargaining with our dead through melancholy, and there is no strength in this attitude. Baudrillard's anthropology is poetic and death stands at the head of the line before anagrammatic dispersion, wit, etc., as a pataphysical solution. The salient point is that Baudrillard's claims are poetic, and merely to recognize them as such does not constitute a critical insight.

Baudrillard is careful in *L'Echange symbolique*, just as he was in *Pour une critique*, to try to deflect the charge that he produces a 'mystical fusion' of terms such as life and death beyond the disjunctive code. There is no nostalgia in his work, he claims, for a 'fusional utopia', nor does he 'play happily' with analogies between the collective events of 'primitive' societies and the autonomic psychic sphere, thereby engaging in a 'profound mystification'. Analogical distance and the distortions of applying production, the unconscious and repression to 'primitive' cultures are erased in the immediacy of symbolic exchange. Although Baudrillard does not want to produce signs of the way in which death may be played against the system in the same manner as our culture conjures death by the signs of survival, death cannot be shown to be silent semiotically, without also being mystical.

HOSTAGE ANTI-VALUE

'Nous sommes tous des otages': this phrase is a refrain in Baudrillard's writings from *L'Echange symbolique* to *La Transparence*. Who or what is holding 'us' hostage? We are all hostages in the sense that the system holds our death in the

balance. My death is out of my hands – it will be minutely administered, officially announced and, in short, coded in a structural economy of death; no matter how I die, my death will be found out.

Throughout 'Ma mort partout, ma mort qui rêve' in *L'Echange symbolique*, Baudrillard elaborates his conception of death in terms of the gift and counter-gift couched in an anti-economic, symbolic obligation to return what one has received (1976: 243–82). The counter-gift is not life. One is completely trapped in 'the biological simulation of one's own body' if, Baudrillard argues, one neither wants to give nor receive death. In his presentation of the symbolic exchange of death, Baudrillard first animates the system's gift of death by evoking the spiritual power of the gift. Even the gift of death issued from the statistical indifference of an anonymous system may be socialized in a radical gesture. Baudrillard imports the idea from Mauss that the thing received has a 'soul'. One would not dare to keep it or refuse to return it, thereby breaking the social bond it establishes and risk bringing its moral and spiritual power against oneself. As a gift, death obliges one to return a counter-gift to the system. The system manifests its superiority by controlling death, in giving a gift that cannot be returned. To accept a gift without returning it in kind or with something even more powerful or valuable is to subordinate oneself to the giver (Mauss, 1973: 269).

Baudrillard is not interested in drawing subtle anthropological distinctions between the Haida and the Maori, between the potlatch and the 'hau' of 'taonga'. Baudrillard's efforts are guided by the following sentiment expressed by Mauss: 'In our times, the old principles react against the rigors, abstractions, and inhumanity of our codes' (1973: 260). The symbolic violates the code and shortcircuits capitalist–exchangist relations. Deleuze and Guattari also turned to Mauss for much the same reason in *Anti-Oedipus* (1977: 185ff). They praised Mauss for 'at least leaving open' the question that debt was not reducible to a structural exchange, that it challenged the idea of exchange and could become the basis for an alternative definition of society. But Deleuze and Guattari do not accept Baudrillard's idea of a non-structural exchange since exchange remains the conceptual basis of the definition of society rather than their notion of inscription.

How can one possibly eclipse the power of the system? Baudrillard writes:

> We are all hostages. This is the secret of the hostage taking: we all dream, instead of dying ridiculously in the end, of receiving death, and of giving death. To give and to receive is a symbolic act (it is the symbolic act par excellence) which rids death of all the indifferent negativity that it has for us in the 'natural' order of capital.
>
> (Baudrillard, 1976: 253)

If the semiurgical system has kidnapped the symbolic, how does one respond? 'In order not to be taken, take others hostage': Baudrillard suggests we are all terrorists (1982a: 6–7).

If the system controls death to such a degree that it seeks to prevent certain forms of it, the counter-gift must exploit precisely these forms. Death is socialized by the symbolic. It must not come to one from an abstract, impersonal force ('nature', 'science', 'state'). Death exists as a social relation between persons. It is 'anti-natural' or, as Baudrillard prefers, artificial and sacrificial. Death is a social relation established through ceremony and artifice. By partaking of the accidental, the bitter pill of death control may be spat back at the system which distributed and accounted for it in relation to several general equivalents so as not to lose any of its value. Accidental death cannot be controlled, and therefore it has for Baudrillard a 'symbolic yield'. But accidents are not so accidental, Baudrillard specifies, because this is the name bestowed upon them by the system in order to be able to calculate and distribute them in its official records, to entomb them statistically. The 'symbolic particularity' of the accident is found in its social and sacrificial character. Here, death can be given and received.

The ritual execution of a hostage has a 'symbolic yield 100 times superior to that of the automobile death, itself already 100 times superior to that of natural death' (Baudrillard, 1976: 253). Industrial accidents, it is said, have no symbolic import – this is no different from their existing value in the system. The death of a hostage is 'totally undeserved and thus totally artificial, therefore perfect from the sacrificial point of view'. Baudrillard's rough tally of 'yield' reveals the danger of the example of a hostage's execution since the highest work of the system is also 'executed' (literally accounted for) in this event. Such 'tallying' is completely normalized in the economic hostages of developing countries and individual investors as much as blackmail is generalized by bankers and insurance agents. What, then, does the terrorist act demonstrate? Why are we all terrorists, anyway?

In *L'Echange symbolique*, the ritual execution of a hostage was said to have a high symbolic 'yield'. By the time we reach Baudrillard's reflections on the hostage taking in *La Transparence du Mal*, the analysis of death as a counter-gift has fallen away. The question of the meaning and import of the hostage taking remains central to Baudrillard's theorizing from the perspective of the symbolic, even if the symbolic has come to take new forms beyond the gift. Death is replaced by the power to designate Evil, to reintroduce an Absolute Evil into a universe defined by its ability to rid itself of all negativity and Evil. Baudrillard's new 'tally sheet' reads this way: if the principle of Evil is *la part maudite*, and every effort is made to expel this devil's share from our artificial paradise of positivity and operational whiteness, symbolic power accrues to the one who can (re)introduce the Evil share, with all the violence of an *effraction* (break and entry), through our Western prophylaxes into a clean, all-American universe.

In the Rushdie affair, Khomeini employed a weapon more powerful than arms, oil and money: the principle of Evil. For Baudrillard, he gave 'spectacular proof of the possibility of a reversal of all relations of force by the symbolic power of a *prise de parole* [speech]' (Baudrillard, 1990: 88). Khomeini's *prise de parole* was a *prise d'otage*. Baudrillard thinks that 'Westerners' (without distinction) are the fanatics – fanatic about our softness, our consensus on the expulsion of evils and viruses, on the rights of 'man', etc. Our societies are for these reasons vulnerable to the 'least viral attack', to the very thing we have lost the ability to tolerate. Such a culture is so thoroughly allopathic that it has systematically endangered itself. Baudrillard further dramatizes Khomeini's decree through an analogy with the opening of a crack in the fuselage of an aircraft; like Cixous and Clément (1986: 96ff), Baudrillard plays on the similarity between *un vol* (a flight) and *un vol* (a theft), and the phrase *vol avec effraction* (robbery or theft with break and entry) suggests the breakthrough of the symbolic:

The effects of fascination, attraction and universal repulsion unleashed by the death decree against Rushdie resemble the phenomenon of the sudden depressurization of an aircraft at the time of a break or a fracture in the fuselage (even if it is accidental, it always seems like a terrorist act). Everything is violently sucked outside, toward the void, in virtue of the difference in pressure between the two spaces. It is enough to open a break, a hole in the ultra-thin layer which separates the two worlds. In the form of taking hostages terrorism is the act par excellence which opens this type of break in an artificial and artificially protected universe (our own).

(Baudrillard, 1990: 90)

There is nothing left to do but to stand guard over the oxygen masks! Baudrillard's complex analogy also presents the hostage as a microbe of sorts. The speech in which the hostage is taken enters through the opening created by Khomeini's speech and infects the Western system; this entry is, it would seem, a reentry since for years multinational capital has either dumped its 'waste' in 'other worlds' or supported specific byproducts of this process.

Khomeini designates what can no longer be tolerated (Evil), and maximizes what has been minimized. An individual such as Rushdie is taken hostage not so much by being taken anywhere but as a result of the West having been taken hostage. This hostage drama provides proof for Baudrillard of 'the ineluctable cowardness of entire collectivities vis-à-vis the least of their members. This indifference of the collectivity has for its correlate the indifference of each individual vis-à-vis the collectivity . . . it is this political misery that the strategy of the hostage reveals without pity' (1990: 92). Baudrillard's theoretical interest in the Rushdie affair not only furthers his ongoing interest and analysis of the hostage form, but conforms perfectly to his repeated introductions of 'archaic elements in a modern context' as a standard critical exercise (from the gift to the fatwa). In both cases Baudrillard isolates what the system cannot tolerate, either in terms of what it cannot prevent, and thus control and exchange, or an external irritant which puts into jeopardy the delicate 'immunological' balances of its prosthetic systems.

'We are all hostages, we are all terrorists', Baudrillard has written in *Les Stratégies fatales* (1983: 44). This is the 'mirror of terrorism', terrorism understood as the image in a distorted mirror of the social and political orders. The hostage is a non-negotiable, inexchangeable pure object, a crystal if you like. The hostage is not a commodity (not as yet); neither alienated as a commodity which becomes a use value for others by entering into the circuit of exchange, nor strictly speaking in the first instance a non-value for its captors. This inexchangeable object symbolizes the death of the scene of exchange as a system of value (Baudrillard, 1983: 54). The hostage takes its revenge, like any fatal object, inasmuch as no one knows what to do with it nor how to get rid of it. What rises from the ashes of the scene of exchange? The hostage renders exchange ob-scene, more visible than visible, with pornographic detail.

When Baudrillard looks into the mirror of terrorism he finds verification of the banality of blackmail, the normality of the hostage taking (nuclear blackmail, OPEC holding oil-importing countries hostage, the blackmail of participation – or as the Government of the Province of Ontario tells its citizens: engage in particip*action* – held out by the social, etc.). The 'fantastic dream' of the impossible exchange has come crashing down with the Gulf War.

In the 'Miroir du terrorisme' in *La Transparence du Mal*, Baudrillard addresses the simulacral character of the European Cup match played in Madrid in 1987 between Real Madrid and Naples before an empty stadium – but broadcast in its entirety on television – in terms of the 'terrorist hyperreality of our world'. Events are decontextualized, defined televisually and take place in a vacuum; before a public, that is, banished for its own safety to the comfort of images. This pure event is a 'kind of surgical anticipation of our future events: an event so minimal that it could not have taken place, but with a maximal amplification on the screen' (1990: 86–7). The future event in question is the Gulf War. It is in these terms that Baudrillard reads the war in *La Guerre du golfe n'a pas eu lieu* (1991).

By the time Baudrillard's book on the war had appeared – the first essay appeared in the French newspaper *Libération* on 4 January and thus predates the UN deadline of 15 January for the withdrawal of Iraqi forces from Kuwait; the second was written relative to February and the beginning of the ground war; a fragment of the third essay also appeared in *Libération* on 29 March some weeks after Iraq's acceptance of the UN ceasefire on 2 March – the North American Baudrillardians had already produced their master's response to the war before it had 'taken place' in his book (for instance, Der Derian, 1991). There is no clearer example of the precession of simulacra.

Baudrillard's first essay, 'La Guerre du golfe n'aura pas lieu', treats the war as a non-event: 'after the hot war (the violence of conflict), after the cold war (the equilibrium of terror), here we have the dead war – the thawing out of the cold war' (1991: 9). As this frozen cadaver thawed, it began to putrefy, making everyone nauseous. There is no future for this stinking corpse of war; not even American technology can resurrect it, since America itself hums with a dead energy and is incapable of assuming power in the form of a struggle. A slaughter is not a struggle. The Gulf War will not have taken place in the ruins of the mutual dissuasion of the superpowers. This balance of terror has become in Baudrillard's estimation an auto-dissuasion, a self-deterrence.

The new 'protagonist of the simulacrum' is the hostage:

> The hostage is the phantom actor, the cipher who occupies the powerless space of the war. Today, it is the hostage on the strategic site, tomorrow the hostage as a Christmas present, the hostage as exchange value and as liquidity. Fantastic degradation of what was the very figure of the impossible exchange.
>
> (Baudrillard, 1991: 11)

All of us were hostages of the media during this non-war (Baudrillard included); all of us were held strategically *in situ* by the screen, just as groups of Westerners were held *in situ* for strategic purposes in Iraq. The strategic site par excellence in the West was the television set.

The dream of a pure inexchangeable object comes to an end with Saddam Hussein. Saddam is 'the capitalist of hostage value'. Baudrillard has forgotten Oliver North's only regret: he tried to put a price on the hostages. The 'arms-for-hostages' imbroglio of Irangate signalled the entry of the hostage into the circuit of capitalist exchange.

All the same, one of the hard lessons Baudrillard learned from the events in the Gulf was that his idea of the hostage as a challenge to the order of exchange was compromised by Saddam and, to be sure, by the subsequent negotiated release of

Thomas Sutherland, Terry Waite, Terry Anderson, *et al.* The personal apology Terry Waite received from his captors was, in Baudrillard's terms, a message to the West: 'We apologize for having captured you.' Waite's further remarks that 'they recognize now this was the wrong thing to do, that holding hostages achieves no useful, contructive purpose' (in Powell, 1991 and Martin, 1991), brings home in spite of itself Baudrillard's thesis that the anti-exchangist gesture without consequences is the 'purposiveness without purpose' of the hostage taking. Yet, on a level of analysis sensitive to the configurations Israeli–Arab–American relations have assumed since the death of Khomeini, the dream of an inexchangeable object is just that: a dream. I do not want to claim that Baudrillard's interpretation of the hostage is in some invocation of *Realpolitik* only a dream, as if dreams had no power. His reading of the hostage has always been in the service of the symbolic, not in the service of *Realpolitik*, nor has he been attentive to the prisoners-for-hostages, policy-for-hostages, human-remains-for-hostages, ransoms, and even the outbreak of 'peace' between Israel and its neighbours, which have punctuated the hostage drama for many years. These facts repudiate the theory only if one believed naively in the first place that the theory was straightforwardly applicable, descriptive, explained certain events, etc. There is no straight gate to the real.

Baudrillard leaves the impression that once upon a time one could pass by way of a logical chain from '*le virtuel*' (in the Aristotelian sense of potential; and not actual, hyperreal) to the actual (real). This is no longer possible because the '*passage à l'acte*' (a term Baudrillard borrows from psychoanalysis; in English it is usually rendered 'acting out', compulsive behaviour marking the emergence of hitherto repressed contents), which would have carried the virtual to the actual, has been tainted by the logic of dissuasion and self-deterrence. Self-deterrence, then, prevents 'acting out'. Events are stuck in a 'hyperrealist logic of the dissuasion of the real by the virtual'.

Saddam is a virtuoso of the virtual. He not only extended 'virtual hospitality' to world leaders and in exchange for these state visits and international legitimation freed groups of foreign nationals, but paralyzed the world momentarily by the virtual death of the hostages. The passage from the virtual to the real cannot be acted out because of 'the fear of everything real, of all real violence, of all *jouissance* which is too real. Against this fear of the real we have erected a gigantic apparatus of simulation enabling us to realize the passage "in vitro" (Baudrillard, 1991: 16). Together with the biological metaphors which support it, Baudrillard's use of 'acting out' suggests a change in his thinking from *L'Echange symbolique* and *De la séduction*, since the depth implied by the unconscious and the problematic bar of repression returns if only implicitly. In the techno-reductionistic readings of 'virtual' which abound, the recognition of the direct and indirect military and multinational sources of funding is often suppressed in favour of the thrills and chills of hyperreality. Baudrillard's reading of the Gulf War may dampen some of these spirits.

In the second essay, 'La Guerre du golfe a-t-elle vraiment lieu?' Baudrillard finds a symbol of what he calls a post-Clauswitzean episode (the non-war of publicity is the absence of politics pursued by other means): a sea bird covered in oil on a beach in the Gulf. This is a symbol 'of what we all are, before our screens, before this sticky and unintelligible event' (1991: 23). The question of the passage to war remains central for Baudrillard. As the generals and other war experts displayed more and more of their artificial intelligence through their 'war-processing' devices, the more difficult it became, Baudrillard contends, for the war to take place. Just as the word processor takes the dramatic uncertainty out of the *'passage à l'acte'* of writing, the war-processor presents scenarios which are too detailed, too complete; the probability of battle is overcalculated and overprocessed into its inverse. All of this preprogramming prevents the *'passage à la guerre'*. Baudrillard seems to have forgotten that the battles by which the American military ravaged Vietnam were not called a 'war' and thus did not require a passage to war in order to become one.

In the second essay Baudrillard attempts to address his differences with his colleague Paul Virilio on the Gulf. Virilio's reflections on the varieties of the so-called 'direct' representation of events and the revolutionary telepresence of observation in 'real time' are turned back into themselves by Baudrillard. The revolution of 'real time' becomes the involution of 'real time', 'an involution of the event in the instantaneity of all things at once'. Baudrillard holds that 'real time' evokes a spectral event, an event which is 'encrusted in information'. In short, the move

toward the 'directness' of 'real time' gives the illusion of progress toward the real event.

While Virilio thinks of the war, we are told, in terms of
apocalyptic escalation, Baudrillard reads it as dissuasive and
virtual. These two apparently irreconcilable positions eventually
converge inasmuch as 'the war and the nonwar have happened
at the same time' (Baudrillard, 1991: 49–50). The simultaneous
event/non-event of this very strange war indicates, as far as
Baudrillard is concerned, that 'the space of war has become
definitely non-euclidean'. It is from the perspective of the unde-
cidability of the war as an event that Baudrillard launches
attacks on anyone who has not interrogated the reality of the
event.

It is in the final essay, 'La Guerre du golfe n'a pas eu lieu', that
Baudrillard considers Iraq's ironic contributions to the New
World Order, especially the service it rendered in its war against
Iran. Iraq 'served to liquidate . . . the most radical form of the
anti-Western challenge' (1991: 99). Even Baudrillard must recognize that 'liquidate' is too strong a word to describe the results of
the Iran–Iraq war.

The consensus manufactured through the American domi-
nated UN gave the Gulf War an unprecedented global and legal
base and a monopolistic hold on democracy. American-style
democracy was brought to bear upon Iraq in the name of the
New World Order: 'the crucial and decisive stake in this entire
affair was the consensual reduction of Islam to the world order'
(Baudrillard, 1991: 98). In the name of the 'democratic' law of the
New World Order, Islam (embodied this time by Iraq) was to be,
as Baudrillard aptly puts it, 'domesticated' so that the radical
challenge which it symbolizes for the West will have been
neutralized or stunned into passivity. The American 'missionar-
ies of democracy' routinely stun their converts, Baudrillard
remarks, by administering jolts of democracy by electroshock.
Does the 'Evil Other' survive the war, at least theoretically?

The consensual and televisual war had as one of its goals the
domestication of the Evil Other and the bloody exorcism of
the challenge it posed to the West. The death of Khomeini
did not erase the decree against Rushdie, although his passing
weakened the phonocentric zeal with which commentators
approached his speeches and the grain of his voice. Baudrillard
once again produces a 'tally sheet': 'The strangest thing is that

the other no longer believes in its powerlessness, but the one who does not believe in its powerlessness is much stronger than the one who does not believe in its power, even if this power was a thousand times superior' (1991: 91). The strength of the weak is a matter of belief. Here, it is based largely on a cliché about the opacity of Americans to themselves (irreducibly other even to themselves). In spite of Saddam's capitulations and the anamorphoses of the symbolic, the radical alterity and irreducibility of Islam and its symbolic power remain intact, at least for Baudrillard, although no one knows who will prevail.

It is evident that Baudrillard's analysis of the hostage as a pure object has in its own terms been undone over time by the Gulf War. It was in his metareporting about the war that Baudrillard was able to bring to closure at least one variety of symbolic exchange. In addition, the symbolic power of the Other was also diminished and almost completely compromised. There still remains in *La Guerre du golfe* an element of hope connected with the possibilities afforded by further manifestations of the symbolic. In the meantime, Baudrillard hedges his theoretical bets with vagueness. It is safe to say that this hope has shrunk considerably since the time of *L'Echange symbolique*. To conclude that Baudrillard's vision is dark, nihilistic and hopeless is unwarranted. This does not obviate the need for an exposition and analysis of the blind spots in his vision, nor does it release him from the murky depths of his repeated valorizations of so-called 'primitive' social systems and rituals.

Baudrillard is forced to retreat into the virtual and to place his concept of the symbolic into the realm of hypothetical possibility. Baudrillard was, after all, one of many thinkers who were caught or rather stuck in the mediatic oil slick of the Gulf. He too had to wallow in the hallucinogenic pleasure of the false, of the lure. While he furiously wrote over the gaps in the coverage of the war and struggled to stay the complete withdrawal of his concept of the symbolic (even in its more recent manifestations), having seen the emergence of hostage value, there are numerous moments of regret in *La Guerre du golfe*. These include a phallocratic regret that the non-war could not afford satisfaction because of his profound displeasure with this interminable striptease; the sterotyping of Saddam as a rug merchant who exists in the 'inverse of real time: the recurrent time of *The Thousand and One Nights*'; and finally, there is most importantly an ungenerous failure to recognize that there is nothing meta-phorical or symbolic about dying in a war which could not take place, or rather, whose place was 'taken' by the American propaganda and war machine.

The rambling essays of Baudrillard's *La Guerre du golfe*, built of numerous analogies presented in the form of aphorisms, are perhaps more coherent than the two volumes of *Cool Memories*, but they are of the same sort: cool and participatory, like tele-vision, although they concern a medium which did as much as it could to hide any critical messages by reflecting incessantly upon itself. The tenses of the essays – (i) future, 'will not have'; (ii) present, 'has it really'; (iii) *passé composé*, 'has not had' or has not taken place – convey Baudrillard's own passage between the negation of the future event of a war which seemed to defy its own inevitability and his judgement, formed on the basis of questioning after the 'reality' of the event and stated from the points of the view of a series of 'presents' each of which seemed to mark the duration of the war, that this 'war' did not pass into the real. These 'time bombs' parallel his concern with the pass-age to war. The question of the 'place' at which the war has not transpired may be answered in part by an appeal to the image of an event suspended in a media lab of disinformation, an infor-mational vat which functioned inversely with respect to the event in its efforts to speed the war along. Baudrillard's con-cerns were brought home with startling clarity by Mordecai Briemberg (1992) when he wrote (in the 'Preface' to a collection of essays and art on the war against Iraq), in the manner in which traditional Arab folk-tellers begin their stories, *Kan wa ma kan*: It was and it was not . . . a war . . . a television spectacle . . . in the Gulf . . . a new world order . . . 43 days long.

PATAPHYSICAL GESTURES

'Pataphysician at twenty – situationist at thirty – utopist at forty – transversal at fifty – viral and metaleptic at sixty – that's my history', Baudrillard remarked in *Cool Memories II* (1990a: 131). The implications of Baudrillard's formative or, if you like, pata-physical years – which never really ended – will concern me here. The influence of the playwright Alfred Jarry (1873–1907), in whose writings the so-called 'science' of pataphysics origi-nated, is very much in evidence throughout Baudrillard's *oeuvre*.

For instance, in a playful aside in an essay on Victor Segalen (to whose work I return in Chapter 4), 'L'Exotisme radicale', in *La Transparence du Mal*, Baudrillard remarks: 'Every acting out is an imaginary solution. This is why *patagonie* rhymes so well with *pataphysique*, which is the science of imaginary solutions. Pataphysic and agonistic. Patagonistic' (1990: 154–5). While Baudrillard often proceeds on the basis of the formal charm of concepts in poetic collision, in this example he brings together, with the assistance of a sketchy definition of Jarry's 'science', his own fascination with the Argentinian region which he has visited and photographed (but perhaps knows best through his reading of Bruce Chatwin's exotic travelogues) and an unassuming use of the concept of competition/conflict between protagonists (*agon*), which indicates a general agonistics underwriting and undermining poststructuralist arguments against magisterial discourses.

In both *Amérique* (1986: 229)) and 'Le Destin de l'énergie' in *La Transparence du Mal* (1990: 107), Baudrillard refers to the Perpetual-Motion-Food Bicycle Race in Jarry's *Le Surmâle*. In the former, he likens, through a series of rhetorical questions, 'America' to the Race; that is, during the 10,000 mile, trans-Siberian race between a team of cyclists on a bicycle built for five and an express train, one of the riders expires *en route*. It is, however, in death that he is able to set a pace so remarkable that the cycle outruns the train! Like Jarry's dead cyclist, America is at its most powerful when its time has passed: this power is hysteresial (a physical process in which there is a time-lag between causes and the appearance of their effects; the appearance of the latter depend upon an established pattern of causes). In a reflection on extreme phenomena which implicates both physics and metaphysics, Baudrillard suggests that the chaotic declination of energy, its liberation as it were, is 'a vertiginous process which feeds on itself'. For Baudrillard, Jarry's dead cyclist and New York City are cut from the same cloth: in both cases it is a matter of living off the energy born in the expenditure of energy, of *mobilité cadavérique*.

La Gidouille d'Ubu, the famous gut of Père Ubu, has served Baudrillard well from the time of *L'Echange symbolique* through *Les Stratégies fatales* to *Cool Memories 1980–1985* in its capacity as a symbol of the parodic circularity and the pseudocyesis of power which he thinks defines the spiralling systems of our culture.

Ubu is the central character in the Ubu cycle of plays (*Ubu Roi, Ubu Cocu,* and *Ubu Enchaîné*). The notorious *Ubu Roi* appeared in 1896. *Ubu Cocu* was written between 1890 and 1894 and was only published (posthumously) in 1944, while *Ubu Enchaîné,* written in 1899, was published in 1900. The phrase 'Ubu cycle of plays' is a fanciful formation which alludes to Jarry's love of cycling and the extravagant ways in which the trappings of this sport were integrated into his life and work. Pataphysics is introduced by Ubu and later elaborated by Dr Faustroll in Jarry's 'neo-scientific novel' *Gestes et opinions du Docteur Faustroll, pataphysicien* (written in 1898 and published in 1911; Jarry, 1972).

My goal is not to rehearse the relationship between the work of Baudrillard and Jarry. What Baudrillard learned from Jarry was how to embellish his work with scientific concepts. This 'borrowing' both enriched his prose – but without, ironically, lending it scientific respectability – and reduced some of such concepts (fractal, for instance) to their adjectival value. The poetic value of these rich modifiers rises as they are stripped of their substantive content, decontextualized and strung together in fast succession. As a textual practice, rhetorical science is not peculiar to Baudrillard. A rhetorical science is not to be confused with a so-called postmodern science, since the former is a science fiction practised in the service of the symbolic.

Although there is some debate about the authorship of the urtext of *Ubu Roi* (LaBelle, 1980: 8), it emerged from a farcical puppet play (*The Poles* 1885–87) staged by Jarry and his friends Charles, Henri and Charlotte Morin while they were students at a lycée in Rennes. Ubu was inspired by their physics teacher Félix Hébert, a short man with a magnificent gut which he maintained by means of *petit fours*. The alimentary machine which is Ubu is articulated by an immense *gidouille* (syn. *giborgne*); Jarry's two pairs of neologisms, the other combination being *boudouille* and *bouzine*, signify digestive, sexual and excretory functions and organs (Arrivé, 1972: 201–10) – a crude retention–evacuation device not unlike Baudrillard's description of Beaubourg. Recall that it was Ubu's excrementitious opening salvo of *Merd(r)e!* on the début of *Ubu Roi* on 10 December 1896 which did a great deal to provoke the riotous catharsis which ensued. The French *merd(r)e* may be rendered in English by the equally bastard (due to the 'r') form of 'shitr' or 'sheeyit', as one finds in certain fanciful translations. Roger Shattuck explains that 'public utterance of the word was, in 1896, unthinkable' (1955: 161), although it was certainly known as *le mot de Cambronne*: '*Braves Français, rendez-vous! Général Cambronne répondit: Merde!*'

Just as Jarry learned his physics, chemistry and mathematics at a lycée in Rennes, Baudrillard would later learn his pataphysics at a lycée in Reims. According to Henri Béhar, there are many traces of Jarry's lessons and curious extracurricular experiments in his work. For instance, the manuscript of *Faustroll* was said to have been written in invisible ink, and thus it was legible only under infrared light; the Perpetual Motion Food had a base of strychnine and alcohol in accordance with an inverted homeopathic principle: if a weak dose is dangerous, then a strong dose is beneficial (Béhar, 1980: 193).

We have before us, then, a substantial gut. But this is not the referent of a 'before' picture. One must not succumb to the urge to hypostatize Ubu, believing that one has found an essential referent of Baudrillard's text. Ubu is essential, but in the following sense. Charles Grivel (1986: 11) asserts that 'Ubu is abdominal': he is and he has his stomach. In a similar vein, Armand Guilmette (1984: 72) thinks that Ubu is his own referent: *Tout Ubu!* With respect to Ubu's sovereign dispensation of justice in *Ubu Roi* iii. 2, for instance, Guilmette writes that 'Ubu is the law. He does not even take the time to decree it, since he has merged with it'. Although I might have used the word 'reify' instead of hypostatize, this term does not connote the accumulation of substances in certain parts of the body, a medical dimension which Baudrillard is careful to build into his account of the obesity of transmodernity. Arrivé has pointed out that the gut-bag is not an object which may be destroyed (Ubu does not have fatty deposits in his belly which may be threatened with swords, diets or the like). On the contrary, the grand paunch and, indeed, Ubu too, are simulacral (Arrivé, 1972: 202). Baudrillard's 'medicine' is paraphysical and Ubu is suspended in an intertextual imaginary of Jarry's theatre and Baudrillard's speculative prose.

In Baudrillard's terms, Ubu is an *ecstatic* form. He potentializes himself, like an obese system, to the nth degree: *Steigerung* triumphs over *Aufhebung* (1983: 38). The spiral of an intense reduplication through which the system produces more of itself carries the sign of Ubu: the figure of the spiral on his *gidouille* was a helical form much beloved by Jarry. It is also the emblem of the Ordre de la Grand Gidouille adopted by the Collège de Pataphysique. A system may be said to be ubuesque due to its hyperplastic spiral into what is more real than the real. Although in some quarters it has become a matter of critical and historical protocol to read poststructuralism and Baudrillard through the seminal texts of the Collège de Sociologie (Richman, 1988), I attend a different college in search of other 'patacessors'.

In Baudrillard's world, all of society's bodies are cancerous. The metastasis of obese systems affects the transfer and enjoins the spiral with the helix inasmuch as it seems for Baudrillard as if bodies rebel against their genetic decrees by pursuing their own delirious ends (1983: 37). 'Metastasis' is a term with applications in both pathology and rhetoric: in the latter, it indicates a swift change in subject matter, as we in fact find in Baudrillard's rapid move from Ubu to DNA; furthermore, it connotes a revolutionary transformation of the sort Baudrillard describes in terms of the destructuration of value which marks the advent of a viral culture.

For Baudrillard, it's as if we are all a little bit Ubu; he is the sign of our *fatalité*. Perhaps, then, we might heed the words of Eluard and Péret (1977): *A chacun sa panse*. Carried, as Baudrillard would like, along the spiral pathway of the *as if*, one meets another biological term central to his writing. 'Hypertely' is the overdevelopment of organisms, which may be manifested by the growth of useless appendages (i.e. extra horns) such as a *gidouille*; in Baudrillard's use of the term it means a hyperend, that which has gone beyond its own ends. This *grosse bedaine* is as vacant and simulacral as any imaginary body part. Now, since there is nothing biological about Ubu, we need not watch our paunches so very closely.

Ubu is the definitive hypostasis of the social. He is a misshapen figure (*gidouille*, retractile ear, three teeth – one of stone, one of iron and one of wood) and a foundational persona of Baudrillard's textual imaginary of the pataphysical *as if*: 'Ubu: the small intestine and the splendor of emptiness. Ubu form full and obese, of a grotesque immanence and a brilliant truth. A figure of genius, replete with that which has absorbed and transgressed everything, shining in the void like an imaginary solution' (Baudrillard, 1983: 79–80). We happen upon Ubu with the same mixture of horror and disgust as one who finds an eye at the bottom of a chamber pot. Effulgent Ubu, brought forth as brilliantly as Granero's eye by the horn of a bull, an imaginary solution to Simone's desire (Bataille, 1970: 56–7).

As a figure of the social, Ubu, too, comes to absorb everything, leaving no remainders. Ubu is also subject to a bar game. The bar which separates a weak from a strong term (nothing/everything, hypo/hyper) becomes inoperative, Baudrillard has argued in 'Quand on enlève tout, il ne reste rien' (1978c), when one considers the problem of *le reste*. What is the remainder/residue of *le reste*, the remains of the remains? There is nothing but a question mark on the other side of the bar: *le reste/?*. Moreover, just as the social, in progressively eliminating by absorbing all of its residues, itself becomes residual, Ubu ends the bar game of drawing distinctive oppositions between substantive and residual terms by becoming a remainder, a substantial one at that; in other words, a shit.

In *Ubu Cocu* i. 3, Pa Ubu introduces himself as a pataphysician: 'Pataphysics is the branch of science we have invented and for which a crying need is generally experienced.' Ubu's personal pseudoscience gathers more symbolic import when it is 'explained' by Dr Faustroll in *Gestes et opinions*. In Jarry scholarship, however, reflections upon this 'science' range from the retort that it 'has received so much unwarranted attention' (LaBelle, 1980: 141), through a systematic delineation of its essential traits (Béhar, 1979: 24), and a biographical fusion of Faustroll and Jarry (Beaumont, 1984: 198), to a Derridean reading in which 'Jarry's desire to escape metaphysics returns today, newly masked under the philosophical thrust of deconstruction' (Stillman, 1983; Dufresne, 1993).

Jarry writes: 'An epiphenomenon is that which is added to a phenomenon' (*Gestes et opinions* ii. 8). In one respect this is a straightforward definition of an epiphenomenon. But an epiphenomenon is a secondary phenomenon that is superfluous and necessary. It is a necessary object of interest for pataphysics since this 'science' studies such things, and superfluous in the sense that it is an added extra. The necessary superfluity of an epiphenomenon brings us back to Baudrillard's diagnosis of transmodernity: in pathology, an epiphenomenon is a complication which arises during the course of a malady and, in Baudrillard's vision, takes a hypertelic form.

Further: 'Pataphysics . . . is the science of that which is added to metaphysics, either within or outside of the latter, extending as far beyond metaphysics as metaphysics extends beyond physics' (*Gestes et opinions* ii. 8). Pataphysics spreads out from its host (metaphysics) like a hypertrophied cell travels over a membranous surface. Pataphysics is a hyperplastic extension of metaphysics which knows no definite limit since one cannot first measure accurately how far metaphysics is beyond physics and thus establish a limit case. No one, not even Baudrillard, knows how far pataphysical systems will travel along the skein of a viral culture.

Pataphysics does not escape metaphysics. It neither disappears into metaphysics nor operates as a postmetaphysics. Instead, it redoubles itself and absorbs metaphysics, thus becoming more metaphysical than metaphysics. Pataphysics is metaphysics' paunch. How does one approach something pataphysically? In his preamble to *L'Echange symbolique*, Baudrillard states that once a system nears perfection it only takes a little push in the right direction to make it collapse (1976: 12). It is only a small epiphenomenal step from the tautologies of capitalism to *la gidouille d'Ubu*; from a sublime operationality to a perfectly ridiculous spherical belly. The science fiction of turning a hyperreal system against itself is pataphysical: an imaginary solution indeed.

By 'DEFINITION: Pataphysics is the science of imaginary solutions, which symbolically attributes to the lineaments of objects the properties described by their virtuality' (*Gestes et opinions* ii. 8). This definition is as unruly as the 'science' it defines, but Jarry suggests that what is attributed symbolically to the observable properties of things is their hitherto unrecognized potency, and it is, then, the work of the pataphysician to pursue willy-nilly – since after all 'there could not be more Pataphysics in this world than there is because it is already the sole ingredient' (Sandomir, 1960: 171) – what lurks or should lurk alongside the obvious. Pataphysics is the science of the accidental particular, of the epiphenomenal exception, although even the pataphysician knows that 'it is said the only science is that of the general' (*Gestes et opinions* ii. 8). In the spirit of pataphysics, Baudrillard presents us with a universe which, in the words of Jarry, 'perhaps must be seen in the place of the traditional one' (*Gestes et opinions* ii. 8).

Both Baudrillard and Jarry shop around in scientific discourses for images and ideas to concatenate, play against and pile upon one another. For Jarry it was the work of Charles-Vernon Boys, William Crookes and Sir William Thomson (Lord Kelvin); Baudrillard dabbles in the work of Mandelbrot and Monod, and manipulates a variety of concepts from contemporary scientific discourses. Baudrillard's motto of sorts, *le cristal se venge*, even suggests Lord Kelvin's *The Molecular Tactics of A Crystal* (1894), read pataphysically, of course. A single example of Jarry's style of reading will suffice. Chapter v. 31 of *Gestes et opinions*, 'Concerning the Musical Jet', consists largely of a fanciful reconstruction from Boys's *Soap Bubbles and The Forces Which Mould Them* (1959; orig. 1902). The musical fountain or jet of Boys is part of a primitive sound and light show described in great detail, which in Jarry's hands becomes a Bishop's stream of urine amplified by a porcelain sounding board.

The mathematical prank is common to the theoretical foundations of the theatres of Jarry and Fernando Arrabal. In *Gestes et opinions* viii. 41, Jarry derives geometrically the surface of God and defines Him in these terms:

God is the shortest distance between zero and infinity.
In which direction? one may ask.
We shall reply that His first name is not Jules, but
Plus-and-Minus. And one should say:
± God is the shortest distance from zero to infinity, in
one direction or the other.
This conforms to the belief in the two principles; but
it is more accurate to attribute the sign + to that of the
subject's faith.
But God, having no dimension, is not a line.
– Notice in effect that after the identity:
$\infty - 0 - a + a + 0 = \infty$
the length a is nil, a is not a line, but a point.
Therefore, definitively:
GOD IS THE TANGENTIAL POINT BETWEEN ZERO AND INFINITY.
Pataphysics is science . . .

Linda Stillman (1983: 31–40) has observed that Jarry's magical *bâton-à-physique* – the physics stick from his *César-antéchrist* and *Gestes et opinions* viii. 39. 1 – is a deconstructive tool, since as it transforms itself into a plus sign from its horizontal position as a minus sign it functions as a spinning signifier in reconciling opposites, not by showing them to be the same-though-different, but instead, equal-but-opposite. God's name is Plus-and-Minus, a conjunction of contraries in Jarry's pata-mythology *and* the arithmetical symbol of probable error. This stick is an unacknowledged patacessor of the bar games of poststructuralism, especially Lyotard's gay bar of *Economie libidinale*. This bar of disjunction – the dividing line with which one draws critical distinctions – is set on its way rotating at great speed, and it is the intensity of this rotation which cancels any disjunctive function it might have had:

> You take this bar which separates this from not-this. That is, any segment whatsoever. You place it in a neutral space, let's say one which is tridimensional in order to facilitate the very crude intuition of the imagination. You give it a movement of rotation around a point on this segment, a movement which presents the following three properties: the rotation occurs along all three axes without exclusion; the central point is itself displaced on the segment in an aleatory way; finally, it is displaced as well in the neutral space we have pre-supposed. Thus, a surface is engendered which is none other than the labyrinthine libidinal band with which we have been concerned: this surface always has for its width the length of the segment, etc. But what is important is not to describe the properties of the band.
>
> (Lyotard, 1974: 24)

Lyotard's gay bar flits – although its passage is 'perhaps absolutely immobile' – over a surface upon which each point is at the same time this and not-this. The temporality of the bar eludes description since one cannot describe it quickly enough; at any instant the bar has already dissolved and reappeared elsewhere, but not in a linear sense of time, nor in terms of a traceable passage. Eventually – and this term is at best dubious – the whirling bar slows down and bars this/not-this. It just happens this way. It is an event.

The bars of Jarry and Lyotard are imaginary demonstrations that a barrier must also be a fine line of inclusion, the site of the collapse of the terms of a binary structure which, no longer articulated by the bar, engage in a non-productive copulation. In

Lyotard's energetics, the bar is a catwalk in the theatre of the sign from the signifier to the signified that is held aloft by the 'religion' of representation. In Lyotard's anti-semiological energetic theatre, the gap between the signifier and the signified must be stripped of its function as a little gate so that the energy of the unconscious may flow freely as such, without the impediment of having to support a work which stands for something else. Deleuze and Guattari's efforts on behalf of the disjunctive synthesis also serve this regime of bar games (1977: 76). Through their emphasis on what logicians call – but schizophrenics teach – the weak disjunction (or . . . or both), one finds the force of an affirmative, non-restrictive, and inclusive relation in the disjunction: 'either . . . or . . . or', as opposed to the strong disjunction of 'or . . . but not both'. Lacan, too, plays at Plus-and-Minus's work with his algorithms of metonymy and metaphor. The *franchissement de la barre* for both Jarry and Lacan raises the question of the subject's faith before 'the cross' and at its axis, a 'religion' if you will of the bar game.

Arrabal defines '*l'homme panique*' in terms of memory and chance – '*le hasard c'est l'homme*', and vice versa. By means of a series of pseudoarithmetical expressions of the 'identities' of memory and chance, Arrabal concludes that: $\sqrt{-1}$ = chance (1973: 44–5). There is no solution to the problem of chance; it is equal to the square root of the imaginary number. Pataphysically, this is an imaginary solution.

I can find no recognition of Arrabal's panic theory in the work of the Canadian theorist Arthur Kroker, whose work has been at the centre of the Canadian 'Baudrillard scene'. That Kroker, Kroker and Cook's *Panic Encyclopedia* (1989) is an encyclopedia at least in name and not a dictionary lends it a certain concreteness and social specificity, even with its denials which capture the mood of non-fulfilment; the book lacks the ideality of completeness and competence which haunts dictionary work. This is a postmodern alphabet light years beyond Harold Innis: 'Not then an alphabetic listing of empirical facts about the modern condition, but a postalphabetic description of the actual dissolution of facts into the flash of thermonuclear cultural 'events' in the postmodern condition' (1989: 15). Baudrillard's contribution 'Panic Crash!' – not to be confused with his earlier essay on J.G. Ballard's novel *Crash* – describes stockmarket crashes, the scenario of nuclear war and the population bomb as catastrophes which are eternally virtual, implosive events circulating in hyperreal circuits, acting in a curious way as protection against the massive and brutal return of the real.

The *Panic Encyclopedia* is not particularly well rounded and covers only some branches of the subject 'panic'; it is, to be sure, radical in the French tradition of Diderot and D'Alembert, and especially so when set against conservative programmes for 'cultural literacy'. The episodes and scenes which are washed over (one might say 'reduced' or 'shrunk') by the waters of panic become abstract moments in a *raz-de-marée* of format and style, allowing one to appropriate and present any matter of concern in an ever expanding new and revised alpha-collage: Panic _____.

According to Catherine Clément, 'the only nourishment that the hermit [Lacan] took with him into the desert was mathematics' (1983: 27). The neo-desert father, critical of all of the disciplinary practices from which he learned so much, played mathematical games with a constitutively defined notational system which he called at various times 'algebraic' and 'algorithmic'. Like Arrabal, Lacan also ran up against the imaginary unit $\sqrt{-1}$ in his distortion of its symbol in $s = \sqrt{-I}$; s is the statement of the 'not inexpressible' operation of what the subject always lacks and cannot think $(S = -I)$, which is equal to the square root of the minus signifier/ego in their reliance upon their respective others for their identities. The square root of -1 looks like the square root of $-I$; the former is expressed as i while the latter is expressed as an operation in the register of I, the Imaginary; here, the solution is not imaginary but rather, in the Imaginary (Lacan, 1971: 317–19). There is no mathematical answer to the square root of the dialectic of ego and other, except by following the march of letters in Lacan's notation (i.e. I is the Ego Ideal and i a point upon this delusory Other). Descombes once observed in a pataphysical spirit that Lacan's graphs, which he used to formalize the fundamental concepts of psychoanalysis, 'are to any authentic formalization what Jarry or Duchamp's "*machines célibataires*" are to ordinary machines' (1986: 178).

Dr Faustroll's side-kick and skipper (of the sieve which served as a boat) Bosse-de-Nage (Bumface) knew only one French phrase: '*Ha Ha*'. In short, A = A, as Faustroll understood it. For Baudrillard, death is the pataphysical event which can push the operational perfection of the tautologous society – 'when the system says "A is A" – over the edge' (1976: 11). In panic logic, as Alexandro Jodorowsky explains (in Arrabal, 1973: 59), one always looks for a further principle:

A est A
A n'est pas A
A est plusieurs A
A n'est pas A mais a été A
A n'est pas A et n'était pas A . . .
A est AA, AAA, AAAAAA, etc.

Perhaps it is just as Ubu surmised in *Ubu Cocu* ii. 4: *Non cum vacaveris, pataphysicandum est*. This is to say that since you are busy you ought to pataphysicate along with your fellows at the Collège, where idle derivations and inconsequential transform-ations are the orders of the day. Indeed, as one expresses the tautology, one also laughs.

When I refer to science as rhetorical, I do not mean to dis-parage it; it is not a question of measuring it against a more legitimate domain. It is uninteresting to claim that the rhetori-cal uses of science from Jarry to poststructuralism must be defined negatively, as invalid, for example. It is with ubuesque verve that Baudrillard claims that there isn't as much pata-physical acid in theory as there perhaps should be. In addi-tion, he tries to guarantee a certain going to extremes by suggesting that pataphysics lies in wait for physics at the latter's undisclosable limit (1983: 93), somewhere beyond cold fusion. Notwithstanding Baudrillard's claims regarding the so-called objective irony of excess which lays in wait, like the God Pan, for science, in general his textual imaginary of the 'as if' and the 'perhaps' is populated by recognizable symbols of 'scientific' work. In some cases, these symbols articulate a speculative construction by giving it an internal coherence of sorts; the science of the Imaginary is not an imaginary science. In other instances, scientific concepts are treated with the dis-respect (both feigned and open direct hostility) that has marked poststructuralist discursive engagements with insti-tutions, disciplines and theories which have presented them-selves in terms of their proximity to truth. Moreover, as pure form, Mandelbrot's fractal may be appreciated aesthetically and used to contribute to the construction of an imaginative intuition of the social, without having to respect any of the protocols of scientific research.

Baudrillard's use of pataphysics signals that one need not lament for 'the revolution'. One should not suppose that he failed to tell us what is to be done. It is bad faith to lament and thus to hang this 'failure' around his neck if one considers the science fictionality of pataphysics. In the absence of a definitive strategy, there are only science fictions of toppling the system by turning it against itself. J.B. Pontalis (1978: 94) reads Baudrillard's description of the computer as a social figure of death in terms of a call for vandalism: smash the computers! While he approves of this 'strategy', Pontalis thinks that it is hopeless since a more powerful computer will 'not fail' to integrate a vandalism invariable into its next program. If one does not read Baudrillard's work through his qualifiers, including pataphysics, one may conclude with Pontalis that computer crime and assaults against computer systems may be eventually neutralized. But if strategy is pataphysical and therefore an act of theoretical violence with no evident practico-political application, a public inutility, one cannot hope to actually smash anything. Pataphysics is weak and tactical.

It may be the case that there isn't as much symbolic, pataphysical acid in theory as there perhaps should be. Once again, 'perhaps', just as 'as if', indicates an imaginary solution which hangs in the Jarry–Baudrillard intertext, where they each lead by example, and shine like Ubu in the void. In the era of the reign of the qualifier, theory rests upon its hedges, without hedging its bets.

After Faustroll 'made the gesture of dying' in *Gestes et opinions* vii. 35, he translated the 'Little Sketches on Pataphysics After Ibicrates the Geometer and his divine Teacher Sophrotatos the Armenian', a dialogue in which Ibicrates explains the physics stick of Pa Ubu. With the gesture of dying Faustroll loses the 'society' of his side-kick and skipper Bosse-de-Nage, whose only words, one may recall, were '*Ha Ha*'. It is surely a pataphysical accident that death is for Baudrillard the very symbolical gesture which pushes the tautologies of the system over the edge, with a belly laugh of symbolic proportions.

Chapter 4

Empty signs and extravagant objects

The French imaginary is populated by complex configurations of *le Maghreb*, *l'Algérie*, and *l'Arabe*. Yet the 'other' of Arabia Deserta exists alongside an equally powerful desert form in French thought: America Deserta. French and Maghrébine literature have been shaped by the disparate ideas, social failures and hopes borne along a continuum from the contradictions of French colonialism in North Africa to the post-colonial tragedy of the popular discourse on immigration in France. The cultural expressions of these phenomena have been subject to critical scrutiny by such organizations as the Centre de Recherches et d'Etudes sur les Sociétés Méditerranéennes and filled the pages of numerous reviews and studies. The recreation of *le désert* pervades the symbolic articulation of the difficult ligature of France and North Africa.

The concept of *le désert* is as diverse and challenging as deserts themselves. The mental desert landscape of French colonial and postcolonial experience owes as much to Saint-Exupéry and the Foreign Legion, as it does to *Casablanca*, Lawrence of Arabia, Islam and the Desert Fathers. There exist, for example, several switching points between the geographic, ethnographic, socio-political, literary and religious axes of North Africa and France in and by the work of the French Algerian writer Albert Camus. Camus's work is a liminal point between colonial (*colonocentriste*, *colonial indigénophile* and similar novels) and postcolonial French literary expression. The influence of landscape is immense in Camus's *Noces*, *L'Eté*, and *L'Etranger*. Important contributions to the literary reconstitution of the spirit and power of the desert are also evident in the work of Camus's fellow writers of the so-called *L'Ecole d'Alger* (Gabriel Audisio, Emmanuel Roblès, *et al.*), and in works by well-known indigenous North African writers working in French (Albert Memmi, Mohammed Dib, Kateb Yacine, etc.), as well as in the so-called *génération de 1962* (Malek Haddad, Assia Djebar, etc.).

Together with this impressive field of symbolic articulations, however, the myth of the American desert plays a significant role in French writing. Baudrillard's mythic operator is the American desert. His desert is empty of meaning, an unnatural and superficial flat for the recording of speed records. America is a lack teeming with simulacra. He is not concerned with the deserts of North Africa, though he is fully aware of the petty racism directed against North Africans in the everyday life of France.

In the first section of this final chapter I want to explore Baudrillard's encounters with America in two phases. In the first phase, I unfold some of the key references in modern French socio-political thought to the *an*ecological myth of *le désert américain*. Baudrillard's trip was, in one sense, a good one because he refused to fuse ethno-allegorically, like Carlos Castaneda (perhaps, on the other hand, it was a bad trip since he didn't bother with Castaneda's hallucinations); neither did Baudrillard drop out in order to take a mind expanding trip by means of Artaud's peyotism. That is to say, Baudrillard refused a kind of mystical fusion associated with the collapse of *exotisme* and the rise of tourism. In the second phase, then, I situate Baudrillard's refusal in terms of the French Sinologist and critic Victor Segalen's theory of *exotisme* in *Essai sur l'exotisme* (1978). The *Essai* is a series of programmatic statements, journal entries, quotations and extracts from letters written by the author in Paris from June 1908 to March 1909, during his voyage through China (November 1909 to January 1914), upon his return to China (April 1917 to October 1918), and in the course of his hospitalization in Brest in 1918. Baudrillard's declarative, yet speculative, aphoristic style owes much to Segalen and is most evident in his explicit writing on him in *La Transparence du Mal*. In literary and theoretical terms, Segalen's importance in Baudrillard's recent writing has begun to parallel that of Jarry. Baudrillard's debt to Segalen, critically unacknowledged hitherto, provides us with a new understanding of *Amérique*. America is for Baudrillard what Japan was for Barthes. Accordingly, Baudrillard did not attempt to understand

America and certainly did not try to fuse with it. To claim that he has misunderstood America is only indirectly to affirm the central hypothesis of Segalen's theory.

In the second section I examine another side of the sign in its most general sense. The object acquires both prominence and a life of its own, if you will, in Baudrillard's writing in virtue of the critique of the sign. Where, after all, does one go after signs have burnt? To objects, of course. The object which would become in Baudrillard's vocabulary a vengeful crystal first appeared in his work in *La Société de consommation* (1970: 305) in the context of a reflection upon the film *L'Etudiant de Prague*. After selling his mirror image to the Devil and witnessing a series of interventions in his affairs made by this double, the student attempts to kill the double, only to mortally wound himself. The pact with the Devil entails for Baudrillard the revenge of the object, understood as the soul, the shadow, and even the products of one's labour. No one can escape a pact with objects in a culture of consumption. Objects haunt and take their revenge upon subjects. But Peirce's lesson that every object is also a sign alerts us to a semiotic paradox: the further Baudrillard ventures away from signs, the closer he comes to aligning, albeit unintentionally, his notion of the crystal with Prague School semiotics of the theatre and the theory of the active, wily prop.

SALT, SAND AND SIMULATION

At numbers 6 and 8 rue Quincampoix in Paris, one finds a curious travel agency. This agency deals exclusively in one kind of destination: it sells desert vacations. One may buy into and travel by caravan through African deserts; go by all-terrain vehicles through the hot and cool deserts of the southwestern United States; one may trek through the deserts of the Andes, or skitter over the surface of the white desert of Greenland by dog-sled. What, then, is a desert? To be sure, our Parisian agent does not think it is only a place where evaporation exceeds rainfall.

A desert is, in short, a sublime space, and it is a Burkean (1958) *and* a Kantian (1960) sublime. This packaged sublimity is wrapped in the empiricism of Burke and the transcendental analysis of Kant. The former is used to convey to the eager traveller how the sensible features of desert forms evoke the passion of astonishment, the most powerful effect of the sublime in nature; through the latter, potential customers discover that the sublime does not subsist in nature, but rather dwells in their minds. Given this strange juxtaposition, a philosophical *mésalliance*, why would one want to travel at all? Since the agency provides numerous samples of sand, stones, photographs, slides, comfortable chairs, etc., one might very well choose to tarry in the agency itself among these different kinds of signs of the desert. However, the desert is said to mean that even in its power and our fear in the face of it, we are superior to it as conscious moral agents on the verge of a relatively safe holiday. After all, our agent says: *'déserts, c'est avant tout et surtout des hommes'*. One is, in a sense, already *there*. As a motto and a way of comporting oneself in the desert, our travel brochure advises that *'on ne "fait" pas le désert, c'est le désert qui vous fait'*. The desert makes the traveller and one is always subject to its whims.

My neo-desert fathers are Alexis de Tocqueville, Jean-Paul Sartre (Camus to a lesser degree), Baudrillard and to some extent Paul Virilio. While none of them resemble the Syrian anchorite Simeon Stylites, for example, they have all sought out *le désert* and done so in America, while on vacation, on desert vacations as it were.

In 1831, Tocqueville arrived in America to undertake a study of the penitentiary system. Upon his arrival in New York, he remarked that 'one sees neither a cathedral, nor a steeple, nor a large building' (1909: 1). New York was monotonous in its horizontality, a feature enhanced by the colour and uniformity of the brickwork of its buildings. Aside from his interest in prisons, he expressed the desire to travel into *le désert*, the wilderness, in order to see *les Indiens*. During his journey from New York to Buffalo, Tocqueville realized that 'it is more difficult than I thought to find the wilderness' (1909: 9). It was not only the case that the wilderness had given way to the settlements of white men, but that the only traces of native people that he encountered were the rivers and valleys which bore the names of their tribes. His hopes for an encounter with native Americans, aroused in large measure by images of the 'last of the Mohicans', were shattered upon his arrival in Buffalo where, as it happened, a large number of native people had gathered to collect payment for land 'sold' to the US government: 'I do not believe I have ever experienced a disappointment more complete than at the sight of these Indians' (1909: 10). This disappointment follows from the prejudice that native peoples *were* something, an idea which appalled Tocqueville.

It was more than prison reform that Tocqueville disseminated in Europe. *Le désert* will linger as an image which is equal to or greater than the reality of the woods and valleys themselves. Tocqueville did not experience the great American deserts: Mojave, Gila, Vizcaino, Painted and Great Salt Lake. For the visitor to America, *le désert* is a mythic form, signs of which are set adrift upon return home. Such signs fit the form, conform to it as it were. Baudrillard, for instance, adopts the desert as his 'mythic operator', the key to reading America. In 'Villes d'Amérique', Sartre carries with him an idea of the American desert, a vague notion for the European but for the American, at least as far as Sartre is concerned, it is supposed to be an 'everyday reality' (1949: 94).

Tocqueville's journey was a disappointment for two reasons. He found white culture where native life and nature should have been, and found his 'natural' natives in white culture, where they should not have been. The issue of the confusion of certain notions of nature and culture is one which also haunts Baudrillard's experience of America in the 1980s as well as the visits of Sartre and Camus in the immediate post-World War II years of 1945–46.

In 'New York, ville coloniale', Sartre remarks that the most modern of cities is *un terrain de camping*: the heart of the city is the heart of nature (1949: 119–21). His campers are unprotected from the city's cruelty and wildness. Camus and Sartre experienced a foul New York, a city which afforded no escape from the elements, whether they were thunderstorms or heat waves; Camus observed that when a rainstorm swept through the streets, the skyscrapers towered up through the grey mist like immense tombstones (1978: 17ff); for Sartre, the stifling heat of summer dropped on the city like an atomic bomb.

In Manhattan, a desert of iron and cement as Camus put it or, as Sartre wrote, a desert of rock which permits no vegetation, one can become accustomed to the skyscrapers to such a degree that they appear to be 'natural', even though one still feels trapped by them, having lost hope that the built skyline might at some point give way to the treeline. Camus, like Karl Rossman in Kafka's *Amerika* (1954), could not adjust to staying in a cement cube (1954: 43).

In Baudrillard's *Amérique*, the high open sky of New York City is indicative of the immense space of the North American continent, the space of thought itself. Sartre also celebrates the sky, pushed far above one's head by the skyscrapers, as pure and solitary as a savage beast. In Europe, Baudrillard writes, the sky is tame: it slopes down near to the ground because there are no buildings that can hold it aloft. The sky of Paris never takes off; it is trapped by the sickly low buildings. Moreover, the European sky is spoiled by the dappled little thoughts of Europeans, Baudrillard ironically thinks (1986: 37). These thoughts pale in the face of the space of thought and the cloud clusters of the skies over America. In America, one may imagine, the sky is as vertiginous as consciousness.

Sartre and Camus use the idea of the desert and observations on length (i.e. the highway along the Hudson River) to set the horizontal against the vertical, developing the other side of Louis-Ferdinand Céline's erect city (1983: 159), and perhaps even reawakening Tocqueville's experience of a very different cityscape *circa* 1831. Sartre's suggestion that New York resembles the great plains of Andalusia, and is as monotonous if traversed on foot, but superb and changing when crossed by automobile, enables one to appreciate the transformative power of the desert metaphor.

Sartre and Baudrillard are fascinated by the marvels of modern demolition, a desert machine which produces parking lots and empty lots. While Sartre came to realize that American cities were originally encampments in *le désert* – in the southwest the desert proper and in the northeast the wilderness – Baudrillard for his part maintains:

> American culture is heir to the deserts. They are not a part of nature as opposed to cities, they designate the emptiness, the radical nudity which is behind every human establishment. At the same time, they designate human institutions as a metaphor of this emptiness, and the work of man as continuous with the desert, culture as a mirage and the perpetuity of the simulacrum.
>
> (Baudrillard, 1986: 126)

Baudrillard not only finds evidence of the desert in the city but treats America in its entirety as a desert. In this respect he is close to Henry Miller in *The Air-Conditioned Nightmare*: The 'desert rat' responds to a question about where the desert begins, with: 'Why, as far I can make out, it's all desert, all this country' (1945: 223). Baudrillard is a desert rat. His hunting grounds are, so he says, the deserts, the freeways, the ghost towns and the downtowns, not the institutions of higher learning.

In Baudrillard's America, the desert delivers one from depth and the heroic oppositions of humanism. It is hopeless, for instance, to set Death Valley against Las Vegas (the former a natural formation and the latter a cultural ensemble). Las Vegas is a mirage of the desert and it is about as stable as an after image. With the so-called collapse of the nature/culture distinction, one epiphanizes heat, the hallucinogenic glaze which hangs over the desert and runs into the city along the highway, chased by ghostly swirls of dust. The casinos of Las Vegas resemble the erosional forms of the desert and the artificial glow of neon washes over the environment like the varnish which appears over the countless pebbles on desert pavement. Culture is as shifty as a dune of pure sand.

America may be hopeless but it deserves credit for it. Such metavulgarity, sterling banality and brilliant superficiality may be an affront to the European intellectual still smitten by critical sense, but even the affront has its charms. America cannot be snubbed, as Baudrillard says, because the revolutions imagined in Europe – against culture, the subversion of meaning and the destruction of representation – have been realized in America (1986: 194). Philippe Sollers makes a similar point in noting that the subjective liberations experienced in Europe during the interwar years were completely grafted onto America around the end of World War II (in Kristeva, *et al.*, 1978: 9). The price of these grafts has been high: the realization of the utopias of European thought has created a massive anti-utopia. America is an anti-utopia because what has been realized is imaginary. The combination of the first and third stages of simulation has resulted in a real fiction. In America, the difference or gap between a utopia as a picture of what is possible and a social world no longer obtains. Baudrillard writes: 'everything here is real, pragmatic, and it all makes you wonder . . .' (1986: 57).

The lightness of Baudrillard's travelling is in part due to his notion of the travels of light. Baudrillard sustains the desert metaphor with two images: *sidereal* America and the charm of disappearing into speed-distance, or the tempographic zone, *la dromosphère*. The former astronomical trope introduces the latter interpretation of the Mach regime as a *sidereal* space of metamovement, *chez* Virilio:

> I looked for *sidereal* America, that of the vain and absolute freedom of the freeways, never the one of the social and of culture – the one of desert-like speed, of motels and mineral surfaces, never the deep America of mores and mentalities. I searched in the speed of the screenplay, in the indifferent reflex of television, in the film of days and nights across an empty space, in the marvellously affectless succession of signs, images, faces, and ritual acts of the road, for what was closest to the nuclear and enucleated universe which is virtually our own right down to the little european cottages.
> (Baudrillard, 1986: 16)

How does one look for sidereal America? Baudrillard is not interested in measuring America's relation to the stars. Instead, he evokes an astral America of starlets and roadside bars and composes an orbit, a speed-scene, with a gearshift, a gas pedal, a windshield marked by stones and splattered insects; in short, he produces a dromospherical simulation in which inanimate objects appear as if they were animated by a violent movement (Virilio, 1978: 324–5). As an *auteur-compositeur*, *Easy Rider* (Denzin, 1991: 131) Baudrillard tracks the orbit of his journey into the non-referential desert of backfiring signs. His journey is at least in part 'driven' by the work of Virilio.

Virilio considers the desert flats to be 'sensible plates for recording the speed record' (1984: 194). While reflecting on Salt Lake City, Baudrillard refers to Bonneville, *Grand désert de sel*, as the site of speed itself and a surface of pure superficiality. Baudrillard travels on these plates of Virilio which were, for a time, the place in America where speed records were 'engraved', and he does so in the mode of Virilio's thought, that of the 'aesthetics of disappearance'. This concept is derived from the picnoleptic seizure, or petit mal, a paradoxical state of wakefulness parallel to sleep during rapid eye movement, or paradoxical sleep. The seizure carries one into a mode of being which Virilio thinks is a 'lost dimension', a missing time without duration which escapes memory. The technological achievements of high speed would, then, like a picnoleptic event, entail the loss of consciousness and perception as the means by which one knows the world and one's place in it. The 'lost dimension' is a dromospherical space defined by acceleration and deceleration.

Baudrillard disappears into the superficiality of America, a space emptied of sense. And if Virilio (1976: 68) is correct that the milieu of the voyage never quite conforms to the space traversed, then when one is in such a space one is in an America which is shorter than usual; in other words, one is in an America of the sidereal day, a day which is shorter than usual. A journey through sidereal America is tracked according to a sidereal rate, a rate at which one's driving apparatus (a car rather than telescope) must be set in order to track American stars and bars.

Virilio's investigations into dromology are based in large measure on his understanding of the implications of supersonic speed. An object moving at such a speed is measured by a Mach meter and assigned a Mach number which is the ratio of its speed through a medium to the speed of sound in the medium. The speed of sound is given as the square root of specific heats (heat capacity at constant pressure, coefficient of velocity) in a perfect gas, the gas constant (thermal resistance) and the absolute temperature. $M=2$ is about 1,480 mph or twice the speed of sound (331.4 m/sec = 1,087.8 ft/sec); a Minuteman III intercontinental ballistic missile has a maximum speed of $M=20$, or approximately 15,000 mph = 24,000 km/hr.

Baudrillard's orbit is an imaginary path since he does not move at supersonic speed. Like Virilio, however, a supersonic jet, missile or land rocket serves him as a hermeneutical vehicle, a conceptual extension which yields a new interpretive framework, one with the desert as its central operator. And if the desert, at the correct time of day – recalling that the speed of sound changes with an increase in the temperature of the air in which it travels – is favourable to speeding (which is the reason why land-based speed records are set at the coolest time of day), offering the least resistance to a well-designed object, one might say that the object is absorbed by the desert since the object-vehicle creates before itself a vacuum which absorbs it, instead of relying upon wind resistance. 'In this way', Baudrillard writes, 'the centrifugal, eccentric point is reached where circulation produces the vacuum that absorbs you' (1986: 28). The land rocket disappears, in a sense, into the empty desert and simply 'figuring' it as such is enough to disappear along with it, at least in Baudrillard's America. It's true that a vehicle can outrun its shock wave, punching a hole in the air, as it were, at the speed of sound, leaving its thunderclap behind. It is good rhetorical physics to posit a vacuum before a vehicle, a hole in the sound barrier, into which one might disappear, having reached a centrifugal limit of sorts (from VITE to VIDE).

Baudrillard and Virilio were among McLuhan's earliest French readers, and they borrow his image of an airplane breaking the sound barrier, at which point 'sound waves become visible on the wings of the plane' (McLuhan, 1964: 27). McLuhan continues: 'The sudden visibility of sound just as sound ends is an apt instance of that great pattern of being that reveals new and opposite forms just as earlier forms reach their peak performance.' For McLuhan, fragmented, mechanical technologies flip over into organic configurations just as they reach their peaks. By the same token, the 'eccentric point' of travel is no longer on the order of appearance, but rather, a moment of disappearance and emptiness.

The desert form is the locus of all the features of Baudrillard's formalist bias. There is, however, little doubt that the desert in all of its diversity is rich in surface effects and forms, even special effects: desert pavement, crescent dunes, mirages, the surreality of moving rocks, etc. The contours, lines, colours, all the effects of dryness, dust, openness and wind, lend them- selves to Baudrillard's unbalanced reading of the surface of things. If the desert 'makes' the traveller, and the latter is unprepared, then one may be relegated to considering the sur- face of things, as the American naturalist and monkeywrencher Edward Abbey (1968: 30–1) found during his first days in Arches National Monument in southeast Utah.

The desert is irreducible to its surface effects. That is to say, enviro-aesthetic formalism or surface reading is a limited way of appreciating a natural place since this approach does not require one to gain knowledge (common sensical, biological–ecological, or the learning of the naturalist) of the place which one seeks to appreciate. An appreciation of the desert requires an under- standing of the ecological relations and processes therein and without a modicum of this knowledge one does not know what to appreciate. There is also a trivial side to this argument since Baudrillard is not interested in the desert as an ecological reality. When he claims to know the desert better than 'they' do, what he 'knows' is a form of pure travelling in an absence, a caricature of what he considers to be the 'American way'. In America, banality is next to epiphany and extreme heat delivers one from sense. What is a desert? Well, it's a garbage dump, a nuclear test facility, a tourist vista, the haunt of criminals and freaks, the host of malignant subdivisions. What is alive in this desert is the freeway, a gigantic pump, inhaling and exhaling up to a speed of 55 mph, as Morin once described it (1970: 50).

At least since his essay 'Design et environnement ou l'Escalade de l'économie politique', Baudrillard has held that ecology volatilizes nature in order to reconstitute it, like orange juice, as environment (1972: 254).[1] As a real referent Nature is dead and environment survives it. Environment is a designed semioaesthetic form for the circulation of signifiers disconnected from their referents. Baudrillard, then, sets himself up as a theorist of the conditions which obtain after nature.

It is naive to believe that the desert eludes the 'cultivation' of nature. Still, there is reason to claim that one requires the insights of the naturalist in order to appreciate that a few inches, perhaps a few feet, below the surface of a dry lake bed, one finds salt water for salt tolerant plants; one may need to discover that certain trees signify potable water; that not all water in the desert is potable, and how one can tell that it is. Simply put, non-formal and non-aesthetic features are necessary for an understanding of the deserts of America. Of course, one does not learn how to appreciate the desert by staying behind the wheel of a car on the highway, looking through the 'lens' of the windshield (or, like Sartre, looking at the desert through the window of an airplane) at what may as well be geographic nullity. The semiotics of water does not become a pressing need along the way from motel to diner, unless of course it is a matter of micturition. Many of the signs one finds in the desert are empty of meaning, as Baudrillard has put it, from the vantage point of the driver's seat.

At the very least, the naturalist gets out of the car, off the road and, with fore- and in-sight, ventures into the desert. The naturalist Barry Lopez describes his procedure in a bit of autoburlesque:

I was crossing the desert. Smooth. Wind rippling at the window. There was no road, only the alkaline plain. There was no reason for me to be steering; I let go of the wheel. There was no reason to sit where I was; I moved to the opposite seat. . . .

I moved to the back of the vehicle . . . and sat by the rear doors. . . . I opened all the doors. The wind blew through. I stepped out; ran away. When I stopped and turned around the vehicle was moving east. I ran back to it and jumped in. Out the drivers door; in through the back. I got out again, this time with my bicycle, and rode north furiously. . . . I lay the bike down and jogged alongside the vehicle. . . . I shifted it into neutral through the open door and turned the key off. I sat in it until it came to rest. I walked back for the bicycle. By a series of strippings such as this one enters the desert.

(Lopez, 1976: xi–xii)

Lopez's striptease parodies both off-road antics and the use of the desert flats as a recording surface for land speed records. He quite literally opens the vehicle up and enters and exits it as if it were a moving, porous membrane. The view of the desert as a mythic operator running along a Virilian vector severely distorts what may be experienced and how it may be imagined. This is, however, an important part of Baudrillard's approach.

How can one 'make' and most importantly be 'made' by the desert if one is neither in a position nor in a condition to accede to its charms, dangers and subtleties? My neo-desert fathers ventured into the *le désert* and overcame the temptation to consider where they were. This vicarious experience of the desert turned out to be an entirely inept victory in ecological terms. Ross (1989: 222ff), for example, has sought to escape Baudrillard's desert by turning to an 'older desert tradition of communal exile' described by Reyner Banham in his *Scenes of America Deserta* (1982). It did not occur to Ross that Banham, like Baudrillard, was a tourist in America and that part of his fascination with desert forms may be attributed to the opportunity they afford to experience and understand simulation.

Let's return to our travel agent. No matter which journey one might undertake, one will be on a road to nowhere. But even this itinerary complicates matters because the road is nowhere. In *L'Ere du vide* (1983), Gilles Lipovetsky defines postmodernity in terms of the desert produced by the forces and services of personalization. From this view, we are all active agents of the desert. 'Personalization' is a symbolic operation defined by the processes of desocialization (from the atomization of the social to the collapse of grand values, institutions and narratives) and desertification (not in the ecological sense but through the vicissitudes of autonomy). The near solipsistic pleasure achieved through solitary pursuits conjures, for Lipovetsky, the image of the neo-desert father. Lipovetsky's neo-desert fathers, his 'great priests of the desert', are *les psy* (psychologists, analysts, etc.). Postmodern France, Lipovetsky tells us through his choice of the 'priesthood', is a desert in which the disaffected, the indifferent and the apathetic all seek advice by confessing to the priests of psychology. What these priests have to offer is simple: they deal in methods of association in order to mend broken communities, and to redirect the postmodern desire for nothing: the desert is 'us'; it neither begins nor ends.

Notwithstanding the enormous popularity of analysis in France, Lipovetsky cannot find anything in this desert in terms of which a community might be said to exist or come to pass. As we have seen, Baudrillard used a similar metaphorical wash in order to desertify America, to empty it without recognizing the associative strength either of the concept itself or of the existing conditions themselves. In ecological terms, the desert takes its revenge by expanding. This expansion is not a march of tropes.

EXOTES LIKE US

Exotisme is first and foremost a general theory of separation. A line of radical exclusion may be placed between all of the conceptual oppositions which Segalen suggested: for example, between Self/Other, men/women, real/imaginary. These barred oppositions uphold Segalen's idea of the 'perception of the Diverse' (Other) as well as the conception of the distance between paired terms. Exotic experience is that of an irreducible and inaccessible alterity. The aesthetic fascination which the *exote* has for Difference is irreducible to the semiurgical and touristic bars of implication.

Segalen was well aware of the many unfavourable connotations of the word *exotisme* – in particular, 'expressions of distant lands' – but he retained it for etymological reasons. *Exo* signifies 'everything which is "outside" the unity of our facts of everyday consciousness, everything which is not our customary "mental tonality" ' (1978: 20). The Diverse (Other) was degraded, according to Segalen, through the gradual deterritor-ializations of tourism and colonialism. For Segalen, there are *exotes* – his own neologism – and *pseudoexotes*: the former have the strength to conceive of all the flavours of the diverse and are born travellers, while the latter are mere tourists, 'procurers of the sensation of the diverse' and the authors of picturesque colonial literature.[2] Baudrillard fancies himself an *exote* and *Amérique* is a prime example of 'radical exoticism'. Baudrillard writes:

> Genuine knowledge is that of what we will never understand in the other, of what in the other ensures that this other is not itself, and thus can neither be separated from itself, nor alienated by our look, nor established in its identity or its difference (never pose to others the question of their identity: it's the same for 'America' – the question of the American identity is never posed, it is the otherness of America which is at stake).
>
> (Baudrillard, 1990: 153)

In lieu of ethnography and ecology, Baudrillard embraces the principle of radical alterity. The Other cannot be seduced; there will be no 'psychodrama of alienation' for Baudrillard. The Other is simply incomprehensible; but, knowledge of this much is genuine. In the above passage Baudrillard makes two points. The first is that the Other is not itself. The second concerns the goal of recognizing the otherness of the Other.

The Other is incomprehensible and impenetrable. The 'acute and immediate' perception of this essential exoticism, Segalen and Baudrillard suggest, may also apply to the Self. This 'interior exoticism' is supported by the Self's and the Other's non-self-identity; the subject, to use a different system of notation, is barred. The subject is, in fine, foreign to itself (desire and transparent self-consciousness are barred). The subject is at least as radically exotic as the object.

My use of the concept of 'interior exoticism' differs from that of Baudrillard's colleague Marc Guillaume in his *La Contagion des passions* – which has the subtitle, *Essai sur l'exotisme intérieur* (1989). Guillaume believes that Segalen's *Essai* indicates a *cou-*

pure in the representation of the Other in the colonial era. As the Other became more and more rare – a rarity manifested in the forms of *exotisme* – due to the degradations of colonialism and policies of assimilation, Segalen sought to resist this process and to recover a strong sense of the essential difference of the Other. Guillaume writes: 'the *coupure* that Segalen indicated at the end of the colonial era is now completely and perfectly visible' (1989: 83). With the decline of the Other through the rise of global homogenization and the resolution of incommensurables, it became necessary to invent the Other as a fiction. The 'society of the spectre' arises, according to Guillaume, through new modes of being and exchanging – that is, communicating – with Others (spectres). This new 'interaction' is defined by anonymity (through the loss of the means of identification), the emergence of an electronically mediated distance between anonymous poles, and a flight into fantasy and simulation provided by telematics and other new 'interactive' technologies. These 'new forms of presence to ourselves and to others' are understood as survival strategies, as ways of adapting to the symbolic incoherence of contemporary culture.

It is not that *Amérique* is merely psychologically, sociologically or ideologically shallow. No, it is exotic because it upholds the otherness of the Other. Most of the 'critical' responses to Baudrillard's *Amérique* have pointed out in some way or another the many ways in which he has simply misunderstood America. But the hypothesis of *exotisme* delivers Baudrillard from understanding, intimacy, familiarity and fluency. Moreover, the *exote* holds 'fusion' in contempt:

> Distaste for trivial exoticism. No longer seeking to abolish oneself before the other. Such is the temptation of Isabelle Eberhardt: fusional form, mystical confusion. She responds to the question how one can be Arab, in becoming Arab, by denying her own otherness. She can only die from it. And it is an Arab who precipitates it in the waves, so as to ruin this apostasy. Rimbaud never merges. His otherness to his own culture is too great, he has no need of mystic diversion.
>
> (Baudrillard, 1990: 154)

The *exote*, then, doesn't fuse; neither playacting nor becoming-an-object will suffice. For the *exote* has Rimbaud's foreignness to his own culture; even better, an authentic '*exote*' was Glenn

Gould at the piano playing Bach. Baudrillard writes: 'Glenn Gould: his bodily trance, completely independent of the perfect technical mastery of his hands which fly over the keys without looking at them, while his head swings with his eyes closed. No pianistic grandstanding. The absolute ear' (1990a: 36). In 1964 Gould abandoned live public performances in favour of the studio. Innovative documentary projects for radio (contrapuntal radio) occupied him for some ten years throughout the 1970s. His now notorious personal quirks (interviews with himself, reviews of books about himself; his media personalities) and fascination with sound and recording technologies were in no way diversions. An *exote* does not abolish himself before the other of the score, the recording technology, his career, the concert audience; he does not play at becoming-the-great-pianist-performer, etc.

Moreover, Isabelle Ehnni, née Eberhardt, is a legendary figure in France and abroad; she is celebrated as a mystic in California, and treated as a protofeminist whose masculine attire, she insisted, only facilitated her desert passages; 'what Carlos Castaneda was to the new mysticism, Eberhardt is to feminism', one critic has remarked. Dubbed 'la Bonne Nomade' by René Louis Doyon in 1923, she would later be called *l'amazone des sables* and *la débauchée*, among other things. Her posthumous literary glory was undoubtedly carried forward by the French desert imaginary of *le Maghreb* and *l'Arabe*, especially in the context of colonial literature and its visions of occupation, exploitation and the brutal reduction of indigenous resistance. Eberhardt at once seemed to repudiate and to succumb to these ideas. The enigma of Eberhardt and her paradoxical standing does not stop here.

Such is the case with respect to her so-called 'conversion' to Islam, which she herself called into question by claiming that she was born a Muslim and thus never changed her religion; having written under the name of Mahmoud Saadi in the French Algerian press, she claimed that her journalism repudiated the charges of her detractors that she was anti-French and anti-semitic; her life assumed mystical proportions after she 'miraculously' escaped an assassination attempt. From this moment forward she believed she was chosen and subsequently began her 'mystical quest'.[3]

In Baudrillard's terms she had what may be called at best a

'passive exotic conscience', a typical *idéologie indigénophile*.[4] Indeed, one of Eberhardt's goals was to fuse with the Other of Islamic North Africa. From another perspective, Baudrillard's use of Eberhardt is consistent with his efforts to repudiate mystical fusion as a self-defence, and as a relevant position in general. Baudrillard directly refers to Eberhardt's death in an uncharitable manner. He seems to have drifted in a mental desert landscape from drowning to revenge (he adds an element of the assassination attempt to her death). Eberhardt died at the age of 27 years in 1904 at Aïn Sefra. It is for the most part assumed that she drowned after having disppeared during a period of torrential rains in Aïn Sefra which overflowed a canal (*un oued*) and flooded the village. Her body was recovered several days later in the silt under the rubble of her house. Still, it is paradoxical that she drowned in a desert. By contrasting Eberhardt with Arthur Rimbaud, Baudrillard lays to rest the popular and completely speculative suggestion, repeated by several French writers, that she was the daughter of Rimbaud.

Baudrillard thinks that 'the worst is understanding, which is only a sentimental and useless function' (1990: 153). How does this claim inform his reading of America? There is no truth of America because the *exote* has no interest in this notion other than in embracing the genuineness of non-understanding, in preserving Difference. Barthes's Japan, one may recall, was a faraway place composed of features from which he invented a system of signs. He did not speak Japanese; rather, he appreciated the irreducible difference of language whose richness was due to the absence of referential alibis and the fundamental emptiness of signification. This 'Japan' was not deep; ultimately, it was full of empty signs whose signifieds had fled from the scene.

For Baudrillard, Americans could not possibly understand themselves to be models of simulation because they suffer from the hypothesis of *exotisme* imposed upon them. Americans, it would seem, are 'savages' since Baudrillard thinks 'if we do not understand the savage it is for the same reason that he does not understand himself' (1990: 153). Americans are savages and foreign to themselves by definition. Further, America is *the only primitive society of today*, Baudrillard writes (1986: 21). It is fundamentally primitive. He crosses America as though it were the primitive society of the future. These so-called 'savages' have been erased by two projections: first, the indigenous peoples of America are considered to have been great. They exist historically. Second, 'savages' in general exist 'as if' in a hypothetical future. Baudrillard thinks that it is perhaps only *les Indiens* who have interpreted the geological signs of the Grand Canyon and Monument Valley. In Navajo country, Baudrillard writes, 'one understands why the Indians required such a powerful magic and so cruel a religion to exorcize such a theoretical grandeur and a geological and celestial event as the desert, in order to live up to their surroundings' (1986: 14). Today, much of Navajo country has become a park, and one finds traces – according to the first exclusion – of a once mighty nation.

Baudrillard adds that the 'experimental attraction' in Arizona called Biosphere 2 is an artificial desert constructed in a natural desert, in Biosphere 1, as it were. This artificial desert of miniaturized ecological systems under glass supports a terrible irony: 'extraterrestrials' are ordered to study survival and virtual immortality in the very place where Native Americans, who were much better adapted, were destroyed (1992: 124). Baudrillard has also advanced the more general and disturbing hypothesis that Native American peoples (without tribal distinctions) have had 'a strange complicity . . . in their extermination [by the Spanish, the Whites, the State, etc.]: it was the only way for them to protect the secret of alterity' (1990: 138). If one does not play the game of a negotiable alterity in a world of universal difference (an ecumenical and structural humanitarianism which is never symmetrical but always violent), then one will be exterminated; even if one plays this game, one remains in an impossible position because extermination will take place by means of differentiation, the most subtle and slowest form of extermination (small 'd' differentiation is never exotic and radical). Baudrillard implicates, on Segalian grounds, the native peoples of the Americas in their extermination. The stakes of this theory are both horrible and unjust. But this is not a straightforward case of blaming the victims. For Baudrillard writes: 'Racism does not exist when the Other is Other, when the Outsider remains outside. It begins to exist when the other is different, that is, when the other is dangerously close' (1990: 133). Nobody, it seems, can escape racism in a world of universal structural differentiation. Even though Baudrillard (1990: 154) praises Barthes's book on Japan, the latter's sense of difference is semio-linguistic and therefore, in strict terms, it succumbs to the faults of structural relations in general. The primitive societies of the future can only escape extermination if their alterity is essential, radical and singular. This is the utopia which may exist after structural differentiation has been destroyed. Even so, those who carry out such exterminations are also condemned, according to Baudrillard, in the long term by their own systems of extermination. Baudrillard's effort here is to push racism to its extreme in order to destroy it. In order to accomplish this critical task, it is necessary to be more racist than racist (the standard Baudrillardian formula of more x than x remains the same), but without knowledge of the consequences or at least the willingness to turn a 'blind eye' to them. In the short term, the effects will be disastrous. In the structural game of differences, all differences are close and nothing is truly exotic; there is neither an Absolute Other nor an incomparable non-structural Difference. These are the dirty secrets of *exotisme*: anti-feminism, anti-egalitarianism, hyperracism and anti-colonialism, but the last only by default.

WILY PROPS AND VENGEFUL OBJECTS

I continue my exploration of Baudrillard's relationship with several traditions in the theatre by examining his controversial concept of the 'revenge of the crystal'. The crystal's revenge has been treated as an anti-human, cynical 'capitulation to reification' by Kellner (1989: 154). From a different perspective, Gane (1991: 69–70) hints at the broader aesthetic context in which the concept belongs by referring to the Underground man's fear of the rise of the Palace of Crystal in Fyodor Dostoyevski's *Notes From Underground*, in relation to Baudrillard's attempt to recover what cannot be accounted for in any political economy. Gane thinks that no such capitulation has taken place because both Baudrillard and the Underground man claim that there is something which cannot be reduced to the crystal palaces of perfection erected by 'progressive humanists'. In Dostoyevski's novel this unclassifiable something is a principle of goodness, while for Baudrillard it is a fatal reversal embodied in the genius and cunning of the pure object or crystal.

Although Gane does little to develop his reference to Dostoyevski, he points out that the Palace of Crystal signifies the complete mastery of human beings by means of scientific reason. Nature and society will, then, be played like 'a sort of piano keyboard or barrel-organ cylinder', as Dostoyevski imagined. But the Underground man insists that human beings do not always act according to the dictates of reason and in their own best interests: 'it is indeed possible, and sometimes *positively imperative* (in my view), to act directly contrary to one's own best interests. One's own free and unfettered volition . . . inflated sometimes to the point of madness – that is the one best and greatest good, which is never taken into consideration because it will not fit into any classification' (Dostoyevski, 1972: 33–4). In Baudrillardian terms, the abstract combinatorial possibilities dictated by the code *inter* human beings in the Palace of Crystal. This palace is perfectly sterile because it has expelled its *part maudite* (accursed share). Every effort is made, Baudrillard thinks, to expel evil from paradisiac palaces of crystal. This search for 'operational whiteness' equals death. Today power accrues to the one who can reintroduce this devil's share into crystalline systems. Indeed, what frightens the Underground man is that it may not even be possible to stick out one's tongue at the 'eternally inviolable' palace. There is, however, something ironic in the very idea of the crystal palace which runs counter to its realization. For the Underground man, the independence of volition is irreducible to the algorithms and mathematical expressions of human desire, whereas for Baudrillard one may say that there is a certain crystal which demonstrates its indifference to the dictates and structures of the palace by pursuing its own interests. Baudrillard does not directly borrow the idea of the crystal from Dostoyevski. Gane's turn to literature in order to track the polysemic crystal indicates, however, the aesthetic context which I will explore in this section.

The story of the object told by Baudrillard may be constructively contextualized and elaborated upon through a reflection on two developments in the theory of drama. In particular, it is Antonin Artaud's theatre of cruelty to which I turn for a source of a theoretical and theatrical context for the notion of the object's revenge. In the second instance, I appeal to the semiotics of theatre of the Prague School (especially the groundbreaking protostructuralist work of Otokar Zich in the 1930s and Jiri Veltrusky's dialectical structuralism of the 1940s) in order to explain how a certain energy and oddity may be said to reside in an object. The fundamental theatricality of Baudrillard's theorization of the object, or what one may call the drama of theory, has led me to consider the theory of drama. In this light, Patricia Mellencamp's remark in her essay on Baudrillard and Herbert Blau seems misleading: 'Baudrillard's is a grey world without theatre' (1985: 144). Given Baudrillard's debt to Jarry, for example, such a phrase seems patently false. What Mellencamp alerts her readers to is the end of theatre as representation, the end of the ironically named 'Baudrillard scene' in the transparency of the obscene. Mellencamp's phrase may be understood in the context of Artaud's turn to objects, gestures and non-linguistic signs. This is a theatre in which the object will have its revenge on Western metaphysics. The relationship between Artaud and Baudrillard may be best understood within the context of the diverse critical positions taken on Artaud's writings by key poststructuralist thinkers.

In 'De système des objets au destin de l'objet', in L'Autre par lui-même, Baudrillard describes a 'double spiral' winding forward from his early engagement with objects in Le Système des objets toward a switching point at which his subject-based theorizing ultimately moved to the side of the object: 'The desire of the subject is no longer at the center of the world. It is the destiny of the object which is at the center' (1987: 69). In what at first appears to be a flight into hyperanthropomorphism, Baudrillard posits a principle of reversibility which plays a game with, primarily but by no means exclusively, the subject/object distinction at the heart of the Western philosophical tradition. In this reversal, the object 'takes revenge'. It is the object's destiny to take revenge on the subject through the 'passions' of indifference, inertia, ironic silence, conformity, etc. The object, then, leads the subject astray; in this way it avenges its subordination and marginalization.

The fatal strategy of the object consists neither in its dealienation and liberation, nor in its (re)production of value-giving intentionality on the model of an ego. The object does not mimic the subject's operations. Rather, it has an 'Evil Genius' and is fatal inasmuch as it is enigmatic. It is this enigmatic quality which enables the object to challenge the subject's will to know, control and conquer its universe. Baudrillard's crystal is neither passive nor a subject. It is not involved in a process of projection and identification (the mirror stage, desire, etc.). The crystal has a destiny rather than a desire to fulfil. This pure object's passions are on the order of irony, inertia and the ruse, while the passions of the subject are invigorating and final (expressing and fulfilling desires and claims).

The crystal is fatal in several senses. First, it is irresistible and will be the ruin of the subject; not only is the object seductive, it remains indecipherable, and as such it fulfils its destiny by thwarting the will to power/knowledge/mastery of the subject. Second, Baudrillard's concept of the object's destiny is buoyed by the crisis of the subject in structuralist and poststructuralist discourses. Baudrillard takes advantage of the 'death of the subject' and the critiques of power, knowledge and history to exploit this moment of weakness by effecting a turnaround on behalf of his special object. He would have his readers believe that the object was only waiting for an opportunity to realize its destiny.

Baudrillard's crystal is a polysemous figure which may be identified with anyone and anything treated, traditionally and otherwise, for better and for worse, as an object. This does not mean the revenge in question is that of the objectified over the objectifiers. Although Baudrillard claims that his pure and fatal object is not a subject, he does admit that it can designate 'people and their inhuman strategies' (1983: 204). After all, there are no terms in his description of the objective passions of the object that are inappropriate for some subjects. They, too, can create confusion, surprise, behave like objects, treat one another as objects, cultivate indifference, believe in destiny, etc. But this is surely not Baudrillard's point since the crystal is neither simply an animal nor a vegetable, and not exactly a mineral. Baudrillard's crystal is a precious thing to be sure, itself unlikely to be crystalline; rather, it is like the ball toward and into which one gazes in order to arouse a myriad of sensations. The crystal is a fetish whose potency is tied to its ambivalence, by which I do not mean the sort of attitude one may take toward the power of a crystal ball.

The crystal suggests the undecidable sponge Derrida found at work in the poetry of Francis Ponge: a zoophyte such as a sponge has a medusant character, he writes, because it is 'neither simply a thing, nor simply vegetal, nor simply animal'. The sponge is an animal plant, full of water and air, and a medium which incorporates and expunges (Derrida, 1984: 68ff). Baudrillard's crystal is just as much a sign of writing as Derrida's sponge. It is precisely the sort of textual operator he needs to effect a writing practice equal to the demands of the symbolic order he has consistently favoured in his theorizing. The crystal is Baudrillard's precious hybrid object, a transparent medium ready to be filled with content like McLuhan's electric light. The crystal is the sort of hybrid in which Baudrillard has always shown interest. An object may be a perfect domesticate, but is a domesticated animal such as a dog a perfect object? For the dog, Baudrillard thinks, is a household 'object', often no more than a piece of sentient furniture, bred for the narcissistic interiors of urban dwellings, absolutely dependent upon its owner whom it exalts, and castrated either physically or symbolically. Like other interior animals, Baudrillard maintains, dogs are a species in between beings and objects (1968: 107–8; 1987a: 138, 194–5). In order to be a perfect object, a dog must always exalt its owner, it must never break down, as it were, enduring like a prized possession. The perfect domesticate is found in a Disney character: the barking ottoman which regains its full share of caninity when the spell over the castle is lifted at the climax of the film *Beauty and the Beast*. There is, then, a bestiary in Baudrillard, but not in the deliteralized sense Gane would have one believe in his Baudrillardian bestiary without animals! (See also Baudrillard's repeated references to beautiful, little translucent scorpions which symbolize evil and whose absence from Biosphere 2 creates a symbolic imbalance (1992: 119–21).)

The identity of the promiscuous crystal fluctuates, drawing the reader of Baudrillard in several directions. Baudrillard's concept of ambivalence (one of the means by which the symbolic moves beyond signification) makes the crystal's identity uncertain. This ambivalence is, most importantly, immanent to the concept of the crystal, and this enables it to function as a lure in Baudrillard's text. Brian Singer – who translated *De la séduction* into English (1990b) – recognized that his own ambivalence about Baudrillard was in the end immanent to the work itself; yet, this is for Singer the work's fascination (1991: 150).

The play of uncertainties is part of what I call the drama of Baudrillardian theory. The inexorable rise of the pure object is the drama of theory. The tactical manoeuvres of Baudrillard's crystal lead me directly into the theory of drama.

Postmodern theatre was born with Artaud's *Le Théâtre et son double* (1964) in the 1930s (McGlynn, 1990). As early as the mid-1920s, Artaud had already conceived of the theatre as a challenge to the spectator, as an event which would instill in the spectator the idea of its profound seriousness and demonstrate that one would no longer be able to leave the theatre unscathed. His experiments with the Alfred Jarry Theatre were decisive for the emphasis he came to place on the theatre as a means for challenging the Western tradition itself, especially the form of a naturalistic theatre which sought to imitate reality. The idea of the 'masterpiece' also became a target for Artaud. In the brief essay 'Sur le théâtre balinais', Artaud – with all the hyperbole of someone who wants to conjure a miracle – highlights the importance of objects and their ineluctable advance against the hegemony of words in a struggle to express themselves in their very concreteness. In this sense the danger, surprise and astonishment experienced by the spectator would, for Artaud, be provoked by things themselves (1964: 100–1).

While the importance of Artaud's contributions to contemporary debates on representation in poststructuralism has been recognized by numerous scholars, this recognition has not equalled uncritical acceptance. For Artaud remains a controversial figure whose ideas are still hotly debated.

In 'The Theatre of Cruelty and the Closure of Representation', Derrida describes this theatre's production of a 'non-theological space' (1978: 235ff). This space is neither opened by means of speech nor is it merely an addition to a dramatic work. By challenging the privileged status of the already written, lived or thought by means of mise en scène itself, Artaud exceeded, in Derrida's words, 'all the limits furrowing classical theatricality (represented/representation, signifier/signified, author/director, actor/spectators, stage/audience, text/interpretation, etc.) [which] were ethico-metaphysical prohibitions, wrinkles, grimaces, rictuses – the symptoms of fear before the dangers of the festival' (1978: 244). This space of festival is opened every time a bar is lifted between the aforementioned paired terms; this bar game may be defined as a *refusal* to re-present a pre-existent text and a *refusion* of hitherto barred terms. The theatre of cruelty has no place for 'the supreme Logos', the man-God; it is not a 'theatrum analyticum', the analytic scene of the return of the repressed. What Derrida saw in Artaud was his courage in the face of recognizing that no theatre could possibly fulfil his desire. Artaud was caught in a struggle to represent what is unrepresentable and to find a space which could be used to demonstrate life to a being whose 'only inhabitable place – locus – is language', as Kristeva has affirmed.

'Modern theatre does not take (a) place', Kristeva writes, for the reason that one is always in language, in a space structured by what she calls the symbolic. In dislodging speech from its dominant role in the theatre and the tradition, Artaud did not take solace in silence. This is not a speechless theatre, even though Kristeva suggests as much in her remarks on Artaud's effort 'to do without language' and his turn to 'colors, sounds and gestures' (Kristeva, 1977: 131). Artaud believed that there is no escaping from language in the theatre, despite one's best efforts. There is only the conscious rigour of a cruelty which is not clouded by the unconscious (a concept for which Artaud had no use), or what Kristeva includes in her concept of the semiotic. Kristeva criticizes various attempts (by Robert Wilson, Yvonne Rainer, Richard Foreman) in the French and American theatres throughout the 1960s and 1970s to realize Artaud's dream of an immediate, communal theatre without the remainders of text, readers and interpreters, and a thrill-seeking bourgeois audience. These efforts could only represent the unrepresentable, remainderless energy of Artaud's conception of such a theatre, caught as they were in the trap of failing by succeeding. They heightened the desire for a place to 'remake language', or at least to reassemble the semiotic and the symbolic once more. The Artaudian 'festival' is not for subscribers.

The 'non-theological space' of Artaud's theatre is, in Lyotard's short essay 'La dent, la paume', thoroughly 'theological'. Derrida's enthusiasm for Artaud is not contagious. Between A and B (i.e. signifier/signified, work/performance, tooth/palm) there is a gap (*nihil*) which must always be bridged by a connection (*religio*). Mind the gap, Lyotard says, because the bar differentiates and connects the theatre with something beyond itself; don't let the bar become a religion of representation. The bar binds the sign; a Marxist-materialist conception of language is the 'religion' of Brecht's epic theatre; and, as Hans Bellmer digs his nails into his palm when he has a toothache, Lyotard thinks that the palm represents the tooth for any *réflexion*, for all *réflexologie* (1973a: 96). Artaud fares no better.

In Lyotard's estimation, what stopped Artaud short of grasp-
ing the reversibility of the pure libidinal energy of a debarred
A/B, was that he had already found a 'religion':

> In order to put intensities to work, he manufactured a 'tool'
> which would serve as a new language, a system of signs,
> a grammar of gestures, a 'hieroglyphics'. This is what he
> thought he found in Eastern theatre, particularly in the
> Balinese and Japanese theatres. He thus remained a Euro-
> pean; he repeated the 'invention' of the agreement of the
> body and the senses, and made the great discovery (at the
> antipodes) of the unity of the libido as Eros and of the libido
> as death drive; he repeated his ethno-logical mise en scène on
> the Eastern stage.
>
> (Lyotard, 1973a: 99–100)

Lyotard surely knows that a theatre of energy is a religion too.
There is, at the end of his essay, only the following question: 'It
[an energetic theatre] has to produce the highest intensity (by
excess or lack) of what there is, without intention. These are my
questions: is it possible? How?' (1973a: 104) Lyotard also asks
one to wait for an answer, even though he has already provided
the means for only a negative response. Artaud's 'orientalism'
was marked, according to Baudrillard, by his 'often scabrous
affinity with magic and exorcism, even orgiastic mysticism'
(1976: 338–9). Scripts, masterpieces and psychology are for
Westerners, Artaud believed, while the *metaphysics in action*
of the Eastern theatres constitutes a new poetics of space.
For his part, Baudrillard has repeatedly denounced various
forms of mysticism (including psychoanalysis) which require
the liberation of an 'original' source of 'energy'.

At this point one may recall the final paragraph of Foucault's
presentation of Deleuze's 'theatrum philosophicum', a passage
impressive for its cruel scenography of wild dancing, explosive
laughter, reversals, blind gesturing and disguises all in the
service of a thought which plays the history of philosophy as we
have known it as mise en scène, as everything that is required in
staging a performance (Foucault, 1977). Ultimately, the positions of Foucault and Deleuze will diverge on the question of
the relation between Artaud's art and madness.

Baudrillard's contribution to poststructuralist debates concerning Artaud's place in the critique of representation is his

emphasis on the object. In 'En finir avec les chefs-d'oeuvre', Artaud comes to consider, in the course of answering a hypothetical misreading of his sense of cruelty as 'blood', 'the much more terrible and necessary cruelty [more than mutual dismemberment] that things can exercise against us. We are not free. The sky can still fall on our heads. The theatre can make us understand this' (1964: 123). Artaud was convinced of the '*revelatory aspect of matter*, which seems all of a sudden to scatter into signs in order to teach us the metaphysical identity of the concrete and the abstract' (1964: 91). This lesson was well learned by Baudrillard. For him, the active manifestations of things display an 'offensive resistance . . . to [their] investigation' (Baudrillard, 1984d: 149). Baudrillard's objects 'take revenge' through a profound reticence. Even science 'underestimates [the object's] vices, the derision, the offhandedness, the false complicity'. Artaud's things come forth brilliantly, while Baudrillard's objects are rather taciturn. Not all of Artaud's things behaved so well. What Artaud enjoyed in the Marx Brothers' film *Monkey Business* was the degree to which 'things get out of hand . . . objects, animals, sounds, master and servants, host and guests, everything comes to a boil, goes mad, and revolts' (Artaud, 1976: 240).

There is, however, in Artaud's praise of Vincent van Gogh, a troubling aspect of the theatrical celebration of 'things gone mad'. Indeed, if Blau is correct that 'we have made a ceremony out of what Artaud calls "the revenge of things" ' (1965: 247), then Baudrillard may be considered to be the most recent master of ceremonies of a universe in which such revenge has tended to carry over into a madness as chilling as receiving an eye or an ear in the mail. No one should confuse Artaud's enjoyment of The Marx Brothers with his praise for van Gogh. Artaud thought of himself and van Gogh as fellow *aliénés authentiques*; they were superior men whose visionary insights into *le mythe des choses* unfortunately brought them into contact with the repressive regime of psychiatry. Not only did Artaud blame 'dear brother Theo' (van Gogh's brother) and Dr Gachet, under whose care at Auvers-sur-Oise van Gogh spent his last months before he died of a self-inflicted gunshot wound, for precipitating van Gogh's suicide, but he attempts to justify on the basis of his experience as a psychiatric inmate that, in a striking literary confession and anti-psychiatric diatribe, van Gogh was 'suicided by society': 'I myself spent nine years in an insane asylum and I never had the obsession of suicide, but I know that each conversation with a psychiatrist, every morning at the time of his visit, made me want to hang myself, realizing that I would not be able to cut his throat' (Artaud, 1965: 496).

The lives of van Gogh and Artaud cannot be deliteralized and assigned to metaphor. Artaud describes throughout his essay on van Gogh how the painter revealed the 'passion', 'nerve', and the 'tidal wave' of things beyond their 'neurotic destiny'; that is to say, van Gogh had insight into their 'psychotic destiny'. Artaud claimed that it was psychiatry, not these things themselves, which took revenge upon van Gogh and himself.

'Artaud the Schizo', as Deleuze and Guattari have called him, was one of several model 'schizorevolutionary' figures upon whose works and lives their reading of schizophrenia as a liberatory, albeit risky, process was based and developed. Artaud's writings, in fact, inspired Deleuze and Guattari's concept of the body-without-organs, an anoedipal body whose potentialities are realized through intense, inventive connections beside the libidinal limits imposed by capitalism, the signifier, genital sexuality, castration, etc. It is not the dysfunctional 'hospital' schizo driving this interpretation, but the literary schizo denouncing the holy family of psychoanalysis. Artaud – the anti-psychiatry/psychoanalysis protestor, and in his time a 'survivor' of many asylums – made what Deleuze and Guattari refer to as a breakthrough, as opposed to breaking down or being broken down into a clinical entity, beyond 'a neurotic or perverse recoding' (1977: 135) and into a universe of scrambled codes where one circulates or 'schizzes' from bit to bit without a goal.

Deleuze and Guattari would eventually write of Artaud in 'November 28, 1947: How To Make Yourself A Body Without Organs?' in *A Thousand Plateaus* that 'even if Artaud did not succeed for himself [in lifting the roadblocks on his "intensity map"; in his experiments with drugs; no one, not even Artaud, can experiment in peace], it is certain that through him something has succeeded for us all' (1987: 164). (The date in the title refers to the period (22–29 November) during which Artaud was in Paris recording 'To Have Done With The Judgment Of God', from which Deleuze and Guattari quote; this is Artaud's 'radiophonic' experiment to which Deleuze and Guattari refer in passing.) The schizophrenic process of Artaud's experiments makes his oeuvre a privileged reference guide for 'how to' achieve a breakthrough. Artaud himself at times seemed to recognize where he went wrong or not far enough, the point at which desire became dangerous, having been emptied by too many drugs, for example. Deleuze and Guattari's reading of Artaud is tempered by Foucault's questioning of the uneasy relationship between madness and art.

One need only recall Foucault's closing remarks in *Madness and Civilization* regarding Artaud's madness as the *absence of the work of art* to understand the point at which he precluded Deleuze and Guattari's position on Artaud. Artaud's madness was, even for Foucault, nonetheless appreciable, infinite in its dimensions, itself reiterating the art work's absence like an insistent signifier:

> Madness is the absolute break with the work of art; it forms the constitutive moment of abolition, which dissolves in time the truth of the work of art; it draws the exterior edge, the line of dissolution, the contour against the void. Artaud's oeuvre experiences its own absence in madness, but that experience, the fresh courage of that ordeal, all those words hurled against a fundamental absence of language, all that space of physical suffering and terror which surounds or rather coincides with the void – that is the work of art itself: the sheer cliff over the abyss of the work's absence.
>
> (Foucault, 1967: 287)

Deleuze, Guattari and Foucault agree that any meeting of madness and art is dangerous, a game of life and death and living death in an institution; this meeting can destroy the work of art and the artist since it becomes a place into which the artist escapes without an exit. Foucault's sense of the madness of Artaud's oeuvre, or more precisely the latter's 'experience of its own absence in madness', which is evidence at once of Artaud's courage and terror and suffering, is marked by breaks, edges and an abyss; this is a partitioned landscape. There is no breakthrough for Foucault: madness does not pass through the fissures of the work of art. But for Deleuze and Guattari, these fissures are the kinds of lines of escape, becoming and cleavages that the work of art, understood as a tool which facilitates a flight from the signifier, subjectivity, genitality, the walls of reason described in so much French literature, and a plateau which ends in a sheer cliff, can provide. Artaud's 'works of madness', as Foucault called them, were works, but not of art.

In the work of both Artaud and Baudrillard, the object is said to have its revenge on the subject and logocentrism. In a theatrical theory like Baudrillard's, just as in Artaud's sense of theatre, the object diverts attention from the actors, speech and the signifieds of the performance. Baudrillard's pure objects are only 'schizorevolutionary' to the extent that his position on them is anti-psychoanalytic. This is precisely the argument Baudrillard makes in the section 'Le cristal se venge' in *Les Stratégies fatales* (1983: 154ff). Seduction is an anti-psychoanalytic concept in Baudrillard's understanding since it is accounted for neither in terms of desire in the psychic economy of the individual, nor in the reduction to symptoms of all appearances in Freudian dream interpretation and the psychopathology of everyday life. Baudrillard had already pointed in *De la séduction* to the fact that Freud abandoned what is called 'the seduction theory' (that the infantile experiences of adult analysands of rape and other sexually abusive attacks were compatible with nothing other than real, material events) in the service of the unconscious, non-material phylogenetic fantasies of sexual abuse, and of 'seduction' as a screen memory in infantile sexual and psychic development. Baudrillard's notion of seduction bears no relation to 'the seduction theory'. He is primarily concerned with the theory's status as a 'lost object' killed off in the name of 'science' (Baudrillard, 1979: 80ff).

Seduction is, however, an enigma which challenges the truth of analytic interpretation. It has nothing to do with the economy of desire, Baudrillard insists, since it originates beyond the individual and subsists 'elsewhere'. The exteriority or radical objectivity of seductive pure objects is essential to their sovereignty and their 'election' of someone/thing to surprise and to lure into a fatal convergence of circumstances and events. Baudrillard's sense of the play of things is far from the heaving and persecutory world of the psychotic.

Patrice Pavis's question 'Mise en scène ou mise en signe?' (1976: 135) carries me from Artaud's theatricalization of the theatre as mise en scène to the Prague School's semioticization of the object as mise en signe. The aesthetics and structuralism of Zich and Veltrusky respectively provide a further means by which to decode the drama of Baudrillard's theory of the object, which becomes in this context a wily prop.

The object is played by the dramatic forces of the stage which catapult it into a leading role in the performance, among whose many features it stands in a relation equal to or more significant than the actor. It is in terms of a subject-object or actor-prop continuum that Prague School theorists have modelled the force of the sign-vehicles of the stage as they are made to shift along the continuum in a given performance. As Keir Elam has observed in *The Semiotics of Theatre and Drama*, experiments in the modern theatre have often involved the object's acquisition of a force 'in its own right':

> It is notable that many of the so-called experiments in the twentieth-century theatre have been founded on the promotion of the set to the position of 'subject' of semiosis, with a corresponding surrender of 'action force' by the actor: Edward Gordon Craig's ideal, for example, was a mode of representation dominated by a highly connotative set in which the actor had the purely determined function of über marionette. Samuel Beckett's two mimes, *Act Without Words i & ii*, play with the reversal of subjective-objective roles between actor and prop – the human figure is determined by and victim of, the stage sign-vehicles ('tree' . . . etc.) – while his thirty-second *Breath* has the set as its sole protagonist.
>
> (Elam, 1980: 16)

Zich's aesthetic conception of an energetics of dramatic space was an important precursor of the understanding of the dynamism, mobility and transformability of the sign-vehicle. In Zich's aesthetics, dramatic space consists of lines of force which radiate from certain dramatic centres of a performance (i.e. characters) and in their turn, in a given dramatic situation, interact in a variety of ways (Zich, in Kiebuzinska, 1988: 34–5).

Veltrusky's concept of 'action force' may be applied all along the continuum from actor to prop. This application furthers Zich's non-hierarchical assignation of forces by breaking the active-passive division between the one who initiates semiosis and the thing that is acted upon. Veltrusky specifies that 'the prop is not always passive. It has a force . . . that attracts a certain action to it' (Veltrusky, in Garvin (ed.), 1964: 88). A prop can shape action even in the absence of an actor. Although objects may become 'spontaneous subjects equivalent to the figure of the actor', this transformation does not take place through personification. Zich thought that an object such as a wig or hairpiece occupied neither pole of the continuum between the actor's make-up and clothing. Indeed, objects may become subjects, just as subjects may be presented as objects in theatrical configurations.

Baudrillard has sought to 'rediscover the aesthetic force of the world' in the object's passion (1987: 73). The theatre can assist in this 'rediscovery', as Veltrusky himself hoped, by expanding the epistemological horizon of everyday life; that is, by lifting the bar which normally separates subject/things and exercises control over the latter. Baudrillard stretches this idea to its limits through a theatricalization of the world, a reenchantment of things. He converts the passivity of the object into the seat of its passions (*passions indifférentielles, passions inertielles*). In its most impoverished sense, it is the artist's passion which passes into the work. The passion of the work is, however, not an object of one's passionate inclination, but the object's condition. The object may be animated by its passions, as well as being *passionnant*, fascinating, seductive and in this fatal.

Lyotard, one may recall, accused Artaud of purloining his concept of cruelty from Eastern theatrical traditions and once again reinventing the 'East' for the 'West'. This reimaging of the 'East' also applies to Baudrillard whose concept of ceremony is derived from The Peking Opera, 'oriental' ceremonies and cultures in general, the Hindu Book of Manu, etc. The 'ceremony of the world' is Baudrillard's theatre of cruelty, a minutely defined circulation of pure ceremonial signs heavy with obligations which are exchanged with a formal strictness according to explicit rules. Baudrillard's sense of ceremony is non-representational. It is not a stage or a scene, even though certain experiments in theatre have preserved some elements of the symbolic violence of ceremony and ritual. Ceremonial violence is akin to theoretical violence. Both are theatrically cruel since they oppose naturalism and expressionism with a logic immanent to a set of rules. In Lyotard's terms, Baudrillard found the same 'religion' as Artaud in the 'East' and the chain of non-representational signs arranged and connected non-causally. Connections in this universe are all on the level of appearances. Baudrillard maintains, then, an 'empty space' (Lyotard's *nihil*) in the violent brush of weapons in the Peking Opera, the uncross-able darkness of the duel and the river between lovers. This 'gap' is rendered palpable by the efforts to cross it. The gap cannot be occupied because it is the space held open by cere-mony itself, a guard against the promiscuity of direct and free contacts (Baudrillard, 1983: 185ff).

Baudrillard's crystal is in Naomi Segal's (1981: 4) terms a *banal object*. Although I have emphasized the ways in which certain concepts in the theory of theatre may be used to explicate Baudrillard's reading of objects, Segal presents an important parallel reading of the power of commonplace objects in litera-ture. Through both positive and negative narrative encounters with it, a banal object forces a crisis and resolves it. Like Baudrillard's objects, it can display a wilful malevolence – a *Tücke des Objekts* – toward the writer. Neither Segal's banal object, Baudrillard's crystal, nor the wily prop may be thought of as completely passive instruments. The crystal is, then, Baudrillard's (Proustian) madeleine as much as the gnarled roots of existential (Sartrean) drama.

Baudrillard's reenchantment of the world is not driven by madness. Artaud might even have scoffed at Baudrillard's neurotic crystals. Today in North America, the crystal's revenge has a specific reference in the context of a New Age subculture whose enthusiastic misappropriation of numerous traditions has brought quartz crystals into a marketplace of saleable and portable mysticisms. This is not the revenge of the pet rock, but of healing crystals! All the same, the reasons for Baudrillard's use of the term *cristal* are quite transparent. Crystal is not only a variety of glass (leaded) with a high degree of brilliance. It is a hyperreal object of sorts in its own right since it is by definition more transparent and heavier than ordinary glass; crystal, then, is glassier than glass.

A new domestic order recently established itself in the United States with an inaugural evening of entertainment. This is not supposed to be just another Pepsi generation, although a new advertising campaign for a Pepsi product (clear and caffeine free) made its début on television with the Clinton government. The television advertisement for Crystal Pepsi ('Right Now') was created by Phil Dusenberry for the BBDO agency, whose advertisements for Pepsi and Macintosh won numerous ind-ustry awards and set commercial stylistic agendas throughout the 1980s. Dusenberry is best known for his soft-sell documentary which resembled a Pepsi commercial for Ronald Reagan's presidential campaign in 1984 (although he also worked for Reagan in 1976 and 1980). The appearance of Dusenberry's new Pepsi advertisement on the eve of the Democrat(ic) takeover of power in Washington is precisely the sort of objective irony at the heart of things which continues to fascinate Baudrillard. The revenge of the Crystal Pepsi reveals a horrible irony: political change is diminished by its association with a new soft-drink whose last 'generation' fit together perfectly with Republican politics (Dusenberry worked for Reagan, Bush and a variety of conservative groups). The Palace of Crystal Pepsi renders political change irrelevant, and even dangerous. Crystal Pepsi takes its revenge on another generation by dragging its conservative past into the present.

In addition, the crystal plays a role in Baudrillard's attack on the commodity. He asks his readers of *Les Stratégies fatales* to forget Marxian hieroglyphics. How, after all, can one hope 'to get behind the secret' of a crystal since it is more transparent than glass? Yet, if the crystal serves Baudrillard's purpose of parodying 'opacity' and the interpretive claims which render it transparent, it also serves well as an example of what for Baudrillard Marx paradoxically accomplished: Marx made the commodity more transparent than glass – a crystal. This was a great accomplishment, unfortunately crushed, writes Baudrillard, by 'Marxian dogma'. The crystalline commodity, however, retained for Baudrillard's Marx a 'disquieting strangeness' in virtue of 'its challenge to the judicious arrangement of things, to the real, morality, utility' (1983: 135, n. 1). In rendering the commodity transparent, Marx momentarily glimpsed the enigma of pure objects. By the same token, too much transparency can itself be opaque and enigmatic since it enables one to see nothing but paradoxes, with respect to which one's only response may be a decidedly un-Baudrillardian ambivalence.

In aligning Baudrillard with the conceptually relevant precursors of Artaud, the Prague School and Segalen, I have not re-paired him. Rather, I have regrouped the influences on his concept of the crystal and shown that it bears the mark of the theatrical and literary traditions which have addressed similar concepts but in different contexts and under different circumstances. By reworking for himself the active object and complementing his reading of Segalen, Baudrillard attempts to ensure by definition the object's incomprehensibility, and therefore its exoticism, while at the same time impairing the subject's control over the object(ive) universe. Only a true *exote* forsakes such control, and the truth of the *exote* is stained with reactionary principles.

Conclusion
Signs of Baudrillard

Baudrillard established his reputation in North America and won over a large segment of its critical audience during the 1980s. His arrival came about in large measure through the efforts of the Telos group which published two important trans-lations (*The Mirror of Production* and *For A Critique ot the Political Economy of the Sign*), articles and book reviews in the 1970s and early 1980s. Despite the fact that much of Baudrillard's work served to *épater les Marxistes*, it was through the com-bined activities of American, Canadian and Australian theorists and translators working from diverse leftist positions that Baudrillard's work was widely disseminated. This is surely a testimony to Left-leaning scholarship.

A great deal of effort has been expended by those thinkers working in the tradition of the Frankfurt School to bring Baudrillard into some kind of line with their theoretical and practical concerns. There is at once both ample and obvious evidence that Baudrillard has deep roots here *and* that he has wrenched these roots from their ground. The central question is whether Baudrillard articulates a form of oppositional practice in his work, especially in his concept of hypersimulative activity, the hyperconformity of the masses. The answer to this question, however, does not exhaust the issue of Baudrillard's 'politics'. On the one hand, Levin claims that: 'all of Baudrillard's work is a meditation on Marx's theory of commodity fetishism. This makes Baudrillard a critical theorist' – even though it does not give him a sense of counterpraxis (1984: 37). For Steven Best (1989), there are three societies with three correspond-ing masters: commodity/Marx; spectacle/Debord; simulacrum/Baudrillard. To these pairs may be added three related kinds of understanding: Marxist, neo-Marxist, and post-Marxist. As a post-Marxist, Baudrillard has no ground upon which to fashion an oppositional practice. Although there are numerous examples of the attempt to show that Baudrillard does not establish a political discourse relevant to counterpraxis, and that he wallows in the 'revolutionary diversions' of a 'negative politics' (Valente, 1985), dissenting voices are also in evidence.

On the other hand, Briankle G. Chang contends that Baudrillard 'continues the practical project of Althusser . . . Williams . . . Hall . . . and others' (1986: 159). By positioning Baudrillard in this way, Chang can claim that hyperconformity is a form of humour by means of which the masses devour the messages of the media but remain incompletely socialized. As Philip Haywood puts it: 'the output of the mass media can be analogized as a cacophony which increases in a direct inverse relation to the silence of the masses' (1984: 132). Kroker claims that Baudrillard is the true successor of the tragic tradition in critical theory and he thinks that Baudrillard presents the political alternative of hyperconformist simulation, of 'resistance-as-object' (1985). Kroker's effusive promotion of Baudrillard as 'the last and best of all the Marxists' has worried Kellner, for whom 'it seems a mistake for Kroker to situate Baudrillard in Marx's tradition' since Kroker and Baudrillard have abandoned Marx's revolutionary project (1987: 128). In a manner worthy of both Kellner and Kroker, Chris Doran (1990) develops a pseudo-formal demonstration of Baudrillard's thesis that 'all dissent must be of a higher logical type than that to which it is opposed' (hence, hyper-logic) by appealing to the 'veracity of working-class parole' against the simulation of working-class experience by social science. Among critical theorists, then, there is no agreement on whether Baudrillard has what one might call, generously or otherwise, a 'politics of opposition'.

During the same period, Baudrillard's influence in the art world began to spread and mature, informing particular artistic practices and critical readings. Other European intellectuals, of course, also arrived to seek their fortunes and witness the simulacra of their realized utopias, even if they did not accept Baudrillard's vision. Eco's popular success as a novelist translated into critical success for his collection of essays (most of which were from the 1960s and 1970s) entitled *Travels in Hyper-reality* (1986).

What Baudrillard did ostensibly for the art world was to provide a poetico-theoretical language with which to describe a state of affairs that certain of its members sensed and sought to render critically: the art world had become no more than the exchange of sign-commodities and these signs no longer signified anything other than their own exchange value. The process by which a painting loses its meaning and even its visibility is described by Baudrillard in his essay 'L'Enchère de l'oeuvre d'art' in *Pour une critique*. The conversion of economic exchange value into sign value rests upon the understanding that consumption entails the production of differential sign value and the latter's exchange. What has not been generally recognized in the Baudrillard-inspired art literature is his idea of the symbolic value of the art auction, this potlatch-like circulation of objects which accrue value through their very circulation and afford legitimacy and prestige to those who possess them. Symbolic exchange, however, is reduced to sign exchange value by the aesthetic function of a work.

The best example of Baudrillard's influence on an individual artist is perhaps the American painter Peter Halley. In an interview, Halley explains how Baudrillard gave him the gift of (in)sight: 'it was Baudrillard who allowed me to understand what I was doing with those day-glo colors I had been using. All of a sudden I began to see them as hyperrealization of real color and I don't think I could have conceptualized that without Baudrillard' (Cone, 1986 and Halley, 1986: 126). Surprisingly, only three years earlier, Halley (1983) was still wondering about the consequences for both the artist and the audience of being seduced by Baudrillard's shimmering world. For his part, Baudrillard dashed the hopes of those engaged in simulist art, neo-geo and the like by distancing himself from them (Heartney, 1987 and Baudrillard, 1986b). The conjunction of seduced and abandoned was never more fitting. At least since the 'Game with Vestiges' interview (Baudrillard, 1984g), Baudrillard has with some consistency offered his opinion that he finds the contemporary art scene, and postmodern art in particular, inferior to the modernist forms produced as recently as the immediate post-World War II period (including surrealism), because of the absence of a radical *raison d'être* and a sense of danger. While he has not warmed to American artists other than Warhol and Barbara Kruger (Baudrillard's untitled catalogue essay for

Kruger's show at the Mary Boone Gallery in New York in 1987 describes an evil genius of advertising who has victimized us all; Baudrillard, 1987c), he has with critical enthusiasm supported the work of his colleague, the Italian painter Enrico Baj, albeit with an important qualification. In his 'Baj ou la monstruosité mise à nu par la peinture même' (Baudrillard, 1980b), Baj's humorous and ironic play with materials in his sculptural paintings has a sarcastic edge to it which Baudrillard appreciates because it transcends surrealism. Baj displays the brutal, derisory and indeed monstrous character of signs themselves in his manipulation of materials. But it is not only the 'monstrosity of the pictorial event' which interests Baudrillard. In 1963, Baj cofounded with Raymond Queneau the Milanese Pataphysics Institute and never tired of *la logomachie jarryenne*.

From the perspective of Baudrillard's *Les Stratégies fatales*, it is hopelessly nostalgic to lament the vicissitudes of exchange value and the ever-receding horizon of use value. Baudrillard's Baudelairean fantasy culminates at the moment when a work of art becomes 'more commodity than commodity', an exaggerated expression of the fact of the commodity. If Baudrillard's tactic of pushing a given object (i.e. a work of art) over the edge in an ironic, non-dialectical, deconstructive 'potentialization' ('more x than x') at one time seemed like a bold gesture which raised exaggeration to a critical principle, it became over time a tiresome formula for many artists and art critics alike. While Baudrillard's work has been immensely influential in the 'postmodern' art scene, there have always been cracks in the armour of his influence.

If one were to gather together all of the terms which take the prefix *hyper* in the texts of Baudrillard, one would not only have a large collection, but a veritable *hypermarché* of signs. Even with only a fragment of this collection in hand, one might linger in the medico-biological section and serve oneself signs denoting abnormal growth. As self-serving as this activity may appear, it would enable one to establish the domains of research whence Baudrillard's operative concepts have come (pathology, biology, geometry, etc.), sketch a figure of the social structure provided by his elaborations upon the theme of *hyper-* (obese, cancerous, etc.), and describe his fanciful, and hyperbolic, concatenations of *hyper*s. Los Angeles is a kind of hyperspace or more spatial than space, a cyberspace if you like or, to put it simply, a maze in which postmodernists are always losing their way and for this reason call for maps of various kinds; the city has a great ex-urban or hyperurban paunch hanging over its limits into the desert like a useless, hypertelic *gidouille*.

When Eco travels in hyperreality, he is for the better part of his journey in the US. During his trip into 'an America of furious hyperreality', he uncovers a truncated process of semiosis in which iconic signs such as holograms have lost their ability to refer to their objects. Eco believes that objects *qua* referents are considered in Peirce's semiotics in discussions of icons and indices, even though Peirce's objects are irreducible to referents. On the one hand, Eco's point is semiotically redundant if one recalls that icons show something of but do not lead one to a 'referent' at all. In addition, Eco's sense of a semiotic mutation in America does not follow from the icon's bi-directionality nor its relative muteness. On the other hand, for Eco the technique of holography – an optical process which yields a virtual image of a visual field in three dimensions – 'could prosper only in America, a country obsessed with realism, where, if a recon-struction is to be credible, it must be perfectly iconic, a perfect likeness, a "real" copy of the reality being represented' (Eco, 1986: 4).

In this America it is easy, we are told, to forget that the perfect likeness is just a likeness because the real is achieved by means of the perfect fake. Like Baudrillard, Eco uses the figure of the hologram – the most theoretically elastic technology before Virtual Reality systems proper – to suggest the dreamy tri-dimensionality of an America. If icons were completely indiffer-ent about their objects, one would then have a straight gate to the Peircean hyperreal. The object may be restricted, but not necessarily so, to a referent at the nexus of the triadic relation of sign–object–interpretant. The Peircean semiotician may in fact show a studied indifference toward the issue of whether or not a given web of semiosis has a real or a true dimension correspond-ing to it. One may ricochet around for some time in Peircean semiosis by considering the immediate and dynamic objects of signs since the dynamic object has a kind of collateral existence as a 'real' thing brought to the attention of an interpreter by the sign, although it does not depend on the sign in the same manner as an immediate object.

Baudrillard's 'misunderstanding' of America as a hologram

signalled his then current optical 'focus'. The hologram is one of many figural devices he has used to suggest the perfect simulacrum (pantograph, photograph, cinematograph, hologram, VR . . .). These devices have not been employed in a rigorous developmental schema. They have all explained, in virtue of their respective degrees of resolution and simulative capacities, how simulacra 'kill' and subsequently replace their original objects. Tridimensional simulation is more powerful metaphorically and literally more exact than a pantographic blueprint. Baudrillard also likes to shop around in scientific discourse. In the hands of Eco and Baudrillard, the hologram signifies America and helps to generate the hyperreal.

America is a peculiar semiotic production and it is the main ingredient in all recipes for the hyperreal. For every *hyponyme* (which will ironically consist of specific *hypers-*) there is the generic *hyperonyme* of hyperreality: for Eco and Baudrillard, the generic hyperonyme is hyperreality; their respective hyponymes include hypericons, hyperbolic formulae; hyperplasia, hypertelia, hyperspace, etc. For a given hyponyme, there is a domain of research, a 'home' discipline to which it may be traced and from whose resources it may be eventually fortified. Concepts are 'borrowed': hyperplasia is borrowed from pathology, hyperspace from mathematics; hyperbole from rhetoric, hypericons from Peircean semiotics, etc. For each domain of derivation, there is a figure of America which may be established on the basis of a given cluster of hyponymes: from optics, one uses dreamy, virtual, holographic; from pathology, descriptors such as obese, cancerous, and viral are put into play. These are some of the operations by means of which one may semiotically produce the hyperreality of America.

Something is *hyper* when it is excessive and exaggerated. It is always more and more: in the 1980s yuppies worked more and more, spent more and more, etc. But what drove this kind of going to extremes? The hyperreal is more real than the real, just as hypertely is in part more final than final. What makes the real *hyper* is that it is more, *plus réel*, and so much more so that there appears to be no way to turn back to a previous condition of less than *hyper*. In some cases, the more one turns back, the more hyperreal nostalgia becomes (the phenomenon of more 'sixties than the 'sixties; even though, as Grace Slick once remarked, if you claim to remember the sixties, you couldn't possibly have been there). But this is not the same abundance that Eco found in America: 'In America, you don't say, "Give me another coffee"; you ask for "More coffee"; you don't say that cigarette A is longer than cigarette B, but that there's "more" of it, more than you're used to having, more than you might want' (1986: 8). Eco's 'more' suggests something akin to a big helping; the size of American things is anti-ecological. Baudrillard's version of obesity is fatter than fat. American obesity is not the flab of idleness but the annihilation of a system's limit in its attempt to digest whatever surrounds it. This is a structural obesity which does not diminish to the profit of anything less than itself in its giddy spiral of self-potentialization.

As the dynamic object of numerous attempts in European culturology to signify America, this nation cannot be said to depend upon a given sign of it, unlike its immediate object or meaning. Baudrillard's complex sign *Amérique* – the original Grasset edition bears a photograph of what may be the skyline of Montréal or Minneapolis – has generated numerous interpretants of itself and its dynamic object America. Baudrillard's genuine 'misunderstanding' of this object underlines the semiotic point that the interpretants generated by this sign give a radically incomplete and imperfect representation of America, and will continue to do so. This semiosis has an element, one may say, of the runaway virus of the fourth order of simulation.

Baudrillard's response to what he considered to be the cold horrors of the code's legibility, transparency and machinic manipulation by cyber-semioticians across the disciplines, echoed the critical remarks on simulacra and structure made by Henri Lefebvre in the early 1960s (1971: 203–4). The philosophy of structure, Lefebvre argued, is technocratic and risks producing nothing more than a simulacrum of the world. Consciously or not, this 'philosophy' simulates humankind by rendering it 'cybernetic'. This representation of the engineering of communication contributed to a context in which anti-semiological bar games could and would flourish, despite the fact that the bar games of poststructuralism departed in letter and in spirit from Lefebvre's mode of critique.

Saussure's bar of implication – Baudrillard called it the bar of structural copulation – and Lacan's bar of repression which refused a fusional Saussurean line, are without question the basic bars upon which poststructuralists play their games; Lacan too played the Saussurean bar. Lyotard's gay bar embodied the spirit of Jarry's whirling pataphysical stick and played ambiguously with the stroke between this/not-this. Immediately following upon their praise for Hjelmslev's linguistics, Deleuze and Guattari recommended Lyotard's *Discours, figure* (1971) as 'the first generalized critique of the signifier' conducted with a bar game called 'the figural'. Once the signifier and the signified have been crushed and the bar disbarred, the signifying chain is opened to asignifying fluxes. Lest one misread Deleuze and Guattari, their praise for Lyotard is quickly dampened by the return of the signifier of lack in his theorizing (1977: 243–4). Some of Baudrillard's strokes of seduction, inasmuch as they were played around the bar, coupled and uncoupled at will and for this reason may be considered fickle. But the important lesson is that Baudrillard, like Deleuze and Guattari, employed 'Peircean' processes even after semiological signs would have burnt, and brought his theory of the object's revenge into line with proto-Prague School semiotics, in spite of himself. Baudrillard's concept of the symbolic must in the end destroy Peircean signs as well since they are implicit in his description of the orders of simulacra.

The power bar held sway over the life/death dichotomy by barring the return of death. This archetype of every control bar – keeping its consequent term down – possesses the means, like a censor, to control social communication. Along with Saussure's bar, it was subjected to numerous barbs in *L'Echange symbolique*. Several years earlier in *Pour une critique*, Baudrillard had installed a strong bar between general political economy/symbolic exchange in order to erect a monument which would come to be toppled with the violence of an *effraction*; that is to say, the symbolic, and later an Evil Other, would break into the semiological world of value and the code in order to destroy them.

The bars – an anagram, after all, of 'Barthes' – of Baudrillard were stroked, erected, broken and lifted in the service of a barless, anti-semiological imaginary of the symbolic. Baudrillard's understanding of the symbolic is irreducible to any of the thinkers from whom he borrowed seminal concepts. The manifestations of the symbolic circulate in a non-structural and weak manner. All of his care taken to maintain the register of hypoweakness, however, gave itself over to the standard of duel and agonistic social relations expressed through the concepts of potlatch, *Witz*, anagram, and death, themselves delivered with seductive strokes, and pataphysical acid. I described in some detail Baudrillard's struggle to avoid an irreversible move in the direction of either strong theory or mysticism; his balancing act, I argued, was ultimately unsuccessful, but not completely disappointing.

Baudrillard does not know his own strength. What sort of strength is implied in the 'injunction' *Oublier Foucault*? (1977a). Is there any stronger theoretical statement in Baudrillard's work than this? In this forgettery there is also a return of the grotesque. A familiar image resurfaces: Ubu. *Ubu lié à Foucault*. *Oublier Foucault* was never a dismissive gesture such as *Oubliez Foucault* would have been. Rather, *c'est un pilier de bar*: one could spend one's life propping up a bar to be sure, and in a way this is what Baudrillard believes Foucault did. He propped up the bars which structure the irreversible agencies of power and sex ('irreversible' in the senses of progress and production as opposed to symbolic cancellation and reversibility). For Foucault's theorizing displays in Baudrillard's eyes a horrible beauty: it manifests what it describes; it is full of methodological spirals chasing after the successive spirals of power and sex. The spiral, of course, is the emblem of the Collège de Pataphysique and it is the figure by means of which Baudrillard represents the shape of Foucault's analyses. Although *Oublier Foucault* is full of spirals, this does not mean that Foucault's work is sufficiently pataphysical. Foucault does not follow the pataphysician's spiral into the abyss in which his objects of interest perish and acquire power only in their death and their simulation. Foucault's spirals are less jarryesque than molecular. Recall that Baudrillard attacked cyberneticists precisely because they inscribed the genetic code everywhere. If Jarry's spiral brings a bemused grin to one's face, then the helix should make one laugh at those who appeal to 'molecularity' as a revolutionary concept. Baudrillard would have us laugh at Foucault, Deleuze and Guattari and Lyotard because the 'molecular' is a matrix of control rather than liberation, the Law splintered into molecular bits. Baudrillard attempts to invert by pataphysical means the view that Foucault's remarkable, meticulous and magisterial analyses produced truths about their objects and a method which could be reproduced and applied by his followers as they themselves spiral around the fixed points of Foucauldian referents the death and disappearance of which recede from view as their beautiful circling unfolds.

Foucault's project was, in Baudrillard's view, carried along by its own obsolescence and blindness to new simulacral forms of the referents to which he clung and whose anamorphoses he traced – from cyclopean panopticism to an ubuesque polyhedral march of crabs in all directions – but whose demise he did not question. Baudrillard's reference to Ubu's polyhedra symbolizes the fragmentation and dispersion of power and conjures Jarry's figure of the scientist Achras in *Ubu Cocu*. Achras breeds and studies polyhedrons (multifaceted solids). Some of these are so fractious as to deserve slaps on all of their faces! Like polyhedrons, power remains a solid (real presence) in spite of its multifacetedness and the need to take numerous positions in order to perceive of all its facets and points.

Foucault was too strong a theorist. If he had been more pataphysical he would have been weaker and therefore more acceptable to Baudrillard. For his part, the strength of Baudrillard's claims against Foucault is mitigated by the Ubu form and recurring figure of the spiral since they mock rather than critique, refigure rather than analyze, and most importantly, they rely upon the assistance of symbolic reversibility as seduction. Baudrillard cannot resist replacing production with seduction. Baudrillard's critique rests on the application of his oft-repeated weak concepts: power is exchanged in the reversible, non-accumulable cycle of seduction. For all of its implied but positive weakness, this set of concepts, as I have argued, is unstable, because its members acquire the strength of the theories against which they are supposed to offer tactical alternatives.

The very idea of an asemiotic imaginary is incoherent in Peircean terms, given the infinite progress of semiosis. It is quite understandable, on the other hand, if one wants to escape a world saturated with Saussurean signs; to escape, in other words, a system requiring escape. Lyotard's critique of Baudrillard raised an important unresolved issue regarding the claim that the gift is not semiological. The gift and counter-gift relation – the sumptuary destruction of goods and the symbolic reciprocity of an expenditure equal to or greater than the initial ritual destruction of riches – plays awkwardly at disbarring itself. The desimulation of this structural couple involved a critique of (com)munication theory in the name of agonistic reciprocity. Anti-semiology is anti-monopolistic. But it is also spiritual since the gift and counter-gift relation is a spiritual mechanism of exchange and an obligation no one in this domain can afford to ignore. Even so, signs of richness are destroyed in order to initiate and/or further symbolic exchanges. In symbolic exchanges, signs do burn. Baudrillard understands Mauss's work on the potlatch in terms of the destruction – by fire or other means – of the material signifiers of the signifieds of wealth. Now, in spite of Baudrillard and, using Saussure's theory of value as a point of reference, one may claim that these signifiers are exchanged for dissimilar ideas, especially social standing, although such a signified is achieved by means of loss rather than through exchange value. Social standing thus acquired opens onto an exchange defined not only by means of the comparison of similar things in a system, but in virtue of an obligatory response (rather than a digital indifference or an oppositional positioning) in kind or with interest to an initial challenge. Signifiers burn in a struggle for signifieds. The signified is related homologically to use value. It is an astructural notion of use value which serves Baudrillard's purpose of promoting strictly incomparable *consommation*. The agonistic relation which is the struggle for signifieds takes place with all the cruelty of the symbolic. In Baudrillard's agonistic anti-semiology, symbolic relations, while at once evoking the struggles of 1968, so-called direct and immediate communication by means of graffiti, and a poetic anthropology, reinstate strong theory (so closely associated with semiology and structuralism) in the place vacated by the vanquished bars of semio-linguistics and psychoanalysis.

I called on Peircean semiosis to elaborate an ecumenical semiotic approach that was at once conceptually compatible with a critique of the signifier but not bound to the vicissitudes of poststructuralist bar gaming. To put the matter bluntly: one needs to know something of icons, indexes and symbols in order to think critically about simulacra. Peirce's place in critical investigations of poststructuralism has been extremely limited. This marginality is perhaps explained by the predominance of Euro-semiology in poststructuralism itself and the seemingly unorthodox ways in which Peirce's concepts have been used by poststructuralist thinkers in discussions of signs. When his concepts do appear, they are redefined for the purposes at hand, as we saw in the case of Deleuze and Guattari.

Baudrillard still clings to hope. Like the ritual destruction of signifiers, manifestations of symbolic circulation constitute a response to a system which seeks to hold its position once and for all. One plays bar games so as not to be put behind the bars of certain kinds of signs, neutralized, in effect, in the prison of structural simulation. Bar games which lift or weakly stroke a prohibitive bar are less efficacious than those played by means of an *effraction*. In *De la séduction*, Baudrillard draws a distinction between 'Rule' and 'Law' to illustrate the incommensurability of these two logics and develop his idea of the game (1979: 181ff). The Rule–Law distinction, however, reinscribes John Searle's seminal semiotic distinction between regulative (Law) and constitutive (Rule) rules into a duel carried out by all of the tropes of hypoweakness. Briefly, according to Searle, the former 'regulate a pre-existing activity, an activity whose existence is logically independent of the rules. Constitutive rules constitute (and also regulate) an activity the existence of which is logically dependent on the rules' (1969: 34). In the same way, the Law lays down regulative lines (interdictions, prohibitions, repression). These lines are transcendent, irreversible (linear), determinate (finite) and protect the necessary depth wherein truth dwells. The immanent reversibility of constitutive rules of the game, by contrast, hide nothing. In the domain of the Rule, one plays by the rules, or one leaves the game. The game establishes a symbolic pact among its players and is supposed to circumscribe the strong desire for universality attributed to the Law, even though it too has a truth of sorts which is duel, agonistic, primitive, symbolic and remainderless (perfectly balanced). The Rule has the depth of the Law it seeks to destroy. The ritual sure signs of the Rule establish debts of honour. These signs exorcise the Law and abolish meaning by exposing the arrogance of dividing up the world into its smallest meaningful pieces. Humility is part of the game. There is in all of this, Baudrillard admits, a terrible nostalgia for the cruel and intense circulation of sure signs, sumptuary practices and sacred ceremonies. Anti-semiological altercations force isomorphic systems and the bars servicing their internal combinational principles to totter like so many top-heavy edifices.

V.N. Volosinov's *Marxism and the Philosophy of Language* reads like a symbolic battle plan against the Enlightenment project of an abstract objective, rational, self-identical, monological semio-linguistic system. Whereas Guattari criticized the despotic formalism of a binary semiotic economy which censored and inhibited hybrid associations, Volosinov undertook a critique of abstract objectivism in linguistics (Saussureanism) with a view to exposing the simulacral nature of an ahistorical, synchronic system of internally fixed signals. The non-ideological, non-semiotic or 'sub-semiotic' instrumentality of signals in a purely technical code fails to conceptualize a life in language shaped by concrete commmunicational interactions in specific socio-historical contexts. Just as Guattari regretted specific aspects of Hjelmslev's glossematics (this did not deter his rescue of sub-stance and matter), a reader of Volosinov with an interest in polysemiotic relations cannot help but have reservations about Volosinov's glottocentric suppositions (all non-verbal signs are 'baptized' by speech and are therefore inseparable from 'the word'; Volosinov, 1973: 13ff).

The symbolic enters the semiological simulacrum. The Rule exorcises the Law. Unformed semiotic substances (gestural, ritual, etc.) and material fluxes decentre the semiotic circles of content/expression, signifier/signified and deform perfectly formed and closed signifying chains. Semio-dialogic under-standing explodes the static recognition of signals by concep-tualizing the generative process of language. This may not constitute a 'golden legend' of anti-semiology, but these examples do contextualize Baudrillard's long-standing efforts to address the problems posed by signs, among which he dwells uneasily. The clearest and most enduring signs of Baudrillard are those marking his struggles against signification in the name of symbolic exchange.

Notes

Unless otherwise indicated, translations are my own.

INTRODUCTION

1 Prior to the appearance of his translations of Weiss, however, Baudrillard assembled a series of quotations and photographs (Burri, 1963) which follow the socio-historic problematic of the irreal effects of the modernization of the Federal Republic of Germany and the theatre of the confrontation of a once divided country. It was not until 1983–84 in West Germany itself that Baudrillard's mature reflections on the fate of the real became widely disseminated, primarily in virtue of a discussion published as *Der Tod der Moderne* (Baudrillard *et al.*, 1983m). Although several of his works appeared in German in the late 1970s, it was only in the mid-1980s that the Baudrillard industry blossomed in West Germany.

In the period, then, from 1964–68, Editions du Seuil published Baudrillard's translations of four plays by Weiss. These translations represent only a fraction of Weiss's substantial output as a playwright and a social critic. The first play *Pointe de fuite* (1964) was followed by the well-known work which staged the imaginary encounter of Sade and Marat, a fantasy which took its cue from the fact that Sade did deliver the memorial address at Marat's funeral after the latter's assassination in 1793. The dramatic encounter would be staged by a small troupe directed by Sade consisting of inmates from the very place (Charenton) where he was confined from 1803 to his death in 1814 (*La Persécution et l'assassinat de Jean-Paul Marat représenté par le groupe théâtrale de l'hospice de Charenton sous le direction de Monsieur de Sade*, 1965). *L'instruction, oratorio en onze chants* (1966) preceded the important text *Vietnam Diskurs*, which in translation became *Discours sur la genèse et le déroulement de la très longue guerre de libération du Vietnam illustrant la nécessité de la lutte armée des opprimés contre leur oppresseurs ainsi que la volonté des Etats-Unis d'Amérique d'anéantir les fondements de la Révolution* (1968). The method by which Weiss expressed his support for the people's war of liberation in the

Discours belongs to the tradition of what is called 'political theatre', of which Brecht's didacticism is a leading example; Baudrillard translated Brecht's portrait of the exile as a dialectician, *Dialogues d'exilés*, in 1965. The *Discours*, however, begins with Weiss's 'Notes sur le théâtre documentaire'. Documentary theatre attempts to lay bare the dissimulations of power by taking, first of all, select cuts into existing documentary material (radio broadcasts, government documents, photographs, interviews, etc.). The fragments which result from such cuts are edited in the fashion of a collage which serves as a useful example, a 'model schema' of current events. The analysis of and reflection upon this model reveals the latent conflicts and falsifications of these events, as well as bringing the public into this theatre's critical inquest on an equal footing with the accuser and the accused. The radically democratic, quasi-legal underpinnings of this process are most evident when Weiss suggests that it may take the form of a tribunal which extends and even completes debates and inquiries *a posteriori*.

Baudrillard's translations placed him squarely in the oppositional intellectual culture of the period, although his other activities during the 1960s did a great deal more to define his own theoretical positions. Baudrillard's most pressing concern at the time was to find a Parisian publisher for his own work, *Le Système des objets*. It was Gallimard that published *Le Système des objets* in the same year as his translation of Mühlmann's collection of comparative sociopsychological analyses of *les mouvements nativistes*, under the provocative title of *Messianismes révolutionnaires du tiers monde* (1968). If Baudrillard's political sympathies were at any time in question, his work on the translation of Engels's *Le Rôle de la violence dans l'histoire* (1971) for Editions Sociales would have dispelled them, although one must be careful not to align his choice of work as a translator too closely with the content of the work in question.

2 What, then, was *Utopie*? The first issue of *Utopie, Revue de sociologie de l'urbain*, appeared in May 1967. I have examined the first seven issues up to August–September 1973, entitled 'Lutte de classe mise à nu'. Over these six years, Hubert Tonka served as managing editor, although this continuity was not reflected in the review's membership, which shifted substantially during the first issues until a core group of four remained: Isabelle Auricoste, Baudrillard, Michel Guillou and Tonka; I note in passing that the construction in the late 1980s of the Parc de la Villette in northeast Paris has produced a flurry of intellectual activity including Baudrillard's brief 'Préface' to this ecstatic urban form in Auricoste and Tonka's study *Parc-ville Villette* (Baudrillard, 1989) and discussion with French architect Jean Nouvel (Baudrillard, 1987j).

For Baudrillard, *Utopie* was of a *genre situationniste*. He applies this term to the review so as to align its general orientation with the character of the oppositional politics of the period, and at the same time he designates the review's political-theoretical antecedents in the revolutionary urbanism articulated in the proto-Situationist and early writings of Guy Debord in the 1950s. *Utopie* did not figure largely in the Situationist International. A certain 'pro-Chinese [Jean] Baudrillart' [sic], however, is listed among those 'decrepit modernist institutionalists gnawing their meagre bones at the professorial chairs of Social Sciences at Nanterre' in a Situationist tract of 1967 ('Our Goals and Methods in the Strasbourg Scandal', in Knabb (ed.), 1981: 211). In a very general way, *Utopie* may be said to have 'constructed situations' which sought to lessen the alienation brought about by urban planning, among which one may count the exposition of *structures gonflables* presented in May 1968 at the Musée d'Art Moderne de la Ville de Paris. Baudrillard still recycles this utopist conception. In *Cool Memories II*, he wrote: 'The rights of Man have an inflatable structure. The [French] Revolution and its commemoration have become inflatable structures' (Baudrillard 1990a: 31). This image expresses well the paradoxical fullness and emptiness of the spectacular ideologies of consumer society. One might recall that in Italian design *circa* 1967, the inflatable armchair 'Blow' appeared on the scene alongside numerous proposals for pneumatic objects such as housing units. These objects, like Baudrillard's use of the concept, were conceived along the same critical lines.

Few editorial statements of the review's reason for being were published. If one compares and contrasts the statement on 'Utopie dialectique' from the first issue with the untitled set of definitions which were published in *Utopie* 4 (1971), the critical locus remained, despite other important changes, relations between concepts. In accordance with the statement on 'Dialectical Utopia', 'it is in the uncrossed interval (*l'intervalle non franchi*) which exists between theory and praxis that we want to place ourselves'. The bar between theory and praxis is not crossed. It is never as simple a matter as that since the bar may be 'crossed' by opening up a space, a space which is still not a place, except in a utopian sense; this in between is also a *u-topos* fit for *Utopie*, since it is 'where' the revolutionary subject wants to place itself. Understood dialectically through the unfolding of an urbanism, 'the existing order is a *topos*. The critique and analysis of it enables one to elaborate the utopia'. The destruction of the existing *topos* by revolutionary means 'permits theoretically a total realization of the *utopia*'. This utopia thus becomes a revolutionary *topos*, which in turn will provoke a critique, etc. By 1971, theory and praxis had given way to the sign in *Utopie*'s effort to situate itself: 'In the topics of the sign, utopia is the gap, this fault, this emptiness which passes between the signifier and the signified and subverts all signs.' The so-called in-significant line between the signifier and the signified is the non-place by means of which one deconstructs the sign. Revolutionary politics has not only been supplanted by anti-semiology, but the *topos* has become a *topics*, a general domain of signs whose revolutionary potential must be freed and actualized. *Utopie* had entered the era of the political economy of the sign. The passage to the topics of the sign was accompanied by this refusal:

'Utopia has been suspended in idealism by a century and a half of triumphant historical dialectical practice. Today it begins, in its rigorous indefiniteness, to supplant all the revolutionary definitions and to return all the models of the revolution to their bureaucratic idealism' (*Utopie* 4: 3). What becomes of utopia when this suspension is lifted? In keeping with *Utopie*'s anti-semiological theorizing, and the critique of politics and Marxism in particular, utopia acquires a kind of vehicular ambivalence which subverts at once the respective places of theory and praxis, signifier and signified, and exposes 'the Revolution as a political simulation model'. The discourse of *Utopie* situates utopia 'beyond the code'. Baudrillard's influence here is decisive since it is the symbolic to which this discourse appeals in the 'beyond'. This is an initial indication of the problem of mysticism in Baudrillard's asemiological musings. The *u-topos* beyond the code, however, is defined in a way which exacerbates this problem. In a Zenic digression, then:

> Utopia is the smile of the *Cheshire* cat, this smile which floats in the air before the cat appears and for some time after it has disappeared. A little before the cat appears, and a little after it has appeared. This smile into which the Cheshire cat disappears, is itself mortal. Utopia is that which, by the abolition of the blade and the disappearance of the handle, gives the knife its *force de frappe*.
>
> (*Utopie* 4: 4)

To use other words, 'utopia is that which, by the deconstruction of the signifier and the signified, gives the anti-sign its *force de frappe*'; that is to say, utopia plays deconstructively with the bar in order to open onto the symbolic.

3 This is the approach taken by Gane (1991). See in particular his chapter 3, 'Baudrillard, Postmodernism, Marxism and Feminism'.

1   BAR GAMES

1 The debate surrounding Saussure's sense of positive terms has been discussed in some detail by Robert M. Strozier (1988). Strozier challenges Samuel Weber's strong interpretation of 'positive' as an isolation of the sign in a simple, rather wooden metaphysics, by reading this term as a tentative suggestion which in no way implies that the sign is a discrete entity; cf. Weber (1976). Weber does not, however, 'ontologize' the totality of the sign. The *move* Saussure made to limit the interminable play of differences by introducing determinate oppositions was, for Weber, necessary and especially fecund for structuralism. While Weber in no way elevates signification above value, he does find in Saussure's introduction of positive facts an implicit judgement about linguistic reality. It is Saussure's determination of indeterminable differences or the system's own displacements which interests Weber.

2   SIMULATION AND SEMIOSIS

1 All references to the writings of Charles Sanders Peirce appear in the body of the text as CP, followed by volume and paragraph number, which refer to the *Collected Works* (1935–66).

2 Deleuze and Guattari cite the work of both Mandelbrot and Robert Brown to distinguish smooth from striated spaces (1987: 486ff); in a different manner, in his 'review' of Mandelbrot's *Les Objets fractals*, Paul Virilio predicts the disappearance of the enterprise of geometry at the hands of the geometer who exercises simultaneously the means to discover and to exterminate the dimensions of the world, given Virilio's understanding of the paradoxical capacities of 'illumination' (1978: 336–7).

3 For a further clarification of this point see Brian Massumi, *A User's Guide to Capitalism and Schizophrenia: Deviations from Deleuze and Guattari* (1992: 154–5, n. 45). In addition, it is evident from the beginning of Kellner's *Jean Baudrillard* (1989) when he refers to the 'French semiologist Ferdinand de Saussure' (Saussure was Swiss and a linguist who dreamt of a science of signs) that the presentation of semiology will be, let us say, brittle. This initial slip is a token of Kellner's discussion of semiology, and it is the sort of position which makes it difficult for him to grasp critically Baudrillard's anti-semiological bar games. On the one hand, Kellner's unfamiliarity with French semiology leads him to contrast Barthes with Baudrillard on the basis of the former's multiplex theory of the code as opposed to the latter's monolithic theory of the code which relies too heavily upon the model of linguistics. Barthes's much commented upon glottocentrism which arose from his inversion of Saussure's idea that linguistics would be a branch of the general science of signs (for Barthes, semiology is a kind of translinguistics) seems to have escaped Kellner. Barthes's brand of 'linguistic imperialism' is confined to a minor tradition in semiotics. Kellner is impressed with the so-called rigour of Barthes's *S/Z* (1970), although none of the five codes (proaïretic, hermeneutic, semic, cultural, symbolic) in this work are subject to an underlying logico-taxonomical organization. The five codes are rather, as Barthes described them, a network, not a list or a paradigm, a mirage of structure, a pure perspective of citation, forces that take hold of the text which is their network. Aiming beyond both sentences and narratives into a gradual, textual analysis, Barthes posits a plural intertextual object marked by, at this point in his career, his ambivalent attachment to structuralist conceptions. The 'voices' of the codes speak contrapuntally and Barthes is concerned with producing their multivalent structuration rather than rigorously reproducing their structures. On the other hand, Kellner acknowledges that Baudrillard's concept of symbolic exchange plays a crucial role in the attempt to exterminate the sign, but he produces a caricature of Baudrillard's complex engagement with semiology.

3   VARIETIES OF SYMBOLIC EXCHANGE

1 Kellner thinks that Baudrillard offers no positive political alternative. In general terms, Kellner does assist us in recognizing the extent to which critical theorists remain undecided on the question of Baudrillard's politics. While he is firm in insisting that Baudrillard offers no strategic political alternative, this firmness obscures the Baudrillard 'scene' and operates on a level too abstract to account for the recognition of the effectiveness of such ideas as hyperconformity on the tactical level. He does not concur with Andrew Ross (1989: 216) for whom 'Baudrillard's strategies . . . can be added to the growing body of parasitical discourses – mimicry, disarticulation, plagiarism – advanced by theorists who have sought to fashion a politics out of the poststructuralist crtitique'. This refusal mistakenly excludes the tactical level. Unlike Certeau in *The Practice of Everyday Life* (1984) – a work which Kellner valorizes without interrogating its claims – Kellner claims that Baudrillard 'completely rules out' self-valorizing activities. For Certeau, consumption is a sphere of self-valorization, although only on the tactical level, as Kellner omits. Certeau's concern is with the anonymous heroes of popular culture and the oppositional character of certain everyday practices.

When Kellner comes to consider hyperconformity, he rightly refuses to afford it any strategic value and looks to Certeau for an alternative. Certeau's concept of *la perruque* – ripping-off or 'borrowing' – is neither pilfering nor sabotage nor absenteeism. Rather, it is the use of 'company equipment' and to a lesser degree 'company materials' on 'company time' for one's own creative ends: '*la perruque* may be as simple a matter as a secretary's writing a love letter on "company time" or as complex as a cabinet maker's "borrowing" a lathe to make a piece of furniture for his living room' (1984: 13). The weak make use of strategic sites as they seize occasions on the wing in a wide variety of acts. Witticism, skilful interjections, making or scoring points against one's interlocutor and turning back a line of argument advancing toward one are all examples of tactical moves in speech and writing. One may count hyperconformity among tactical alternatives. Consider, however, the brilliant ruse unfolded by Hiroshe Takashi's (1984) eco-peace group in Japan as an instance of the tactical force of hyperconformity. By hyperconforming to the propaganda of the nuclear industry in Japan, Takashi's group forced an admission of the dangers of nuclear energy from the industry by means of the convincing simulation of the possibility of constructing nuclear power stations and waste disposal facilities in downtown Tokyo. This tactical victory, based on the principle of a homeopathic exaggeration, did not pretend to put an end to the nuclear problem in Japan. But such is the local wiliness of tactics. In a way, and in spite of himself, Kellner indirectly confirms the tactical status of hyperconformity by drawing our attention to Certeau's work on minor acts of resistance. This awry confirmation of tactical weakness does not satisfy my overall critical aims.

4 EMPTY SIGNS AND EXTRAVAGANT OBJECTS

1 The reference in French is not to orange juice but to meat. Levin's translation is for a North American English readership raised on various forms of concentrated beverages such as Florida orange juice and reconstituted fruit drinks; Baudrillard refers to the reconstitution of nature as a simulation model 'comme on le dit du beefsteak préalablement haché' (1972: 254). Baudrillard may be also referring to the introduction into France from Switzerland in the early 1970s of synthetic beefsteak.

2 Segalen's explicit target is Pierre Loti, pen name of Julien Marie Viaud. As Robert Laliberté points out in L'Imaginaire politique de Victor Segalen (1989: 22), Segalen was an anti-colonialist by default inasmuch as his political position was based on his contempt for the stereotypes of colonial literature. On the other hand, Yvonne Y. Hsieh in Victor Segalen's Literary Encounter With China: Chinese Moulds, Western Thoughts (1988: 17–18), contends that certain of Segalen's metaphors which he used in his description of China reveal his Euro-centrist and colonialist suppositions.

3 See Eberhardt's response to the editor of La Petite Gironde of 27 April 1903 in Yasmina (1986: 8–11).

4 In his Le Roman colonial en Algérie avant 1914 (1984), Alain Calmes situates her writing in a chapter called 'Le Roman colonial indigénophile'. Unlike the colonocentriste group, the writers in this 'subgenre' did not form an association. Their writing, however, plays a moderating role by indirectly reflecting anticolonialist ideology.

Bibliography

Abbey, Edward (1968) *Desert Solitaire*, New York: Ballantine.

Allen, Michael (1988) 'Marsile Ficin, Hermès et le Corpus Hermeticum', in *Présence d'Hermès Trimégiste*, Paris: Albin Michel.

Allen, Richard (1987) 'Critical Theory and the Paradox of Modernist Discourse', *Screen* 28/2: 69–88.

Annear, Judy (1984) 'FUTUR*FALL', *Studio International* 197/1007: 42.

Aristotle (1941) *Rhetoric*, W.R. Roberts (trans.), in R. McKeon (ed.), *The Basic Works of Aristotle*, New York: Random House.

Arrabal, Fernando (1973) *Le Panique*, Paris: Union générale d'éditions.

Arrivé, Michel (1972) *Les Langages de Jarry*, Paris: Klincksieck.

Artaud, Antonin (1964) *Le Théâtre et son double*, Paris: Gallimard.

—— (1976) *Selected Writings*, New York: Farrar, Straus and Giroux.

Aubert, Jean (1969) 'Le Système des objets', *L'Homme et la société* 11: 229–30.

St Augustine (1958) *The City of God*, D.B. Zema and G.G. Walsh (trans.), Washington, D.C.: Catholic University Press of America.

Ballion, Robert (1971) 'Sur la société de consommation', *Revue française de sociologie* XII/4: 557–68.

Banham, Reyner (1982), *Scenes in America Deserta*, Salt Lake City: Peregrine Smith.

Barnouw, Jeffrey (1981) 'Signification and Meaning: A Critique of the Saussurean Conception of the Sign', *Comparative Literature Studies* XVIII/3: 260–71.

Barthes, Roland (1964) 'Eléments de sémiologie', *Communications* 4: 91–144.

—— (1970) *L'Empire des signes*, Genève: Editions d'Art Albert Skira.

—— (1970) *S/Z*, Paris: Editions du Seuil.

Bataille, Georges (1933) 'La Notion de dépense', *La Critique sociale* 7: 7–15.

—— (1970) *Oeuvres complètes I*, Paris: Gallimard.

Baudrillard, Jean (1962) 'Les Romans d'Italo Calvino', *Les Temps modernes* 17/2 (192): 1,728–34.

—— (1962a) 'La Proie des flammes', *Les Temps modernes* 17/2 (193): 1,928–37.

—— (1962b) 'Uwe Johnson: La frontière', *Les Temps modernes* 18/1 (199): 1,094–107.

—— (1967) 'Marshall MacLuhan, *Understanding Media: The Extensions of Man*', *L'Homme et la société* 5: 227–30.

—— (1967a) 'L'Ephémère est sans doute . . .', marginal comments in Jean Aubert, 'Explication: devenir surrané', *Utopie* 1: 94–7.

—— (1968) *Le Système des objets*. Paris: Gallimard.

—— (1968a) 'Henri Lefebvre, *Position: contre les technocrates*', *Cahiers internationaux de sociologie* XIIV:176–7.

—— *et al.* (1968b) 'Débat: La Transgression est-elle un mode d'action politique?', *Communications* 12: 159–74.

—— (1969) 'Le Ludique et le policier', *Utopie* 2/3: 3–15.

—— (1969a) 'La Pratique sociale de la technique', *Utopie* 2/3: 147–55.

—— (1969b) 'La Morale des objets: Fonction-signe et logique de classe', *Communications* 13: 23–50.

—— (1969c) 'La Genèse idéologique des besoins', *Cahiers internationaux de sociologie* V/47: 45–68.

—— (1970) *La Société de consommation*, Paris: S.G.P.P.

—— (1970a) 'Fétichisme et idéologie: La réduction sémiologique', *Nouvelle Revue de psychanalyse* 2: 213–24.

—— (1971) 'Requiem pour les média', *Utopie* 4: 35–51.

—— (1971a) 'ADN ou la métaphysique du code', *Utopie* 4: 57–61.

—— (1972) *Pour une critique de l'économie politique du signe*, Paris: Gallimard.

—— (1972a) 'Le miroir de la production', *Utopie* 5: 34–58.

—— (1973) *Le Miroir de la production, ou l'illusion critique du matérialisme historique*, Tournai: Casterman.

—— (1975) 'Le Crépuscule des signes', *Traverses* 2: 27–40.

—— (1975a) *The Mirror of Production*, Mark Poster (trans.), St. Louis: Telos.

—— (1976) *L'Echange symbolique et la mort*, Paris: Gallimard.

—— (1976a) 'Quand Bataille attaquait le principe métaphysiquement de l'économie', *La Quinzaine Littéraire* 234 (Juin 1–15): 4–5.

—— (1976b) 'Crash', *Traverses* 4: 24–9.

—— (1976c) 'La Réalité dépasse l'hyperréalisme', *Revue d'ésthetique* 1: 139–48.

—— (1977) *L'Effet Beaubourg*, Paris: Galilée.

—— (1977a) *Oublier Foucault*, Paris: Galilée.

—— (1977b) *Le Trompe-l'oeil*, Documents de travail et pré-publications, Urbino: Universita di Urbino.

—— (1977c) 'L'Histoire! Un scénario rétro', *Ça* 12/13: 16–17.

—— (1978) *A l'ombre des majorités silencieuses ou la fin du social*, Fontenay-sous-Bois: Cahiers d'Utopie.

—— (1978a) *Le P.C. ou les paradis artificiels du politique*, Fontenay-sous-Bois: Cahiers d'Utopie.

—— (1978b) *L'Ange de stuc*, Paris: Galilée.

—— (1978c) 'Quand on enlève tout, il ne reste rien', *Traverses* 11: 12–15.

—— (1979) *De la séduction*, Paris: Galilée.

—— (1979a) 'Rituel-loi-code', in Michel Maffesoli and André Bruston (eds), *Violence et transgression*, Paris: Editions Anthropos.

—— (1979b) 'Le Horizon sacré des apparences', *Cahiers confrontations* 1: 115–22.

—— (1980) 'Desert Forever', *Traverses* 19: 54–8.

—— (1980a) 'The Implosion of Meaning in the Media and the Implosion of the Social in the Masses', Mary Lydon (trans.), in K. Woodward (ed.), *The Myths of Information: Technology and Post-Industrial Culture*, London: Routledge.

—— (1980b) 'Baj ou la monstruosité mise à nu par le peinture même', in *enrico baj*, Paris: Filipacchi.

—— (1981) *Simulacres et simulations*, Paris: Galilée.

—— (1981a) *For A Critique Of The Political Economy Of The Sign*, Charles Levin (trans.), St Louis: Telos.

—— (1981b) 'La Cérémonie du monde', *Traverses* 21–2: 15–17.

—— (1981c) 'Beyond the Unconscious: The Symbolic', Lee Hildreth (trans.) *Discourse* 3: 60–87.

—— (1981d) 'La Sociologie? une thérapeutique', G. Pessis-Pasternak (interview) *Magazine littéraire* 174 (Juin): 68–9.

—— (1982) 'The Beaubourg Effect: Implosion and Dissuasion', R. Krauss and A. Michelson (trans.), *October* 20: 1–13.

—— (1982a) 'Otage et terreur: l'echange impossible', *Traverses* 25: 2–13.

—— (1982b) 'La Forme sismique', *Cahiers confrontations* 7: 11–14.

—— (1982c) 'Fatality or Reversible Imminence: Beyond the Uncertainty Principle', Pamela Park (trans.), *Social Research* 49/2: 272–93.

—— (1983) *Les Stratégies fatales*, Paris: Grasset.

—— (1983a) *Suite vénitienne* (Sophie Calle, photographer) and *Please Follow Me*, Paris: Editions de l'Etoile.

—— (1983b) *Simulations*, Paul Foss, Paul Patton and Philip Beitchman (trans.), New York: semiotext(e).

—— (1983c) *In The Shadow Of The Silent Majorities*, Paul Patton, Paul Foss and John Johnston (trans.), New York: semiotext(e).

—— (1983d) *Suite vénitienne* (Sophie Calle, photographer) and *Please Follow Me*, Dany Barash and Danny Hatfield (trans.), Seattle: Bay Press.

—— (1983e) 'What Are You Doing After The Orgy?', Lisa Liebmann (trans.), *Artforum* (Oct.): 42–6.

—— (1983f) 'Nuclear Implosion', P. Beitchman (trans.), *Impulse* (Spring/Summer): 9–11.

—— (1983g) 'The Precession of Simulacra', P. Foss and P. Patton (trans.), *Art & Text* 11: 3–47.

—— (1983h) 'The Ecstasy of Communication', John Johnston (trans.), in H. Foster (ed.), *The Anti-Aesthetic, Essays on Postmodern Culture*, Port Townsend: Bay Press.

—— (1983i) 'Une entrevue avec Jean Baudrillard', Guy Bellavance (interview) *Parachute* 31 (June/July/August): 26–33.

—— (1983j) 'Les Séductions de Baudrillard', Patrice Bollon (interview), *Magazine littéraire* 193 (Mars): 80–5.

—— (1983k) 'Dropping Out of History', Sylvère Lotringer (interview), *Impulse* (Spring/Summer): 10–13.

—— (1983l) 'Le Maniérisme d'un monde sans manières: un entretien avec Jean Baudrillard', *Le Nouvel Observateur* (Fév. 18): 72.

—— *et al.* (1983m) *Der Tod der Moderne: Eine Diskussion*, Tübingen: Gehrke.

—— (1983–84) 'Zelig', *Skrien* 132–3: 15.

—— (1984) 'The Structural Law of Value and the Order of Simulacra', Charles Levin (trans.), in J. Fekete (ed.), *The Structural Allegory*, Minneapolis: University of Minnesota Press.

—— (1984a) 'Astral America', Lisa Liebmann (trans.), *Artforum* (Sept.): 70–4.

—— (1984b) *The Evil Demon of Images*, The Mari Kuttna Lecture on Film, Paul Patton and Paul Foss (trans.), Annandale: Power Institute.

—— (1984c) 'L'Enfant-bulle', *Traverses* 32: 15–17.

—— (1984d) 'Média et information: stratégie d'objet et ironie objective', in Derek De Kerckhove and Amilcare A. Iannucci (eds), *McLuhan E La Metamorfosi Dell'Uomo*, Roma: Bulzoni Editore.

—— (1984e) 'Die Fatalität der Moderne: Interview mit Jean Baudrillard', in Gerd Bergfleth *et al.* (eds) *Zur Kritik der palavernden Aufklärung*, München: Matthes & Zeits.

—— (1984f) 'Jean Baudrillard', in *Entretiens avec Le Monde 3. Idées contemporaines*, C. Deschamps (interview), Paris: Editions la découverte.

—— (1984g) 'Game With Vestiges', S. Mele and M. Titmarsh (interview), *On The Beach* 5:19–25.

—— (1984–85) 'Intellectuals, Commitment, and Political Power: An Interview with Jean Baudrillard', M. Shevtsova (interview), *Thesis Eleven* 10–11: 166–74.

—— (1985) *La Gauche Divine*, Paris: Grasset.

—— (1985a) 'L'An 2000 ne passera pas', *Traverses* 32: 15–17.

—— (1985b) 'Modernité', in *Encyclopedia universalis*, Corpus 12, Paris: Encyclopedia Universalis France.

—— (1985c) 'Der Ekstatische Sozialismus', *Merkur* 39/1: 83–9.

—— (1985d) 'The Masses: the Implosion of the Social in the Media', Marie Maclean (trans.), *New Literary History* 16/3: 577–89.

—— (1986) *Amérique*, Paris: Grasset.

—— (1986a) 'Pré-texte', in *Masses et post-modernité*, J. Zylberberg (directeur), Paris: Méridiens Klincksieck.

—— (1986b) 'Interview with Jean Baudrillard', C. Francblin (interview), *Flash Art* 130 (Oct./Nov.): 54–5.

—— (1987) *L'Autre par lui-même. Habilitation*, Paris: Galilée.

—— (1987a) *Cool Memories 1980–1985*, Paris: Galilée.

—— (1987b) *Forget Foucault*, Nicole Dufresne (trans.), New York: semiotext(e).

—— (1987c) 'Untitled', in *Barbara Kruger*, New York: Mary Boone/ Michael Weiner Gallery.

—— (1987d) 'Please Follow Me', P. Foss (trans.), *Art & Text* 23/4: 103–14.

—— (1987e) 'A Perverse Logic', *UNESCO Courier* (July): 7–9.

—— (1987f) 'USA 80's', Mark Polizzotti (trans.), *semiotext(e) USA* 13: 47–50.
—— (1987g) 'From *Amérique*', J.G. Strand (trans.), *The Literary Review* 30/3: 472–82.
—— (1987h) 'Softly, Softly', *New Statesman* (6 March): 44–5.
—— (1987i) 'Au-delà du vrai et du faux, ou le malin génie de l'image', *Cahiers internationaux de sociologie* LXXXII: 139–45.
—— (1987j). 'Entretien avec Jean Baudrillard and Jean Nouvel', in P. Goulet (ed.), *Jean Nouvel*, Paris: Electa France.
—— (1988) *The Ecstasy of Communication*, Bernard and Caroline Schutze (trans.), New York: semiotext(e).
—— (1988a) *Jean Baudrillard: Selected Writings*, M. Poster (ed.), Stanford: Stanford University Press.
—— (1988b) *America*, Chris Turner (trans.), London: Verso.
—— (1988c) 'Hunting Nazis and Losing Reality', *New Statesman* (19 February): 16–17.
—— (1988d) *Xerox and Infinity*, Agitac (trans.), London: Touchepas.
—— (1988e) 'Orte Der Urbanen Ekstase', *du* 12: 92–5.
—— (1988f) 'Jean Baudrillard: Politics of Performance: Montand, Coluche = Le Pen?', P. Archard (interview), *New Political Science* 16/17: 23–8.
—— (1988g) 'Argentina', (photographic collage) *Museumjournaal* 33/5–6: 330–3.
—— (1989) 'Préface', in Isabelle Auricoste and Hubert Tonka (eds), *Parc-ville Villette*, Paris: Editions du semi-cercle.
—— (1989a) 'Essay von Baudrillard', in *Peter Weibel, Inszenierte Kunst Geschichte*, Wien: Hochschule für Angewandte Kunst.
—— (1989b) 'Panic Crash!', Faye Trecartin and Arthur Kroker (trans.), in A. and M. Kroker and D. Cook (eds), *The Panic Encyclopedia*, Montréal: New World Perspectives.
—— (1989c) 'The Anorexic Ruins', David Antal (trans.), in D. Kamper and C. Wulf (eds), *Looking Back On The End Of The World*, New York: semiotext(e).
—— (1989d) 'Baudrillard: le sujet et son double', F. Ewald (interview), *Magazine littéraire* 264 (Avril): 18–23.
—— (1989e) 'Politics of Seduction', S. Moore and S. Johnstone (interview), *Marxism Today* (January): 54–5.
—— (1990) *La Transparence du Mal. Essai sur les phénomènes extrêmes*, Paris: Galilée.
—— (1990a) *Cool Memories II*, Paris: Galilée.
—— (1990b) *Seduction*, Brian Singer (trans.), Montréal: New World Perspectives.
—— (1990c) *Fatal Strategies*, Philip Beitchman and W.G.J. Niesluchowski (trans.), New York: semiotext(e).
—— (1990d) *Cool Memories*, Chris Turner (trans.), London: Verso.
—— (1991) *La Guerre du golfe n'a pas eu lieu*, Paris: Galilée.
—— (1991a) 'Transpolitique, transsexuel, transesthétique', in J. Lamaneux (ed.), *Droits, liberté, démocratie*, Actes du Colloque International de l'Association Canadienne des Sociologues et des

Anthropologues de langue française tenu dans le cadre du 57 Congès de l'ACFAS, UQAM 1989, Montréal: Association Canadienne française pour l'Avancement des Sciences, Coll. Cahiers Scientifiques, no. 75.

—— (1991b) 'L'Amérique ou la pensée de l'espace', in *Citoyenneté et urbanité*, Paris: Editions Esprit.

—— (1991c) 'The Reality Gulf', *Guardian* (11 January): 25.

—— (1992) *L'Illusion de la fin ou La grève des événements*, Paris: Galilée.

—— (1992a) W. Stearns and W. Chaloupka (eds), *Jean Baudrillard: The Disappearance of Art and Politics*, New York: St Martin's Press.

Bauman, Zygmunt (1988) 'The Second Disenchantment', *Theory, Culture & Society* 5/4: 738–43.

Beaumont, Keith (1984) *Alfred Jarry: A Critical and Biographical Study*, New York: St Martin's Press.

Béhar, Henri (1979) *Jarry, le monstre et la marionnette*, Paris: Librarie Larousse.

—— (1980) *Les Cultures de Jarry*, Paris: Presses Universitaires de France.

Benison, Jonathan (1984) 'Jean Baudrillard on the Current State of Science Fiction', *Foundation* 32: 25–42.

Bennington, Geoff (1988) *Lyotard, Writing the Event*, New York: Columbia University Press.

Benoist, Jean-Marie (1978) *The Structural Revolution*, London: Weidenfeld and Nicolson.

Benveniste, Emile (1966) *Problèmes de linguistique générale*, Paris: Gallimard.

—— (1969) 'Sémiologie de la langue (1)', *Semiotica* I/1: 1–12.

—— (1969a) 'Sémiologie de la langue (2)', *Semiotica* I/2: 127–35.

Best, Steven (1989) 'The Commodification of Reality and the Reality of Commodification: Jean Baudrillard and Postmodernity', *Current Perspectives in Social Theory* 9: 23–51.

Blau, Herbert (1965) *The Impossible Theatre: A Manifesto*, New York: Collier.

—— (1982) *Bloodied Thought: Occasions of Theatre*, New York: Performing Arts Journal Press.

Bollon, Patrice (1990) 'Le Temps d'après l'orgie', *Magazine littéraire* 277 (Mai): 101.

Bonnal, Marité (1986) *Passages*, (photographies de J. Baudrillard), Paris: Galilée.

Borradori, Giovanna (1987–88) ' "Weak Thought" and Postmodernism: The Italian Departure from Deconstruction', *Social Text* 18: 39–49.

Boys, Charles Vernon (1959) *Soap Bubbles and the Forces Which Mould Them*, Garden City: Doubleday.

Brecht, Bertolt (1965) *Dialogues d'exilés*, J. Baudrillard (trans.), Paris: L'Arche.

Briemberg, Mordecai (1992) (ed.), *It Was, It Was Not: Essays and Art on the War Against Iraq*, Vancouver: New Star Books.

Burke, Edmund (1958) *A Philosophical Enquiry into the Origin of Our Ideas of the Sublime and the Beautiful*, London: Routledge.

Burri, René (1963) *Les Allemands* (textes réunis et présentés par J. Baudrillard), Paris: Robert Delpire.

Calinescu, Matei (1979) 'Marxism As a Work of Art: Poststructuralist Readings of Marx', *Stanford French Review* III/1: 123–35.

Calmes, Alain (1984) *Le Roman colonial en Algérie avant 1914*, Paris: L'Harmattan.

Camus, Albert (1978) *Journaux de voyage*, Paris: Gallimard.

Carrier, David (1988) 'Baudrillard as Philosopher or, The End of Abstract Painting', *Arts magazine* 63/1 (Sept.): 52–60.

Céline, Louis-Ferdinand (1983) *Journey To The End Of The Night*, R. Manheim (trans.), New York: New Directions.

de Certeau, Michel (1980) 'On the Oppositional Practices of Everyday Life', *Social Text* 3: 3–43.

—— (1984) *The Practice of Everyday Life*, S.F. Rendall (trans.), Berkeley: University of California Press.

Chang, Briankle G. (1986) 'Mass, Media, Mass-Media-tion: Jean Baudrillard's Implosive Critique of Modern Mass-Mediated Culture', *Current Perspectives in Social Theory* 7: 157–81.

Cixous, Hélène and Clément, Catherine (1986) *The Newly Born Woman*, Betsy Wing (trans.), Minneapolis: University of Minnesota Press.

Clément, Catherine (1983) *The Lives and Legends of Jacques Lacan*, A. Goldhammer (trans.), New York: Columbia University Press.

Cone, Michèle (1986) 'Peter Halley', *Flash Art* 126 (Feb./March): 36–8.

Crookes, William (1897) 'Discours sur le changement d'aspect des lois de l'univers qui serait la conséquence d'un simple changement dans la taille de l'observateur', *Revue scientifique*.

Csicsery-Ronay, Istvan (1988) 'Cyberpunk and Neuroromanticism', *Mississippi Review* 47–48: 266–78.

—— (1991) 'The SF of Theory: Baudrillard and Haraway', *Science-Fiction Studies* 55: 387–404.

D'Amico, Robert (1981) *Marx and the Philosophy of Culture*, Gainesville: University Presses of Florida.

—— (1990) 'Packaging Fog', *Telos* 83: 205–8.

Debord, Guy (1983) *The Society of the Spectacle*, Detroit: Black & Red.

Delacampagne, Christian (1990) 'Le Retour du mal', *Le Monde* (Mars 9).

Deleuze, Gilles (1983) 'Plato and the Simulacrum', R. Krauss (trans.), *October* 27: 45–56.

—— (1988) *Le Pli*, Paris: Minuit.

Deleuze, Gilles and Guattari, Félix (1970) 'La Synthèse disjonctive', *L'Arc* 43: 54–62.

—— (1977) *Anti-Oedipus*, R. Hurley, M. Seem and H.R. Lane (trans.), New York: Viking.

—— (1987) *A Thousand Plateaus*, B. Massumi (trans.), Minneapolis: University of Minnesota Press.

Denzin, Norman K. (1991) '*Paris, Texas* and Baudrillard on America', *Theory, Culture & Society* 8/2: 121–33.

Der Derian, James (1991) 'Videographic War II', *Alphabet City* 1: 4–12.

Derrida, Jacques (1973) *Speech and Phenomena*, David B. Allison (trans.), Evanston: Northwestern University Press.

—— (1974) *Of Grammatology*, Gayatri Chakravorty Spivak (trans.), Baltimore: The Johns Hopkins University Press.

—— (1978) *Writing and Difference*, A. Bass (trans.), Chicago: University of Chicago Press.

—— (1981) *Positions*, A. Bass (trans.), Chicago: University of Chicago Press.

—— (1984) *Signéponge/Signsponge* Richard Rand (trans.), New York: Columbia University Press.

Descartes, Rene (1951) *Meditations*, L. J. Lafleur (trans.), Indianapolis: Bobbs-Merrill.

Descombes, Vincent (1986) *Objects Of All Sorts: A Philosophical Grammar*, Lorna Scott-Fox (trans.), Baltimore: The Johns Hopkins University Press.

—— (1989) 'The Quandaries of the Referent', in Thomas M. Kavanaugh (ed.), *The Limits of Theory*, Stanford: Stanford University Press.

Dick, Philip K. (1964) *The Simulacra*, London: Methuen.

Doran, Chris (1990) 'The Working Class As Zombie: Simulation and Resistance in the Late Twentieth Century', *Canadian Journal of Political and Social Theory* 14/1–3: 126–47.

Dostoyevski, Fyodor (1972) *Notes From Underground* (1864), Jessie Coulson (trans.), Harmondsworth, Middlesex: Penguin.

Dufresne, Todd (1993) 'Derrida, Jarry, Nietzsche: Introducing a Deconstructive Pataphysics, Contra Heidegger', *re: POST* 1: 26–33.

Eberhardt, Isabelle (1986) *Yasmina* (choisies et présentées par Marie-Odile Delacour et Jean-René Heleu), Paris: Lianai Levi.

Eco, Umberto (1972) *La Structure absente*, U. Esposito-Torrigiani (trans.), Paris: Mercure.

—— (1976) *A Theory of Semiotics*, Bloomington: Indiana University Press.

—— (1986) *Travels in Hyperreality*, San Diego: Harcourt Brace Jovanovich.

Elam, Keir (1980) *The Semiotics of Theatre and Drama*, London: Methuen.

Eluard, Paul and Péret, Benjamin (1977) *52 proverbes mis au goût du jour*, Toronto: Oasis.

Engels, Friedrich (1971) *Le Rôle de la violence dans l'histoire*, J. Baudrillard, P. Stéphane and E. Bottigelli (trans.), Paris: Editions Sociales.

Enthoven, Jean-Paul (1990) 'Les Dérèglements du réel', *Le Nouvel Observateur* (Mars 1–7): 28–9.

Faurschou, Gail (1990) 'Obsolescence and Desire: Fashion and the Commodity Form', in H. Silverman (ed.), *Postmodernism – Philosophy and the Arts*, New York: Routledge.

Fellenberg, W. von (1985) 'Parallel Bars, Parallel Worlds', Rudolf Rible (trans.), *Art & Text* 18: 93–9.

Foster, Hal (1986) 'Signs Taken For Wonders', *Art in America* 74/6 (June): 80–91, 139.

Foucault, Michel (1967) *Madness and Civilization: A History of Insanity in the Age of Reason*, Richard Howard (trans.), London: Tavistock.

—— (1977) 'Theatrum Philosophicum', in Donald F. Bouchard (ed.), *Language, Counter-memory, Practice*, Ithaca: Cornell University Press.

—— (1988) 'The Prose of Actaeon', in Pierre Klossowski, *The Baphomet*,

Sophie Hawks and Stephen Sartarelli (trans.), Hygiene, Col.: Eridanos.

Frankovits, Andre (ed.) (1984) *Seduced and Abandoned: The Baudrillard Scene*, Glebe, NSW and New York: Stonemoss Services and semiotext(e).

Freud, Sigmund (1976 [1900]) *The Interpretation of Dreams*, James Strachey (trans.), Harmondsworth, Middlesex: Penguin.

—— (1986 [1905]) *Jokes And Their Relation To The Unconscious*, James Strachey (trans.), Harmondsworth, Middlesex: Penguin.

Frith, Simon (1988) 'What is a Washing Machine?' *New Stateman and Society* 115/2,984 (June): 23–4.

Gablik, Suzi (1988) 'Dancing with Baudrillard', *Art in America* 76/6 (June): 27–9.

Gallop, Jane (1981) *Intersections: A Reading of Sade with Bataille, Blanchot and Klossowski*, Lincoln: University of Nebraska Press.

—— (1985) *Reading Lacan*, Ithaca: Cornell University Press.

Gane, Mike (1990) 'Ironies of Postmodernism: Fate of Baudrillard's Fatalism', *Economy and Society* 19/3: 315–33.

—— (1991) *Baudrillard: Critical and Fatal Theory*, London: Routledge.

—— (1991a) *Baudrillard's Bestiary: Baudrillard and Culture*, London: Routledge.

Garvin, Paul L. (1954) 'Review of *Prolegomena To A Theory Of Language*', *Language* 30/1: 69–98.

—— (ed. and trans.) (1964) *A Prague School Reader on Esthetics, Literary Structure and Style*, Washington: Georgetown University Press.

Gibson, Ross (1984) 'After FUTUR*FALL', *Art & Text* 16: 82–92.

Giradin, Jean-Claude (1974) 'Toward a Politics of Signs: Reading Baudrillard', David Pugh (trans.), *Telos* 20: 127–37.

Godel, R. (1957) *Les Sources manuscrites du Cours de linguistique générale de Ferdinand de Saussure*, Genève: Droz.

—— (1966) 'De la théorie du signe aux termes du système', *Cahiers Ferdinand de Saussure* 22: 53–68.

Goux, Jean-Joseph (1990) *Symbolic Economies: After Marx and Freud*, J.C. Gage (trans.), Ithaca: Cornell University Press.

Greimas, A.J. (1987) *On Meaning*, P. Perron and F.H. Collins (trans.), Minnesota: University of Minnesota Press.

Greimas, A.J. and Courtés, J. (1979) *Sémiotique dictionnaire raisonné de la théorie du langage*, Paris: Hachette.

Grivel, Charles (1986) 'Les Représentations jarryesque', *Revue des sciences humaines* LXXIIIV/203: 5–28.

Guattari, Félix (1975) 'Sémiologies signifiantes et sémiologies asignifiantes', in *Psychanalyse et sémiotique*, colloque tenu à Milan en mai 1974 sous la direction de Armando Verdiglione, Paris: Union générale d'éditions.

—— (1977) *La Révolution moléculaire*, Fontenay-Sous-Bois: Recherches.

—— (1979) *L'Inconscient machinique, essais de schizo-analyse*, Paris/Fontenay-sous-Bois: Encres/Recherches.

Guillaume, Marc (1989) *La Contagion des passions*, Paris: Plon.

Guilmette, Armand (1984) *Gilles Deleuze et la modernité*, Trois Rivières: Les Editions du Zéphyr.

Halley, Peter (1983) 'Nature and Culture', *Arts Magazine* 58/1: 64–5.

—— (1986) 'Frank Stella and the Simulacrum', *Flash Art* 126 (Feb./ March): 32–5.

Harris, Roy (1987) *Reading Saussure: A Critical Commentary on the Cours de Linguistique Générale*, London: Duckworth.

—— (1988) *Language, Saussure and Wittgenstein*, London: Routledge.

Hayward, Philip (1984) 'Implosive Critiques: A Consideration of Jean Baudrillard's *In The Shadow Of The Silent Majorities*', *Screen* 25/4–5: 128–35.

Heartney, Elanor (1987) 'Reluctant Prophet', *Art News* 86/7 (Sept.): 18.

Hebdige, Dick (1988) 'Banalarama, or Can Pop Save Us All?' *New Statesman & Society* 1/27 (Dec. 9): 29–32.

Hefner, Robert (1977) 'Baudrillard's Noble Anthropology: The Image of Symbolic Exchange in Political Economy', *sub stance* 17: 105–13.

Hjelmslev, Louis (1969) *Prolegomena To A Theory Of Language*, F.J. Whitfield (trans.), Madison: University of Wisconsin Press.

—— (1971) *Essais linguistiques*, Paris: Editions de Minuit.

Hoberman, J. (1989) 'Lost in America: Jean Baudrillard, Extraterrestrial', *Voice Literary Supplement* (March): 15–16.

Hsieh, Yvonne Y. (1988) *Victor Segalen's Literary Encounter With China: Chinese Moulds, Western Thoughts*, Toronto: University of Toronto Press.

Hughes, Robert (1989) 'The Patron Saint of Neo-Pop', *The New York Review of Books* XXXVI/9 (1 June): 29–32.

Jaccard, Roland (1990) 'Baudrillard arpenteur du néant', *Le Monde* (Sept. 28).

Jacob, André (1985) 'La Gauche Divine', *L'Homme et la société* 75–6: 266–7.

Jacob, François (1974) *The Logic of Life: A History of Heredity*, B.E. Spillman (trans.), London: Allen Lane.

Jakobson, Roman (1960) 'Closing Statement: Linguistics and Poetics', in T.A. Sebeok (ed.), *Style in Language*, Cambridge: The M.I.T. Press.

—— (1971) 'Retrospect', in *Selected Writings II*, The Hague: Mouton.

—— (1985) 'Structuralisme et téléologie', in *Selected Writings VII*, Berlin: Mouton.

Jarry, Alfred (1945) *Le Surmâle*, Paris: Fasquelle.

—— (1965) *Selected Writings*, R. Shattuck and S.W. Taylor (eds), New York: Grove.

—— (1968) *The Ubu Plays*, C. Connolly and S.W. Taylor (trans.), London: Methuen.

—— (1972) *Oeuvres complètes I*, Paris: Gallimard.

Joseph, Dave (1977) 'Critical Images of Marx's Naturalism', *Critique of Anthropology* 4/13–14: 197–202.

Kafka, Franz (1954) *Amerika*, W. and E. Muir (trans.), New York: Schocken.

Kant, Immanuel (1960) *Observations on the Feeling of the Beautiful and the*

Sublime, J.I. Goldthwait (trans.), Berkeley: University of California Press.

Kellner, Douglas (1987) 'Baudrillard, Semiurgy and Death', *Theory, Culture & Society* 4: 125–46.

—— (1989) *Jean Baudrillard: From Marxism to Postmodernism and Beyond*, Stanford: Stanford University Press.

—— (1989a) 'Boundaries and Borderlines: Reflections on Jean Baudrillard and Critical Theory', *Current Perspectives in Social Theory* 9: 5–22.

Kelvin, Lord (Sir William Thomson) (1894) *The Molecular Tactics of a Crystal*, Oxford: The Clarendon Press.

Kester, Grant (1987) 'The Rise and Fall? of Baudrillard', *New Art Examiner* (15 November): 20–3.

Kiebuzinska, Christine (1988) *Revolutionaries of the Theatre: Meyerhold, Brecht, and Witkiewicz*, Ann Arbor: UMI Research Press.

Klossowski, Pierre (1970) *La Monnaie vivante*, (photographies de Pierre Zucca), Paris: Eric Losfeld.

—— (1985) 'On The Collaboration of Demons in the Work of Art', P. Foss (trans.), *Art & Text* 18: 9–10.

—— (1985) *Cahiers pour un temps*, présentation Andréas Pfersmann, dirigée par Jacques Bonnet, Paris: Centre Pompidou.

Klossowski, Pierre and Monnoyer, Jean Maurice (1985) 'In The Charm of Her Hand', *Art & Text* 18: 42–8.

Knabb, Ken. (ed. and trans.) (1981) *Situationist International Anthology*, Berkeley: Bureau of Public Secrets.

Koerner, Konrad E.F. (1972) *Bibliographia Saussureana*, 1870–1970, Metuchen, N.J.: The Scarecrow Press.

Krampen, Martin *et al.* (eds) (1981) *Classics of Semiotics*, New York: Plenum.

Kristeva, Julia (1977) 'Modern Theatre Does Not Take (A) Place', A. Jardine and T. Gora (trans.), *sub stance* 18/19: 131–4.

—— (*et al.*) (1978) 'The U.S. Now: A Conversation', P. Cohen (trans.), *October* 6: 3–17.

—— (1980) *Desire in Language*, L.S. Roudiez and T. Gora (trans.), New York: Columbia University Press.

Kroker, Arthur (1984) 'The Arc of a Dead Power: Magritte/Baudrillard/ Augustine', *CJPST* 8/1–2: 54–69.

—— (1985) 'Baudrillard's Marx', *Theory, Culture & Society* 2/3: 69–83.

—— (1988) 'Panic Value: Bacon, Colville, Baudrillard and the Aesthetics of Deprivation', in John Fekete (ed.), *Life After Postmodernism: Essays On Value and Culture*, Montréal: New World Perspectives.

Kroker, Arthur and Cook, David (1986) *The Postmodern Scene: Excremental Culture and Hyper-Esthetics*, Montréal: New World Perspectives.

Kroker, Arthur, Kroker, Marilouise and Cook, David (eds) (1989) *Panic Encyclopedia*, Montréal: New World Perspectives.

Kruger, Barbara (1990) *Love for Sale: The Words and Pictures of Barbara Kruger*, (text by Kate Linker), New York: Harry N. Abrams.

LaBelle, Maurice Marc (1980) *Alfred Jarry: Nihilism and the Theatre of the Absurd*, New York: New York University Press.

Lacan, Jacques (1966) *Ecrits I*, Paris: Editions du Seuil.

—— (1971) *Ecrits II*, Paris: Editions du Seuil.

—— (1977) *Ecrits. A Selection*, A. Sheridan (trans.), New York: W.W. Norton.

Lacoue-Labarthe, Philippe (1977) 'Theatrum Analyticum', *Glyph* 2: 122–43.

Laliberté, Robert (1989) *L'Imaginaire politique de Victor Segalen*, Québec: Institut Québécois de Recherche sur la Culture.

Lefebvre, Henri (1971) *Au-delà du structuralisme*, Paris: Editions anthropos.

Levin, Charles (1980) 'De la séduction', *Telos* 45: 198–202.

—— (1984) 'Baudrillard, Critical Theory and Psychoanalysis', *Canadian Journal of Political and Social Theory* 8/1–2: 35–51.

Levin, Charles and Kroker, Arthur (1984) 'Baudrillard's Challenge', *Canadian Journal of Political and Social Theory* 8/1–2: 5–16.

Linker, Kate (1984) 'From Imitation to the Copy to Just Effect: On Reading Baudrillard', *Artforum* XXI/8 (April): 44–7.

Lipovetsky, Gilles (1983) *L'Ere du vide*, Paris: Gallimard.

Lopez, Barry (1976) *Desert Notes*, New York: Avon.

Lugan-Dardignan, Anne-Marie (1986) 'Réflexions du simulacre', in *Pierre Klossowski: L'Homme aux simulacres*, Paris: Navarin.

Lyotard, Jean-François (1971) *Discours, figure*, Paris: Klincksieck.

—— (1973) *Dérive à partir de Marx et Freud*, Paris: Union générale d'éditions.

—— (1973a) *Des dispositifs pulsionnnels*, Paris: Union générale d'éditions.

—— (1974) *Economie libidinale*, Paris: Minuit.

—— (1975) 'For a Pseudo-Theory', Moshe Ron (trans.), *Yale French Studies* 52: 115–27.

—— (1977) *Rudiments païens*, Paris: Galilée.

—— (1978) 'On the Strength of the Weak', R. McKeon (trans.), *semiotext(e)* iii/2: 204–14.

—— (1979) *La Condition postmoderne: rapport sur le savoir*, Paris: Minuit.

—— (1983) *Le Différend*, Paris: Minuit.

—— (1984) *Tombeau de l'intellectuel et autres papiers*, Paris: Galilée.

—— (1984a) *The Postmodern Condition: A Report on Knowledge*, G. Bennington and B. Massumi (trans.), Minneapolis: University of Minnesota Press.

—— (1988) *Peregrinations: Law, Form, Event*, New York: Columbia University Press.

Lyotard, Jean-François and Thébaud, Jean-Loup (1985) *Just Gaming*, W. Godzich (trans.), Minneapolis: University of Minnesota Press.

de Man, Paul (1979) *Allegories of Reading*, New Haven: Yale University Press.

Mandelbrot, Benoit (1975) *Les Objets fractals: forme, hasard, dimension*, Paris: Flammarion.

Mannoni, O. (1969) *Clefs pour l'imaginaire*, Paris: Editions du Seuil.

Maras, Steven (1989) 'Baudrillard and Deleuze: Re-viewing The Postmodern Scene', *Continuum* 2/2: 163–91.

de Margerie, Diane (1979) 'L'exotisme du moi', in *regard/espaces/signe: victor segalen*, colloque organisé par E. Formentelli, Nov. 2–3, 1978, Paris: Musée Guimet.

Marin, Louis (1977) 'Disneyland: A Degenerate Utopia', *Glyph* 1: 50–66.

Martin, P. (1991) 'Shia Kidnappers Winners in Game of Terror', *The Globe & Mail* (5 December).

Martinet, A. (1942–45) 'Au sujet des *Fondements de la théorie linguistique de Louis Hjelmslev*', *Bulletin de la société de linguistique de Paris* 42: 19–43.

Marx, Karl (1954) *Capital I*, S. Moore and E. Averling (trans.), Moscow: Progress.

—— (1973) *Grundrisse*, Martin Nicolaus (trans.), New York: Vintage.

Marx, Karl and Engels F. (1977) *Manifesto of the Communist Party*, S. Moore (trans.), Moscow: Progress.

Massumi, Brian (1992) *A User's guide to Capitalism and Schizophrenia: Deviations from Deleuze and Guattari*, Cambridge, Mass.: A Swerve Edition.

Mauss, Marcel (1973) *Sociologie et anthropologie*, Paris: Presses Universitaires de France.

McCaffery, Larry (1988) 'The Desert of the Real: The Cyberpunk Controversy', *Mississippi Review* 16/2–3: 7–15.

McGlynn, Fred (1990) 'Postmodernism and Theatre', in H.J. Silverman (ed.) *Postmodernism – Philosophy and the Arts*, New York: Routledge.

McLuhan, Marshall (1964) *Understanding Media: The Extensions of Man*, New York: McGraw-Hill.

Mellencamp, Patricia (1985) 'Seeing is Believing: Baudrillard and Blau', *Theatre Journal* 37/2:141–54.

Merleau-Ponty, Maurice (1964) *Signs*, Richard C. McCleary (trans.), Evanston: Northwestern University Press.

Miller, David James (1987) 'For A Critique of the Political Economy of the Sign', *Humanities and Society* 11/1: 118–20.

Miller, Henry (1945) *The Air-Conditioned Nightmare*, New York: New Directions.

Miller, John (1987) 'Baudrillard and His Discontents', *Artscribe* 63 (May): 48–51.

Monod, Jacques (1970) *Le Hasard et la nécessité*, Paris: Editions du Seuil.

Morin, Edgar (1970) *Journal de Californie*, Paris: Editions du Seuil.

—— (1988) *La Vie de la vie, la méthode. Tome II*, Paris: Editions du Seuil.

Morris, Meaghan (1987) 'Asleep At The Wheel', *New Statesman and Society* 113/2,935 (26 June): 28–9.

Moss, Roger (1982) 'The Case for Sophistry', in B. Vickers, (ed.), *Rhetoric Revalued*, Birmingham: Centre for Medieval and Early Renaissance Studies.

Mosset, Olivier (1990) *Olivier Mosset* (text by J. Baudrillard), Bern: Bundesamt für Kultur.

Mourrain, Jacques (1990) 'The Homogenization of America', *Canadian Journal of Political and Social Theory* 14/1–3: 120–5.

Mühlmann, Wilhelm E. (ed.) (1968) *Messianismes révolutionnaires du tiers monde*, avec la contribution de Alfons M. Dauer, Wolfgang H. Lindig, Erika Sulzmann et Helga Uplegger, J. Baudrillard (trans.), Paris: Gallimard.

n.a. (1988) 'A French Thinker in the Land of the Unreal: Jean Baudrillard's America', *The Economist* 309/7,578 (26 November): 99–100.

Nietzsche, Friedrich (1968) *Twilight of the Idols and The Anti-Christ*, R.J. Hollingworth (trans.), Harmondsworth, Middlesex: Penguin.

O'Neill, John (1982) 'Looking Into The Media: Revelation and Subversion', in Michael Hyde (ed.), *Communication, Philosophy and the Technological Age*, University, Alabama: University of Alabama Press.

de P., B. (1969) 'Notes bibliographiques: Le système des objets', *Revue française de sociologie* X/1: 97.

Panoff, Michel (1976) 'Bibliographie: Le miroir de la production', *Revue française de sociologie* XVII/1: 117–19.

Pavis, Patrice (1976) *Problèmes de sémiologie théâtrale*, Montréal: Presses de l'Université du Québec.

—— (1987) *Dictionnaire du théâtre*, Paris: Messidor/Editions Sociales.

Pefanis, Julian (1991) *Heterology and the Postmodern: Bataille, Baudrillard, and Lyotard*, Durham: Duke University Press.

Peirce, C.S. (1935–66) *Collected Papers of Charles Sanders Peirce*, Charles Hartshorne, P. Weiss and Arthur W. Burks (eds), Cambridge: Harvard University Press.

Penley, Constance and Ross, Andrew (eds) (1991) *Technoculture*, Minneapolis: University of Minnesota Press.

Plato (1961) *The Collected Dialogues of Plato*, Edith Hamilton and Huntington Cairns (eds), Princeton: Princeton University Press.

Pontalis, J.B. (1978) 'On Death Work in Freud, in the Self, in Culture', in *Psychoanalysis, Creativity and Literature*, A. Roland (ed.), New York: Columbia University Press.

Poster, Mark (1981) 'Technology and Culture in Habermas and Baudrillard', *Contemporary Literature* 22/4: 456–76.

Powell, E.A. (1991) 'Waite Says Hostage Crisis is Nearing End', *The Globe & Mail* (19 November).

Privitello, Lucio Angelo (1990) 'This Evening's Porcelain', *Canadian Journal of Political and Social Theory* 14/1–3: 106–12.

—— (1990a) 'Mutual Vertigo', *Canadian Journal of Political and Social Theory* 14/1–3: 113–19.

Racevskis, Karlis (1979) 'The Violence of a Catastrophical Strategy', *Diacritics* 9/3: 33–42.

Radermacher, Ludwig (1951) *Artium scriptores*, Wien: Rudolf M. Rohrer.

Ratcliff, Carter (1989) 'The Work of Roy Lichtenstein in the Age of Jean Baudrillard's and Walter Benjamin's Popularity', *Art in America* 77/2: 111–21, 177.

Rauch, Irmengard and Carr, Gerald F. (eds) (1989) *The Semiotic Bridge: Trends From California*, Berlin: Mouton.

Reader, Keith (1987) *Intellectuals And The Left In France Since 1968*, London: Macmillan.

Reijnders, Frank, Bloem, Marja and Groot, Paul (1988) 'De oors-
    prong van Europa, de verschijning van Amerika, en de verdwijning
    van de Indiaan. Over Baudrillard en siderall Amerika', *Museum-
    journaal* 33/5–6: 334–40.
Richman, Michèle (1988) 'Introduction to the Collège de Sociologie:
    Poststructuralism Before Its Time', *Stanford French Review* XII/1: 79–95.
Roderick, Rick (1989) 'Beyond a Boundary: Baudrillard and New
    Critical Theory', *Current Perspectives in Social Theory* 9: 3–4.
Rorty, Richard (1985) 'Le cosmopolitisme sans emancipation, en
    réponse à Jean-François Lyotard', *Critique* XLI/456: 569–80.
Ross, Andrew (1989) 'Baudrillard's Bad Attitude', in Dianne Hunter
    (ed.), *Seduction and Theory: Readings of Gender, Representation, and
    Rhetoric*, Urbana and Chicago: University of Illinois Press.
Rotman, Brian (1987) *Signifying Nothing: The Semiotics of Zero*, London:
    Macmillan.
Rubenstein, Diane (1989) 'The Mirror of Production: Baudrillard and
    Reagan's America', *Political Theory* 17/4: 582–606.
Ruwet, Nicolas (1973) *An Introduction to Generative Grammar*, Norval
    S.H. Smith (trans.), Amsterdam: North-Holland Publishing.
Sandomir, I.L. (1960) 'Opus Pataphysicandum: Inaugural Harangue',
    Evergreen Review 4/13: 169–73.
Santamaria, Ulysses (1979) 'Jean Baudrillard: Critique of a Critique',
    Critique of Anthropology 4/13–14: 179–95.
Sartre, Jean-Paul (1949) *Situations III*, Paris: Gallimard.
de Saussure, Ferdinand (1966) *Course in General Linguistics*, Wade
    Baskin (trans.), New York: McGraw-Hill.
—— (1985) *Cours de linguistique générale* (édition critique préparée par
    Tullio De Mauro), Paris: Payot.
Savan, David (1976) *An Introduction to C.S. Peirce's Semiotics, Part I*,
    Toronto Semiotic Circle Working Papers and Pre-publications,
    Toronto: Victoria University.
Scherpe, Klaus (1986–87) 'Dramatization and De-dramatization of
    "the End": the Apocalyptic Consciousness of Modernity and
    Post-Modernity', Brent O. Peterson (trans.), *Cultural Critique* 5:
    95–129.
Schreber, Daniel Paul (1980) *Memoirs of My Nervous Illness*, Ida
    Macalpine and R.A. Hunter (trans.), Cambridge: Harvard University
    Press.
Searle, John (1969) *Speech Acts, An Essay in the Philosophy of Language*,
    London: Cambridge University Press.
Sebeok, T.A. (1975) 'Six Species of Signs', *Semiotica* 13/3: 233–66.
—— (1979) *The Sign & Its Masters*, Austin: University of Texas Press.
Segal, Naomi (1981) *The Banal Object: Theme and Thematics in Proust,
    Rilke, Hofmannsthal, and Sartre*, Bithell Series of Dissertations, Vol. 6,
    Leeds: Institute of Germanic Studies.
Segalen, Victor (1978) *Essai sur l'exotisme, une ésthetique du divers*, Paris:
    Fata Morgana.
—— (1983) *Equipée, voyage au pays du réel*, Paris: Gallimard.

Shattuck, Roger (1955) *The Banquet Years: The Arts in France 1885–1918*, London: Faber & Faber.
Siertsema, Bertha (1965) *A Study of Glossematics. Critical Survey of Its Fundamental Concepts*, The Hague: Martinus Nijhoff.
Singer, Brian (1991) 'Baudrillard's Seduction', in A. and M. Kroker (eds), *Ideology and Power in the Age of Lenin in Ruins*, Montréal: New World Perspectives.
Starobinski, Jean (1979) *Words Upon Words: The Anagrams of Ferdinand de Saussure*, Olivia Emmet (trans.), New Haven: Yale University Press.
Steiner, Peter (ed.) (1982) *The Prague School: Selected Writings 1929–1946*, Johann Burbank, *et al.* (trans.), Austin: University of Texas Press.
Stillman, Linda Klieger (1983) *Alfred Jarry*, Boston: Twayne.
Strozier, Robert (1988) *Saussure, Derrida, and the Metaphysics of Subjectivity*, Berlin: Mouton.
Takashi, Hirose (1984) 'Nukes Next Door', *CJPST* 8/3: 61–9.
Tertullian (1959) *De Spectaculis*, in *Disciplinary, Moral and Ascetical Works*, Rudolph Arbesmann (trans.), New York: Fathers of the Church.
Thomson, Sir William (Lord Kelvin) (1890) *Mathematical and Physical Papers*, vol. III, London: C.J. Clay & Sons.
—— (1894) *The Molecular Tactics of a Crystal*, Oxford: The Clarendon Press.
de Tocqueville, Alexis (1909) *Voyage en Amérique*, Boston: D.C. Heath.
Todorov, Tzvetan (1982) *Theories of the Symbol*, C. Porter (trans.), Ithaca: Cornell University Press.
Tristani, Jean-Louis (1969) 'Le Système des objets', *Cahiers internationaux de sociologie* XLVII: 12–14.
Utopie (1967) 'Utopie dialectique', *Utopie* 1: 54–5.
—— (1968) *Structures gonflables*, catalogue de l'exposition réalisée par Utopie, Paris: Musée d'Art Moderne de la Ville de Paris.
—— (1971) n.t., *Utopie* 4: 3–4.
Valente, Joseph (1985) 'Hall of Mirrors: Baudrillard on Marx', *Diacritics* 15/2: 54–65.
Vander Gucht, Daniel (1987) 'L'Autre par lui-même', *Cahiers internationaux de sociologie* LXXXIII: 428.
Vattimo, Gianni (1988) *The End of Modernity*, J.R. Snyder (trans.), Baltimore: The Johns Hopkins University Press.
Vattimo, Gianni and Rovatti, Pier Aldo (eds) (1983) *Il pensiero debole*, Milano: Feltrinelli.
Veblen, Thorstein (1925) *Theory of the Leisure Class*, London: Allen & Unwin.
Vidich, Arthur J. (1991) 'Baudrillard's America: Lost in the Ultimate Simulacrum', *Theory, Culture and Society* 8/2: 135–44.
Vine, Richard (1989) 'The "Ecstasy" of Jean Baudrillard', *New Criterion* 7/9: 39–48.
Virilio, Paul (1976) *Essai sur l'insécurité du territoire*, Paris: Stock.
—— (1978) 'La Dromoscopie ou la lumière de la vitesse', *Critique* XXXIV/37: 324–37.
—— (1984) *L'Horizon négatif*, Paris: Galilée.

—— (1989) *War and Cinema: The Logistics of Perception*, Patrick Camiller (trans.), London: Verso.

—— (1991) *The Aesthetics of Disappearance*, Philip Beitchman (trans.), New York: semiotext(e).

—— (1991a) *The Lost Dimension*, D. Moshenberg (trans.), New York: semiotext(e).

Volosinov, V.N. (1973) *Marxism and the Philosophy of Language*, Ladislav Matejka and I.R. Titunik (trans.), New York and London: Seminar Press.

Weber, Samuel (1976) 'Saussure and the Apparition of Language: The Critical Perspective', *Modern Language Notes* 91: 913–38.

—— (1977) 'The Divaricator: Remarks on Freud's *Witz*', *Glyph* 1: 1–27.

Weiss, Peter, (1964) *Pointe de fuite*, J. Baudrillard (trans.), Paris: Editions du Seuil.

—— (1965) *La Persécution et l'assassinat de Jean-Paul Marat représentés par le groupe théâtrale de l'hospice de Charenton sous le direction de Monsieur de Sade*, J. Baudrillard (trans.), Paris: Editions du Seuil.

—— (1966) *L'Instruction, oratorio en onze chants*, J. Baudrillard (trans.), Paris: Editions du Seuil.

—— (1968) *Discours sur la genèse et le déroulement de la très longue guerre de libération du Vietnam illustrant la nécessité de la lutte armée des opprimés contre leurs oppresseurs ainsi que la volonté des Etats-Unis d'Amérique d'anéantir les fondements de la Révolution*, J. Baudrillard (trans.), Paris: Editions du Seuil.

—— (1970) *Notes On The Cultural Life Of The Democratic Republic Of Vietnam*, London: Calder and Bryars.

Wernick, Andrew (1984) 'Sign and Commodity: Aspects of the Cultural Dynamic of Advanced Capitalism', *Canadian Journal of Political and Social Theory* 8/1–2: 17–34.

Wieviorka, Michel (1990) 'La Société, système vain selon Jean Baudrillard', *La Quinzaine Littéraire* 551 (Mars 16–31): 25.

Zurbrugg, Nicolaus (1988) 'Baudrillard's *Amérique*, and the "Abyss of Modernity" ', *Art & Text* 29: 40–63.

Name index

Subject index

acronyms 49–50
aesthetics of disappearance 124–6
agonistics 73–4, 81, 105, 159–60;
  see also symbolic exchange
Air-Conditioned Nightmare, The
  (Miller) 123
aliénés authentiques 143
America 42–3, 52, 102, 105, 118ff,
  127–8, 149–50, 155–8;
  Americans 133–4; Native 120–1,
  134
Amerika (Kafka) 122
anagram 84–8, 159
anathema 85
animals 138–9
anthropology xiv, xx, 10–11, 13,
  17, 93–4; see also potlatch
Anti-Oedipus (Deleuze and
  Guattari) 58, 61, 94
art 154–5

bar games: energetics 141–2; gay
  112, 159; implication 2, 16;
  Lacanian 11, 13, 15, 22, 26–7,
  62, 113, 158; pataphysical xxi,
  111–12; poststructuralist 17;
  power xxi, 1–2, 17, 27, 159;
  psychoanalytic 16–17; radical
  exclusion 2, 14; Saussurean 15,
  17–18, 20–1, 24–7, 62, 158;
  strong xxi, 2, 16–17, 159
Baudrillard, titles cited: *Le
  Système des objets* xi, xiii, 137,
  166; *La Société de consommation*

xiii, 50, 119; *Pour une critique de
l'économie politique du signe* xiii,
xiv, 2–4, 36, 93, 154; *Le Miroir
de la production* xiv, xv; *The
Mirror of Production* 152;
L'Echange symbolique et la mort
xv–xvi, 1, 16, 41, 44, 47, 81, 84,
91, 93, 96, 101–3, 105, 110;
L'Effet Beaubourg xvi; *Oublier
Foucault* xvi, 160; *Le Trompe
l'oeil* 45; *A l'ombre des majorités
silencieuses* xvi, 10; *L'Ange de
stuc* 45; *De la séduction* xvi, 32,
37, 101, 139, 163; *For A Critique
Of The Political Economy Of The
Sign* 39, 152; *Les Stratégies
fatales* xvii, 97, 105, 146, 155;
The Evil Demon of Images 31ff;
Amérique xvii, 42–3, 105, 118,
122, 131; *L'Autre par lui-même*
137; *Cool Memories 1980–1985*
xvii, 104–5; *Selected Writings* 2;
La Transparence du Mal xv, 44,
96, 98, 105, 118; *Cool memories
II* xviii, 104, 167; *L'Illusion de la
fin* xvii; *La Guerre du golfe n'a
pas eu lieu* xvii, 98, 103–4
Beauty and the Beast 139
Bel and the Dragon 30
biology 48–50
Biosphere 134, 139
body: money 33–4; obese 155–6;
  sign 20ff; ubuesque 105ff